GENTLEMEN OF FORTUNE

ALSO BY PAUL FERRIS

Novels

A Changed Man
Then We Fall
A Family Affair
The Destroyer
The Dam
Very Personal Problems
The Cure
The Detective
Talk to me about England
A Distant Country

Reporting

The City
The Church of England
The Doctors
The Nameless: Abortion in Britain Today
Men and Money: Financial Europe Today
The New Militants: Crisis in the Trade Unions

Biography

The House of Northcliffe: the Harmsworths of Fleet Street
Dylan Thomas
Richard Burton

GENTLEMEN OF FORTUNE

The world's merchant and investment bankers

PAUL FERRIS

Weidenfeld and Nicolson
London

CONTENTS

INTRODUCTION

The world's merchant and investment bankers may seem a large mouthful to bite off, let alone chew. As a community they are not easily defined, except that you know them when you see them. They are not the ones who cash cheques; they are the fixers and dealers of the system. But at least there are not too many of them. Their officer-class probably totals no more than fifteen or twenty thousand in the principal centres. I talked to several hundred in Europe, Asia and the United States. I read their magazines and newspapers, sat around their offices and trading floors, ate in their restaurants and private dining-rooms, and tried to catch the flavour of their working lives as they beaver away to the greater glory of capitalism. For better or worse, it is the system that nourishes most of the West and much of the East. One might as well try to see what its acolytes are up to.

Financial institutions and the people who work in them have not gone short of publicity in recent years. But the arts and crafts of the business are still a mystery to most of us outside. I first met Mammon in the flesh a quarter of a century ago in London when I wrote a book called *The City*. Looking back, the place as it was seems almost genteel now. Wall Street has had its own transformation. So have the financial districts of Tokyo and Hong Kong. Mankind's needs seem to have grown more pressing. Rampant wealth needs a lot of expertise; even rampant poverty means the investment banker being paid for his advice. Finance has been reshaped and internationalised. The deals to be fixed are bigger and cross more frontiers. Easier air travel and communication have made most people and places accessible. Concorde flights across the Atlantic are packed with bankers, often going over for the day. Financial firms that had never heard of one another twenty years ago are now locked in daily competition.

Investment bankers are inclined to brush aside the word 'aggressive' and suggest that 'positive' sounds better. But 'positive' is a word from one of their own advertisements. The investment banker, the capitalist-at-large, casts a long shadow. He operates in brutal times where the rich desire to be super-rich, the merely affluent are haunted by failure, and the world's poor have to fight every inch of the way. High finance, like pornography or foreign travel, is no longer the perquisite of an elite. Newcomers elbow their way into the business. The world is there, waiting to be cracked open. Or so they hope. Perhaps we all have grown more greedy: anxious to keep what we have, or acquire what we haven't got. Investment bankers live with the same values as the rest of us. They hardly expect to be loved – most of them are too realistic – but they don't like to be blamed for operating and benefiting by a system that they didn't invent, merely inherited.

The new type of giant investment bank that features prominently (though by no means exclusively) in this account is an American invention, an engine for raising capital and trading securities around the world. It exemplifies the system in action – telephones ringing, computers churning, jaws resolute, smells of aftershave and jet fuel drifting past. Anyone who likes capitalism should find the giants irresistible. Anyone who doesn't may still find them usefully provocative. The Japanese have embraced the concept; the French and Germans are represented. The British have taken the plunge, appropriately enough, through the ambitions of a man with the right name: a Rothschild, the Hon Jacob.

I am indebted to many people for their time and patience. Some of their names appear in the text. Others preferred to be anonymous. A full list of those who helped in one way or another would be difficult to compile, and in the end might be invidious. But my thanks to the unnamed are no less sincere. During many long conversations I found nearly everyone helpful and some positively kind, and made one or two friends. Occasionally investment bankers hint or even say outright that the frenzied bigness of it all these days makes the business less fun than it used to be. But they still seem able to enjoy themselves.

London
1982–4

1
MORGAN ON THE TELEPHONE

Nostalgia and reality — The pride of Morgan Stanley —
Dialogue in the men's room — Invitation to a billion dollar sale —
Predators, great and small — The Word goes out — Dick Fisher's glass box —
The selling concession — Filling and killing — A truly creative lot —
Moral arguments — Phone booths in the twilight —
The varieties of investment bank — Quintessential capitalists

Investment bankers have their golden age like the rest of us. Wall Street
is not famous for nostalgia, but sometimes the stranger catches a breath
of it. A man in his thirties at Merrill Lynch is discussing the investment
banker's daily grind. He comes to the central subject of capital and how
he must persuade industrial corporations to let him raise it for them.
'When Pierpont Morgan was around,' he says, and harks back three-
quarters of a century, 'the banker had the whip hand.' He approves of
that. Who wouldn't, in his place?

In an odd way the investment banker of New York can talk about the
past more easily than can his cousin and counterpart in London, the
merchant banker. There, in the City, history is an occupational hazard.
Long ago they developed the art of living well off deals and schemes:
managers and arrangers doing tricks with money, preferably other
people's. It is what they are still about, though the old sort of game has
been over for years. Power has moved on; the international banker's
language is English but his currency is the dollar. The City has done
well, all things considered. But legends of banking parlours with coal
fires, occupied by partnerships of rich gentlemen in a London at the
centre of the world, are a drag on the market now. Who cares any more?
'Those wonderful old partnerships,' smiles Rupert Hambro, the youngish chairman of his family bank. He says it with irony. Hambros Bank,
though it hasn't been a partnership for generations, clung to the spirit of
unstructured excellence a mite longer than was wise. Mistakes in shipping finance in the 1970s bled it of tens of millions of dollars, a heavy
loss for a bank of that size. But it survived. In the 1980s it has perked up

1

and reorganised and Rupert Hambro takes pains to distance himself and the bank from the less disciplined days when 'things just emerged', when 'you pushed a pigeon out and didn't need to do anything till it came back with a message'. The pigeon is a joke but behind the joke is the reality of change.

The banker's past, anyway, whether in London or New York (or Frankfurt or Paris), was richer only for a handful of Morgans, Rothschilds and Lazards. Wealth is spread more widely now in the investment- and merchant-banking community. There is more of it to go round. It nourishes tribes of fixers and managers in places where investment bankers never trod, Tokyo and Sydney and Hong Kong. It has meant bigger bands of competitors, playing their rough games across continents. The world is greedier than it was and less stable. Tides of money wash around it seeking safe harbours. This is good news for an investment banker, except that he has so many rivals in other countries. Governments are a further inconvenience, waving regulations in one hand and tax demands in the other. It is not an age for a Pierpont Morgan to flourish in.

A few individuals still grow rich in banking, armour-plated with tens of millions which, one is assured by men who ought to know, don't amount to much in the upper brackets of super-wealth. The Wall Street partnership of L. F. Rothschild, Unterberg, Towbin paid six people more than a million dollars each in 1983, plus a share of the profits. Income at this level is usually in the form of salary and bonus, plus some form of retained earnings which become part of the firm's capital and are not immediately accessible. In a good year there are dozens of senior managing directors and partners in Wall Street whose income is near or even above two million dollars. The five or six leading investment banks contain perhaps five hundred partners or managing directors of varying seniority. I asked a banker to estimate how many of them might earn above a million dollars. He thought about a third. But to most of the world's workers the rows of noughts are as meaningless as an astronomer's. The affluence of investment bankers is less interesting than their single-mindedness. The trade has a touch of violence. It cultivates opportunity; it skims off cream. It is a kind of exhilarating plunder.

* * *

Morgan Stanley & Co. is the investment bank that has carried the Morgan name for fifty years. Historically it is the best name in Wall

2

Street. It is well respected because it has adapted to change and gone on making money without losing its aristocratic air. It is also smiled at behind its back for elitism. The core of pure investment banking in the United States is to raise capital by underwriting an issue of securities, as a member of a syndicate formed for the purpose. An invitation to join a syndicate was long declined by Morgan Stanley unless its name appeared in a 'special bracket', with at most three or four others at the head of the list of underwriters. Competitors like First Boston and Merrill Lynch would take what was going. Morgan Stanley, like Elizabeth Taylor, had star billing or none at all. In the smiles was a trace of envy. How nice to be able to afford to indulge one's pride, even to *think* one could afford it. In 1983 Morgan Stanley shed its rule like a creature shedding an old skin. There were too many firms fighting to distribute securities, and Morgan no longer had the old primacy. It began to join syndicates in humbler positions.

To see bankers of any sort in action isn't easy. They may or may not mind having the end-product observed, but the fine shades of negotiation and assessment are kept within four walls. Deciding how best to raise money for a client, or whispering in an industrialist's ear, or playing golf with a foreign politician whose country has money he might want managed, are sensitive matters. Even if the private conversations were accessible they might be less than riveting. When I first went to Morgan Stanley and asked to see things happen, the answer was that I could probably watch it raise capital by issuing securities. These might be in the form of shares (representing money permanently invested in the company, the 'stock' or 'equity', and paying dividends); or bonds (representing money loaned for a period paying a fixed rate of interest). Each piece of business (they told me) has a beginning, a middle and an end; there is a Day One from which consequences flow. Risk-taking is involved. Even the grandest investment bank in the biggest capital market in the world, it was hinted, is like other banks: scratch it and it bleeds money.

While marking time for the right occasion I visited the firm over several weeks, having conversations. I was uncertain how Morgan Stanley would define what the right occasion was. It would hardly be chosen at random. The firm was handling new issues all the time, but no invitation came. I had the fanciful idea of stumbling across an episode I wasn't meant to see. In the washroom off the sales-and-trading floor one afternoon I pricked up my ears at a conversation about London. I didn't know who the two men were. They were talking about something that

3

was due to happen in the City at 10 am next day. That meant before dawn in New York. 'I would be really interested in getting here at five in the morning,' said one of them, without sarcasm. The other combed his hair and said, 'You'd better get some sleep, pal.' I tried to catch his eye in the mirror, below which I was washing my hands, but he was now dancing about in front of a punchbag that hung almost to the floor near the urinals. He jabbed it a couple of times, and a moment later they had gone. The bag was inscribed *Everlast, Choice of Champions*. It looked as though the traders had been giving it a hard time. I never found out what happened at 10 am.

I had talks with Richard B. Fisher, then a senior managing director and a member of the six-person management committee that runs the firm day-to-day. Morgan Stanley is no longer a partnership, but it retains the presence of one; the sixty or so managing directors own most of the firm's stock and are involved in decision-making. (Later that year, 1983, the partner-like directors elected Fisher president, at Morgan Stanley one of two chief executives – the other is chairman, and the firm stubbornly refuses to say that either title is superior; it won't even recognise such a post as 'chief executive', while admitting that 'co-chief executives' is what they are.) Fisher was forty-six and had been there almost half his life; an agreeable man with resolve under the good humour, moving fast down the sales-and-trading-rooms which are his domain despite a limp from childhood polio that makes him use a stick. Most mornings he arrives in the office between seven and eight o'clock, travelling from Brooklyn Heights where he and his family live in a house with high ceilings; it is not far from Norman Mailer's apartment and the famous view across the East River to Wall Street, which on a fine day glitters like the stones of a cemetery.

We had lunch on the premises in a small dining-room, accompanied by one glass of Madeira. It was either that or a dry sherry. 'It's about all Mr Morgan allows us to have,' he said. Even the Madeira was an exceptional treat at lunchtime (at dinner meetings, liquor and wine are served). 'J. P. Morgan wouldn't hear of drink in the bank,' he said, smiling at the lunchtime tradition but content to go along with it. When I looked up John Pierpont Morgan in the firm's library, where they keep a shelf of his biographies, I found he had been dead seventy years, almost to the day.

Morgan Stanley had turned out not to be in the Wall Street district at all. It has computers and various administrative functions there, but its headquarters are in midtown Manhattan, half-way up the Exxon build-

ing. Wall Street is four or five miles to the south. Home for the
securities industry is still the Wall Street area. But commercial banks,
the money-centres like Citicorp and Chemical that take the deposits and
make the loans, have gathered in midtown, to be closer to their corporate clients. Some of the investment houses have joined them. The
taxi-ride from Wall Street to visit a client on Madison or Park takes half
an hour when traffic is bad. Half an hour of investment banker's time is
costly. Besides, the hard new skyscrapers going up in midtown carry
conviction; perhaps their appearance is half the reason for moving, ends
in themselves, piles of even bigger stones to steady the nerves with on
bad days. Do banks ever seem as fragile to bankers as they do sometimes
to strangers? – making their fortunes out of thin air, unpopular in
certain quarters, labelled 'rapacious', potential names for hit-lists
drawn up outside the system by people the system prefers not to think
about. Banks are all targets. So are oil companies. Entry to the Exxon
tower requires a telephone check and the issue of a ticket showing
destination. Guards pace up and down, although a woman at a
cordoned-off entry-point to the elevators is all the illegal visitor would
have to push past; perhaps she has orders to scream.

Safe on the sales and syndicate floor, I waited for Thomas A. Saunders III, described by a colleague as 'our most energetic, effective
investment banker in the new environment'. It was a small conference-
room in a right-angle of the tower, with table and chairs. A sheet of
paper was pinned to an easel, as though part of a presentation. Written
on it in red capitals was BIG DEAL, nothing more. Far below on grimy
buildings near Broadway, electric signs flared at the sun. One, just
readable, said *All American Girls*. Nearby was *Pussycat*. A warship was
going down the Hudson. There was a distant explosion just as Thomas
Saunders III came in, a lean man pumping with vitality. He was sorry to
be dashing about, he said, but 'I've got a little fire going here.' I asked
about the explosion. Don't worry, he said, they are only dynamiting for
a new building at a site on 51st Street. His 'little fire' was a syndication
problem needing urgent attention. We talked for one hour, but he kept
being called away, so the conversation was spread over two. I thought
gratefully of the patient Saunders that evening when a person from
another investment bank, Goldman Sachs, telephoned after a month of
managing not to say Yes or No, to announce that they didn't have time
to talk to me. 'Man,' said the person, 'I am travelling seven days a week.'

The same evening I had a second phone call at the hotel. It was Dick
Fisher to say that if I was doing nothing next day, I might like to sit in on

an issue for American Telephone, where they were the 'lead' or 'book-running' manager. He thought it would happen tomorrow but couldn't guarantee it. Around noon would be fine. Ask for him or Tom Saunders.

I had time for some interviews at Salomon Brothers first, beginning with Richard J. Schmeelk, a sturdy man in a deep blue suit with skin the colour of Caribbean holidays. He was carrying a cup of coffee with a cake perched on the cardboard lid. 'My breakfast,' he said. It was our first meeting. I made some remark about being an innocent abroad in Wall Street, and he said that whenever an out-of-town industrialist or banker walked into his office and told him *that*, he reached for his pocketbook to make sure it was still there. After that I stopped telling people I was an innocent abroad. It was raining when I left Salomon Brothers. A man hurried down Water Street, raincoat buttoned up to a fleshy chin, briefcase dangling from his hand. He might have been forty. I heard him say under his breath, 'I love my Dad.' He wasn't speaking to anybody in particular. Cabs arrived and departed, keeping open the lines of communication to midtown. At five to twelve I was admitted to the Exxon tower, at five past I was sitting next to Saunders at his position on the syndicate desk.

It was, after all, to be a grand occasion; even historic, in Wall Street terms, worth a footnote in a history. The American Telephone and Telegraph Company, the famous AT&T, was raising its last block of equity capital or 'common stock' before having to divest itself, by agreement with the United States Justice Department, of twenty-two local operating companies in the Bell telephone system. 'Ma Bell' had been the world's largest company in private hands, and restructuring it meant that if anything it needed more cash, not less. The company was issuing sixteen million shares in itself (with the option of another 1.6 million if things went well), via Morgan Stanley and four co-managers, supported by a group of more than a hundred investment houses, most of them in the United States but a few in Europe, the underwriters to the issue.

Depending on the exact price at which Telephone shares were being traded on the New York Stock Exchange at the moment of issue – the hinge on which the operation turned – the company expected to receive more than a billion (i.e. one thousand million) dollars, near or even above the record for an issue of shares anywhere. Morgan Stanley and the rest of the syndicate, organised for the purpose of the deal, would guarantee that the company got its money whatever happened. For a

6

brief period, the syndicate would be at risk for the billion dollars of stock. The extent of the risk that underwriters run when issuing securities for an established company is arguable. Those who assume the risk lay stress on what could go wrong, as you would expect them to, and the issuer has to compensate them with a few cents for every share they are allocated. AT&T would pay each manager another few cents a share for managing. Finally, as an inducement to syndicate members, a fee would be built into the price, in the form of a 'selling concession', probably around eighty-five cents a share. This concession would be a major preoccupation. The cost of these items to American Telephone would be upwards of twenty million dollars, deducted by Wall Street from the billion as it shifted from public to company, grease for the wheels. If the underwriting was successful, Morgan Stanley, at the head of the deal, would clear a bit over four and a half million dollars for itself.

The syndicate desk hummed with expectation. Samuel Johnson's mysterious observation, that a man is rarely more innocently employed than in making money, was supported by a certain amount of evidence. They were all absorbed by the matter in hand. The only time I heard anyone take a personal call he said, 'Catherine, you've caught me at a very bad time. Right in the middle of American Telephone. Call you at the close.' Four and a half million dollars concentrate the mind. It was, too, a deal of a traditional kind that cruel competition is bringing to an end. It is companies, not bankers, who call the tune now. Thirty years hence investment bankers will be telling their grandchildren of the golden age that drew to a close in the 1980s. These melancholy thoughts lurked behind the chatter.

Men and women, mostly under forty, many under thirty, sat around a long oval of desk equipped with telephones, notepads and TV screens. Tom Saunders sat in, or mostly stood near, a swivelling armchair at a smaller adjoining desk. A problem had arisen and had been nagging at them all morning. Moody's Investors Service, one of the two leading private agencies that issue credit ratings for corporations and countries, had chosen today to downgrade AT&T in respect of its borrowing by means of bond issues. The reason was the coming divestiture. On one of Saunders' screens at 12.17pm, page 4641 of the Telerate financial information service was quoting a Moody's director as saying that 'from the perspective of credit quality, the break-up of the Bell system must be viewed negatively. The sum of the parts will not equal the whole'. Saunders' Quotron screen, supplying an alternative service, was switched to another facet of the same story. Saunders craned his long neck at it and called to an assistant, 'Neal? What does *this* say? It doesn't say anything.'

They had known for weeks that Moody's was investigating and that a downgrading was on the cards. Morgan and the Telephone Company were still arguing with Moody's the evening before. What no one knew until it happened was when the agency would reach its conclusions, or exactly what they would be. Saunders said that Morgan had calculated the price of AT&T stock would be unaffected whatever the outcome, and that so far the market was bearing them out. The price of Telephone was 66⅛, up three-eighths. But the company's bonds had slipped a little. For decades AT&T and almost all its subsidiaries had basked in 'Triple A' ratings. Now the subsidiaries had come down one or two notches, and in some cases five or six; even the parent had fallen a grade, from Aaa to Aa1. This would cost money. In future the lower ratings would be reflected in the higher interest the company would have to pay on its bonds. In the short term what mattered was the new issue. A flicker in the market, shaving twenty-five cents off the price of Telephone stock, would leave the company receiving four and a half million dollars less than it would otherwise have done.

There were other factors to consider. The market in general was soggy, with stock prices falling here and there. OPEC, meeting in London, was squabbling over oil prices and making investors think depressing thoughts. 'I would love to have them say, "We have an agreement, twenty-eight dollars a barrel or twenty-nine,"' said Saunders. 'That would be very constructive.' He didn't sound optimistic. It was not certain that Morgan Stanley would recommend to the Telephone Company that today was the day. Yet the thing had a momentum, making itself felt. It was more than a week since the company announced that it meant to raise the money (at the time I hadn't noticed). The syndicate was in being. There was a pressure to get on with things, a feeling that deals left too long go stale. A lawyer had gone down to Washington overnight to begin filing a document with the Securities and Exchange Commission, policeman to the industry. This document set out a formula that left AT&T free, within stated limits, to make the issue at will within ten days. News of it would soon leak out. 'Once you file with a formula,' said Saunders, 'you start to tell the market-place that you're getting ready to come.' Did that matter? 'We want to control our destiny. We don't want the Street trading against us with knowledge they shouldn't have.' He pointed down one arm of the room, a dramatic tall bird of a man. 'Our own traders don't know what we're doing yet. Even the co-managers don't.'

I was curious to know how 'the Street' might trade against them. There was no mystery. Aggressive customers could 'short' the stock, selling Telephone shares they didn't own in the hope of being able to buy back similar shares cheaply within hours or days. On the ends of telephone wires were predators, great and small. Their existence made up the capital-raising market but they were not there for charity. They would make it possible for American Telephone to get its money; in the process they would cream off every dollar they could. It was the way the system worked, too obvious to need stating for those inside it, but faintly shocking to the ignorant, like an hotel kitchen seen for the first time.

'Excuse me,' said Saunders, 'this is Telephone coming in, right here.' He picked up a phone and spoke to Larry Prendergast, then assistant treasurer at AT&T, down at the company's headquarters, a marble cavern off Wall Street, at the bottom of Broadway. 'Hey!' said Saunders. 'Yes sir ... OK ... should I get Neal on this? Hold on, I'll put it on 4231.' Neal S. Garonzik – pink shirt, gold-rimmed spectacles – joined the conversation. The three discussed the Moody's report ('everybody keeps going'), the market ('a little heaviness'), the game-plan, as everyone called the strategy ('We're waiting for you to give us a sense of your sensitivities'). I couldn't hear what Prendergast was saying, but the conversation was sparse, as it could afford to be. Long hours of talk had gone into planning the deal, and in any case the Telephone Company was an old client; Morgan Stanley had raised billions of dollars for it since the early 1970s. The outcome was that the syndicate would now be told about the formula that was in the process of being filed in Washington. A balancing act was about to begin, to make sure the underwriters were still interested – it was unlikely they wouldn't be – while leaving all options open, and before the filing with the SEC was official. Nothing could happen until Washington spoke. At breakfast time the lawyer would have walked up to a window with a set of Forms S–3, 'Registration Statement under the Securities Act of 1933', and settled down to wait. The SEC provides a lounge and cafeteria where lawyers can kick their heels.

Garonzik had left the conference call to organise the syndicate-desk staff. 'The Graphic wire's going right now,' he shouted across.

'Hang on one second,' said Saunders.

'Hold it hold it hold it.'

There was a brief discussion about the fact that the formula couldn't be made effective until Morgan Stanley had signed the underwriting agreement on behalf of the syndicate, which in turn couldn't be done until the hundred or more participants had been contacted. Saunders called, 'OK, Neal, send the wire.' He paused and told Prendergast, 'The wire is on its way.' Behind Garonzik a young man curled his fingers into a tube and blew mock trumpet notes 'ta-rah . . . rah!' The Prendergast conversation became light-hearted; action made everyone feel better. 'You're staying in for lunch?' said Saunders, still on the phone. 'OK. I'm going to get something to munch on in a minute. Caviare and cream cheese is what we'd like from you. Send us champagne.' With a line remaining open to the company, Saunders talked to the lawyer in Washington. 'We're going to say in our wire to the underwriters that we expect an answer from them by two. But the process we're going to start here is a massive phone campaign to put 'em in verbally. So we'll let you know, Sandy, when we are ready.'

He called secretaries, making arrangements to sign the underwriting agreement on behalf of Morgan Stanley, then have it sent down by hand to AT&T for the counter-signature of Ginny Dwyer, vice-president and treasurer. In the position next to Garonzik, a woman was saying to an underwriter on the phone, 'We're sending you a Graphic Scanning wire on AT&T – I don't know if you've gotten it yet? It's a formula pricing and it's giving you details and telling you we're going to sign on your behalf this afternoon. We wanted to get your agreement on this.' The noise level was noticeably higher. A voice down the desk said, 'Why, I want to know why?' Everyone seemed to be on the phone, clipped but deferential. 'Hi there, we're sending you a Graphic wire right now. You got it? Oh, you did. Can I get a verbal agreement on that from you?'

The Word was going out. The four co-managers, in for a slice of the management fees but in practice barely consulted on the handling of the deal, would hear and concur – Goldman Sachs & Co., E. F. Hutton & Co., Merrill Lynch White Weld Capital Markets Group, and Salomon Brothers. They would be busy with other deals of their own, though keen for Morgan Stanley to allocate them as large a number of shares as possible in this one, to be sold on through their distribution systems. The rest of the syndicate would similarly take what they were given, and in some cases ask for more. Enthusiasts had been pleading for more shares for days. In the formal underwriting agreement, each was given an 'underwriting amount', from a million shares or more for every co-manager down to 60,000 for a fringe member. But the 'underwriting amount' represents only the number of shares for which a syndicate member is notionally at risk. His underwriting fee, so many cents a share, is based on that amount. The actual number of shares that the syndicate manager finally allocates him, the 'retention', for him to sell on to his customers, may be far more or even far less, down to zero. It depends on the manager's judgement of how well he can do the job, and his own desire (or sometimes lack of it) to have the stock to sell. A man at Donaldson, Lufkin & Jenrette, an aggressive firm, told me they were down for 100,000 shares, after which they made fifty or sixty phone calls over several days, begging for more. 'The book-running manager is God Almighty,' he said, without feeling, as if it was the thing to say. The firm's retention was above 250,000.

The syndicate was carefully put together by Morgan Stanley and the Telephone Company to create a network of obligation. All would later appear standing shoulder to shoulder in a 'tombstone' advertisement, one of thousands that commemorate deals every year and provide lucrative stuffing for financial pages around the world. Traditional American houses like Dillon Read and Smith Barney were there. So were recent hybrids like Prudential-Bache and Shearson/American Express, subject of endless articles about Whither Wall Street? Firms unknown or little regarded in the United States twenty years ago lined up for their helpings, Nikko and Nomura, Daiwa and Yamaichi, the clever Japanese. There was a Rothschild Inc. from New York, a County Bank from London, a Sal. Oppenheim from Cologne, a Banque Nationale de Paris. Not all members of a syndicate perform equally well. When he hears that some firms manage to sell no shares at all, the stranger wonders why they were invited in the first place. But the old-boy network circles the globe. Morgan Stanley was less than keen to gossip about particular names on the list. I ran through it later with a banker at another firm who knows about syndicates. '*This* famous name,' he said, 'can be relied upon to do a particularly miserable job of selling stock. But it originates lots of other business that Morgan probably wants to be in. Here's another with very few salesmen and no ability to distribute. Here's an affiliate of a big Swiss bank. My guess is that the new American Bell will be doing more international business. So it wants to build relations with foreign banks. Hence the Swiss. Here's a couple of names I've had experience of, that I've known to *ask* they be given no retention. It's pitiful, really. Only they make connections.' But even if it was in Morgan Stanley's interest, in a vague sort of way, to invite such dunces, why was it in their interest to accept? 'So that next year they can say, "Last year we underwrote a hundred issues, including the biggest issue in the universe, American Telephone. Of which, if we are honest, we took zero." That's exactly it.' On the tombstone their names would live for ever.

No one in the syndicate area was going to lunch. A woman ate coleslaw with a plastic fork. Coke was being slurped through straws. The rain was beating down outside. Dick Fisher appeared, having come up from Wall Street, wearing a light macintosh and a jaunty hat; he was bone dry. He and Saunders immediately began to talk about Moody's. 'Some security analysts have been saying this is a ridiculous thing,' declared Saunders. 'It's been sweeping back and forth across the tape.'

'Any OPEC news?'

'No OPEC news. We're sitting here waiting for that. And the market is beginning to give some ground. It was up as you know seven or eight bucks, but she's been fading for the last hour. All we've really done is we've started the clock.'

The Telephone price had sagged to $65\frac{7}{8}$. I asked Fisher why they were taking things to the brink on what sounded like a bad day. It was true that they had tipped their hand, he said, that everyone now knew they had it in mind to act if the price was right. But there were pressures. 'We are concerned with the risk in the market-place in general, uncertainty over a fall in the next three or four days. If we get the chance to take a $66\frac{1}{4}$ to $66\frac{1}{2}$ price for Telephone, we'll do it. We've weighed the alternatives. If we keep the cards close to our vest, that may cause us to lose an opportunity. The formula allows us to act at any time. But we've shown our hand. You're right.'

We retreated for sandwiches into a tiny sound-proofed glass box, an extra office built to one side of the trading floor.

'This is Fisher's room,' said Tom Saunders. 'The lean-to.'

'I asked that it be put here.'

'This is the second time we've caught him in it.'

'I can never *get* in it,' said Fisher. 'I was severely criticised for having it built. Now somebody's always using it.'

The Moody's downgrading continued to be worried at in nervous, half-gossipy conversations. It had been worse than expected, said Fisher. But rating agencies took the position that they were like umpires, with a public-service role. The timing was unfortunate and Morgan Stanley challenged the conclusions, but to reappraise the subsidiaries was logical enough, given the uncertainties of divestiture. Pacific Telephone, for example, already rated the lowest in the group, had sunk another category to Baa 1. I said I would have expected an affluent place like California to be rated high, not low. 'Ah,' said Fisher, 'it's mainly because there is state regulation involved. Pacific Telephone is in the worst shape because California regulation for telephone utilities is among the worst in the country from the investor's point of view.' It seemed that California was especially sympathetic to consumers. So the company found it harder to earn what investors regarded as a fair rate of return. We didn't pursue the matter (by the end of the year, Pacific Telephone Co., about to become Pacific Telesis, had an A–3 from Moody's). What did 'fair' mean, anyway? People using telephones in California were one aspect of reality, stock markets putting a price on bonds were another. We all went back to the syndicate area. '"OPEC talks will continue tomorrow,"' Fisher read off a screen. 'Nothing done.' In London it was early evening, the markets were shut, only late stragglers left in the City. But here they were bracing themselves.

Sooner or later, Morgan Stanley and the syndicate would buy the shares from the Telephone Company, paying the market price less whatever selling concession was agreed; this would be the syndicate's inducement to assume responsibility for finding buyers. Assuming the deal was to go through today, Morgan Stanley, as the manager, had two options. It could wait until the New York Stock Exchange closed at four o'clock, and hope that AT&T stock was then trading at an attractive level; $66\frac{1}{4}$ seemed to be the minimum that was acceptable. But the closing price might be unsatisfactory. So the alternative option was for the bank to pounce as soon as, and if, AT&T stock was trading in the market at an acceptable figure. Doing it that way gave Morgan Stanley more room for manoeuvre. It also gave the rest of Wall Street more chance to make money at the bank's expense in whatever hours or minutes remained before the market closed.

The paradox (to the outsider) is that Morgan Stanley, whose object in the deal was to sell Telephone shares into the market at – say – $66\frac{1}{4}$, had to be ready to buy them from the market at $66\frac{1}{4}$ as well. This it would do to 'stabilise' the price, to act as a buyer for all comers so that the value of the AT&T stock would remain at the level of the bid. The SEC would be notified that Morgan Stanley, as manager of the deal, had made a stabilisation bid. The process had to be publicly declared; this didn't happen in J. P. Morgan's day, when banks would manipulate the price of new shares by silent moves behind the scenes, to the disadvantage of investors. The trouble with 'stabilising' was that, by its notice that it would buy Telephone stock at the stated price, Morgan Stanley opened itself to all the sellers of all the Telephone shares in circulation. These shares totalled something over 900 million, worth about $60 billion. It needed only a fraction of these stockholders to decide that the syndicate's price was attractive enough to make them sell, and a blizzard of orders would appear. This could happen the morning after a deal that was done 'at the close'. But it was the hectic, sensitive period immediately following a deal done before the close that posed the sharper risk.

Other things could go wrong. Were they real risks or merely theoretical? The consensus, not stated by anyone in so many words, but emerging from ragged questions and ragged answers, seemed to be that the odds against serious trouble were long, but that long odds had been known to come up. It was not much of an answer, after all. 'The one time they can gang up on an underwriter,' said someone, 'is after you've priced it and own the stock, and the deal starts to come apart. Let's say we go at sixty-six and a quarter today, and the market tone isn't all that good. At a quarter of five, OPEC announce that after all they won't meet tomorrow, they are irreconcilably apart. In other words, we get bad news from the market.' It was true that the syndicate already had orders for all or most of the sixteen million shares. But they were not firm orders, only indications of what the final purchasers might take if they liked the price. Should the stock market fall, the price of the new Telephone stock would be unattractive. The banks, brokers, pension funds and oil companies whose names were on the list had only been 'circled'; they were not committed.

Heads stayed frozen in front of screens, watching the movements of Telephone. From the equity desk, far down the room, you could see them looking across at the syndicate area. Once the deal was priced, they would do the selling. High on the wall beyond them, a frieze of green electric letters and figures was in perpetual motion, the Stock Exchange's tape of latest prices.

Neal Garonzik was never off the telephone now. He said, 'Somebody just took twenty thousand at an eighth.'

Saunders chortled and said, 'We're going to get a quarter in here somewhere, coach.' But he knew the stock was under pressure from speculators, selling it short. He kept throwing back his head to find a last trickle in the cardboard cup of soft drink from lunch. The ice sucked against his teeth.

14

'I still haven't heard if we're effective,' called Garonzik, referring to the lawyer down in Washington and the formula.

'Get to him right now.'

'I've tried to. He isn't answering his beeper.'

Farther down the desk, a woman was still rounding up stragglers in the syndicate. 'I don't know if we're going to price tonight, but it's very possible. Can I get a verbal acceptance from you? Thank you very much.'

Saunders became engrossed in another dialogue with Larry Prendergast. Was the Telephone team coming to Morgan Stanley for the pricing, and if so, when?

'If Bill Cashel [W. S. Cashel Jnr, principal financial officer, vicechairman of the board] wants to come up and be eyeball to eyeball, then clearly, come on. Or we can do it over the phone. But I'm not sure I would like to have you all in transit between 3.30 and 4. I know you've got a phone in the car, but you could be at Canal Street when we should print this thing, and Cashel may not particularly want to do it by phone in an automobile. So think about it a little bit with Ginny, maybe.'

Garonzik called out that the formula registration had been declared effective at 2.30. 'So as soon as we put a price on it,' said Fisher, 'we can lay off our risk.'

Fisher knew that I was committed to another appointment elsewhere in the firm at three. 'The market's up again,' he said, 'but I think we'll wait for the close. I'll send word if anything happens.'

I was not away more than fifteen minutes when a secretary came to bring me back. The mood had changed. Everyone was talking at once. A man shouted down a phone, 'Hey! Get him off! I *need* him.' Garonzik was speaking to syndicate members and to the individual on the Stock Exchange floor who specialises in AT&T, encouraging him to keep the price up. Saunders was trying to get through to the car in which the Telephone team were coming north.

The price wobbled from sixty-six and an eighth to a quarter and back again.

'Sixty-six and a quarter right now, coach.'

'You're not going to get above a quarter, though. You're not going to trade through a quarter.'

'I agree.'

'It's an eighth.'

A moment later it emerged that the main Telephone team hadn't left after all. The top brass were still at 195 Broadway. Saunders braced himself for the big conversation of the day. When it began, I would hear him speak of 'a spread of a dollar thirty'. I missed the significance till later. It was the amount per share that AT&T was prepared to pay to raise its money. This had been provisionally agreed with the company a couple of weeks earlier. The management fee was twenty-four cents, split five ways, with Morgan Stanley receiving the largest share (perhaps seven cents, but no one wanted to tell me). The underwriting fee, which everyone in the syndicate would receive, was twenty-one cents per share of each member's 'underwriting amount', less the expenses of the deal; these would include legal, accounting, advertising and printing costs, and, most important, any losses involved in the process of stabilising. If the total expenses were substantial, there wouldn't be much of the twenty-one cents left. Finally there was the selling concession available to syndicate members as an inducement to sell the securities. This would be the largest item, eighty-five cents a share. In the case of Morgan Stanley, which had allocated itself four million shares, the selling concession alone gave the firm potential earnings of more than three million dollars. But the calculations assumed that the spread would remain fixed at $1.30. A last-minute reduction was possible, in which case it would be the selling concession that suffered; and at 3.20 that afternoon, the company still reserved the right to negotiate. Companies squeeze their bankers when they can. A saving of five cents a share on sixteen million is worth $800,000; as a co-manager said to me later, 'A nickel's a nickel, even at Telephone. It pays a few salaries.'

Saunders was talking to W. R. Cashel and Ginny Dwyer. He said, 'Hello, Bill, how are you? Apologies for a rough day. Ginny, here's the situation right now. Larry – obviously after talking with you – gave us authorisation on sixty-six and three-eighths, to put in a bid and go with a spread of a dollar thirty. We came very close to doing that fifteen minutes ago. Unfortunately the market has turned down quite significantly – the index is now down eight dollars and seventy-one cents. Your stock at the moment is at sixty-six and an eighth. Twenty-five thousand shares just traded at sixty-six and a quarter.'

Garonzik interrupted to say, 'The specialist [on the Stock Exchange] is going to buy a hundred thousand at an eighth.'

'Thank you. The specialist is going to take a hundred at an eighth. We have been working with him all day, and in effect what we're saying to him is, "You take that, and with what we're seeing in the way of interest in the stock, you're going to be in good shape." He's buying stock at sixty-six and an eighth, doing nothing he's not permitted to do. But he'll probably be looking to us at some point to own that hundred thousand shares. And that's fine, we've told him that we're there. I would say, Ginny, that sixty-six and three-eighths is going to be very tough to come by in a down market. With this sort of pressure on the stock now, there's very little chance.'

Garonzik was talking to the co-managers as a matter of form, telling them the deal was on the brink, getting their nod for the final terms. For a minute or two I was out of earshot of Tom Saunders. I wasn't sure afterwards if this was accidental, or if I had been manoeuvred away from his chair. It was the moment when the spread was settled with the Telephone Company, once and for all. This is a delicate area. The investment banker is working for the client but he has to be realistic about the syndicate members, who rely on him as manager not to land them in trouble. It was the following week before a co-manager told me what he thought had happened. He said the Telephone Company, like every other efficient raiser of capital, realised that investment banks could be compelled to cut margins. A year or two earlier, a similar syndicate led by Morgan Stanley had charged $1.55 a share. But since then the company had experimented on a small scale with a technique for auctioning a deal to the cheapest bidder. It ended up paying less than eighty cents a share. So now the company was putting the screws on. Even a $1.30 spread, on a share worth around $66, was cheap. But at the last minute, said the co-manager, he was pretty certain the Telephone Company went for $1.25. It probably wanted to collect a net $65 per share. Since there was no hope of pricing the deal at more than $66.25, a spread of $1.30 would take it below its figure. And if Morgan Stanley had agreed to five cents less? 'Who can tell?' said the co-manager. 'Taking a nickel out of the syndicate's hide could have spoilt the deal. We'll never know. I guess Saunders convinced them.'

The time was just after 3.30. Dick Fisher was telling me that all things considered, Telephone stock was doing well to hold up in a falling market. The solemn features of Tom Saunders poked towards us and Garonzik. He said, 'We have authorisation to do a quarter less a dollar thirty. They've turned it over to us. I want to step in and stabilise.'

Garonzik, hand welded to telephone, swayed towards Saunders and said, 'Let's commence right now. Take it at a quarter, Tommy.' Saunders must have nodded because Garonzik shouted down the telephone, '*Commence!* Stabilise at a quarter.'

It was 3.32 exactly. Dick Fisher said, 'That was it.'

'That was it?'

I wasn't sure what I had been expecting; nevertheless, it seemed decently momentous, an achievement with vibrations you could feel, as if the spirit of endeavour worked for bankers as for rock climbers or even poets. Excitement flowed, making everyone flushed and powerful. Men and women walked over from other parts of the room.

'We are stabilising.'

'Let her roll.'

'At a quarter?'

'My, we are priced!'

From the equity section came applause and some cheers, which lasted ten seconds. Saunders informed the company over the phone that the deal was launched. 'We own it,' he said to Fisher. 'We've got it.' Success meant not owning their share of it longer than they had to. All the underwriters would be doing the same, phoning as if their lives depended on it. On the equity desk, salesmen hit the buttons of direct-wire connections to institutions which had been circled for stock. Morgan is a wholesale and institutional firm, dealing chiefly with other professionals. Some of the issue, probably about a quarter, would eventually find its way to individual investors, who have a soft spot for Telephone. But all Morgan cared about now was banks, pension funds, insurance companies and other bulk buyers. The big ninety-button keyboards were alive with calls. 'We're going back to the accounts,' said Fisher, 'and since the deal is effective with the SEC, we can insist on an answer. We call it *fill or kill*. He either takes the stock he's been circled for or he doesn't. If he says, "Give me ten minutes," it's up to our salesman to decide. If we hadn't set up the formula in Washington, the accounts would have been able to wait overnight because registration wasn't effective. So that turned out to be a very important technical decision. We own the stock. We're at risk now. We've done the job for the company, they've gotten their price. Now what we have to do is manage our position.'

Jimmy Gantsoudes, in charge of institutional equity sales, was talking to his salespersons – in the same room, in San Francisco (where it was still mid-morning), in Chicago. 'I want 'em filled,' he was saying, the words quick-firing in bursts. 'I'm short here. I've got to know where I stand. I want to hear back from you. This thing is a dynamic situation, we can't sit around here for five hours. If they're not good, give me my stock back. I want 'em filled. Why am I short?'

18

From the selling point of view, all seemed in order. The more cries of
'I need some stock!' the sooner it would be over. Dick Fisher said,
'We've had two drops so far, two accounts have turned stock back to us,
one for fifty thousand shares, one for twenty-five thousand. But we
have new buyers, too.' He asked had I heard that Morgan Stanley had
bought 300,000 shares at 66¼ to stabilise in the last seventeen or eighteen
minutes. It was now 3.50, ten minutes before the New York Exchange
closed. I said No, and was that bad? 'We'll buy more,' he said. Anson
M. Beard Jr, a managing director in sales and trading, joined the
conversation. There were 900 million Telephone shares that guys like
us owned, he said. 'Some guy will say, "Hey, sixty-six and a quarter
looks like a good price, we'll sell it."' I pondered this, aware of people
going into huddles, looking at the clock. As fast as one lot of salesmen
were disposing of the newly-issued Telephone shares, another lot were
buying Telephone shares in general. Anyone in need of cash knew that
Morgan Stanley had set itself up to pay the world 66¼ per share. So
stabilising was expensive; that was why it ranked as a charge on the
syndicate as a whole, and came out of the twenty-one cents a share for
underwriting. I had heard 'firepower' talked about. This was the
firepower they needed to keep buying. 'Incidentally,' said Fisher, 'we
went into the deal short of Telephone stock. We allocated the underwriters more than we had for sale. So to buy half a million is no
problem. Now, if we were to buy a million and a half here this afternoon, that begins to get a little dicey.' Two minutes later Neal Garonzik
told him they had bought more than a million and three-quarters. 'Jeez,'
said Fisher, 'that's a lot of stock.' He was telling me they were in good
shape to handle it when Anson Beard came over in case we hadn't heard.

'We're going to set another record. We bought a million eight
already.'

'Neal just said.'

'So before the shouting's over, we'll go above the two million three we
bought, when was it, last June.'

He had good nerves, too. In the last twenty-eight minutes of trading
that afternoon, Morgan Stanley bought 2,400,000 shares. They didn't
like it. 'It's a lot of stock to buy in half an hour,' said a salesman when the
room was calm again. 'Customers know what's going on. They say, "My
God, the stock's coming out of the woodwork, this deal is going to come
apart." Not to blow our horn, but it's one of the things that Morgan
Stanley does – stand there to the end, until we can't buy any more
stock.' But wasn't that what any syndicate manager had to do? 'I don't

want to give a Morgan Stanley commercial here, but you can't imagine how often, *bang*, a syndicate pulls away. We'll buy stock till the cows come home. And every share we buy we have to put back out again, so we're buying [from outside the syndicate] at $66\frac{1}{4}$, but passing it back to syndicate members at $66\frac{1}{4}$ less the eighty-five cents selling concession, for them to resell at $66\frac{1}{4}$. So it's costing eighty-five cents a share, charged against the syndicate as a whole.' That was where the firepower went, millions of dollars worth. It was said that some of the underwriters were secretly selling stock back to Morgan Stanley in order to repurchase it five minutes later at a profit of eighty-five cents a share, pirates within the syndicate. But that sort of thing was hard to prove.

I had assumed there must be some regulation to stop shares going round and round, having eighty-five cents creamed off them every time Morgan Stanley took them in and sold them out again; there seemed to be regulations for most things. But regulations were to protect the public, not the professionals. It was a matter of profits for the nimble, versus Wall Street's uneven code of private ethics plus Morgan Stanley's ability to police the deal by refusing to handle orders if it suspected that smart operators were playing tricks. The paths that stock can take at such moments are apparently infinite. While the process of stabilising the deal continued, all members of the syndicate would receive the 85-cents-a-share allowance for the stock they took from the manager, Morgan Stanley, and sold. Firms of broker-dealers, not members of the syndicate, also could apply to Morgan Stanley for shares, and might get an allocation. None of these firms, whether inside or outside the syndicate, was allowed to pass on the allowance to buyers. But there was nothing to stop a potential institutional buyer from designating particular firms within the syndicate from whom it wanted to do the buying. If institution A told Morgan Stanley that it wanted to buy a hundred thousand shares from syndicate member X, it gave $85,000 worth of business to X. Morgan Stanley would supply X with the shares at the eighty-five cents discount, and X would make the sale. It would be a legitimate way for the institution to compensate investment bank X for services (typically, research services) rendered or to come.

Variants of the technique could be used on a large scale or a small, greasing all manner of wheels in the machine. Everyone expected favours. Issuing shares was a ritual with gifts. 'Look,' said a manager at a syndicate firm, 'imagine I'm an institution. You're a salesman at a firm that has an allocation of Telephone stock. I call you up and say I'd like

20

you to sell me ten thousand Telephone. You buy them from the syndicate less eighty-five cents, and sell them to me at the full price. That's eight thousand five hundred dollars for you. As it happens I don't want ten thousand Telephone any more than I want a hole in the head. I've already sold them on through a discount [cut-price] broker-age, so it's only cost me a nickel a share. They bang them back in the bid for all I know. It's only cost me ten thousand nickels, that's five hundred dollars. The big gainer is you, the salesman. When I come to you next week for shares in a hot issue, you have your allocation, and guess who you'll give some of them to? There are always ways in which people will behave that aren't particularly beneficial to the Telephone Company or Morgan Stanley.'

Some of the methods used to move stock round and round, creating 85-cents-a-time obligations, sail close to the wind. Those were the ones that upset Tom Saunders. 'I've seen the games they can play,' he said, 'but I sure haven't seen 'em all. They're a truly creative lot when it comes to finding a new way of laundering stock, and you getting it back. A lot of it comes back from Europe. That's a standard place for doing it. They can put it through what appears to be a legitimate buyer. It's a very simple game.' That was why policing the deal was important. 'Well,' said Saunders later, 'they say all cats are black at night, but you do know the difference. We know which institutions play the game and which don't. You choose very carefully who you sell it to. There were some underwriters asking for a lot that we didn't give any. There were some institutions that could have asked and we'd have sent them away. Know your customer. There's a lot of who's doing what to whom.'

On the afternoon of the deal, they were glad to see four o'clock at Morgan Stanley. Next morning Saunders was awake before dawn and at his desk by 7.30 after five miles in his tracksuit; he is a running man. The syndicate desk talked to every underwriter to see where they stood, anxious to avoid more of the previous day's discomfort, where 'you put this stock out and it comes back and bites you'. The most important decision was the price at which Morgan Stanley should open the stock. Under the rules, it could lower the bid but not raise it. By lowering the price to all comers, the bank would make it less attractive to the pirates and creative thinkers who were getting ready for another day's specula-tion. But if the price was lowered too much, holders of the stock might take fright. It would undermine confidence, the market price would fall and soon Morgan Stanley's price would look expensive.

The deal would effectively collapse. In the end it was decided to reduce the bid by twenty-five cents to $66 exactly – 'to be honest,' said Saunders afterwards, 'the best decision we made in this whole deal.' The bank had to buy in heavily for a few hours, but the worst was over. Stock rained on it when the New York Exchange opened at ten o'clock. In thirty minutes or so it bought nearly half a million shares more. Then the pressure eased. A second wave caught it at lunchtime, and within an hour it had to buy a further two or three hundred thousand. Its firepower was almost exhausted. 'If we'd been forced to keep buying,' said Jimmy Gantsoudes, 'we might have had to back away. But once again the buyers started to fill in.' At the end of the afternoon, Morgan Stanley formally ended its stabilising function. The closing price that afternoon, a Friday, was a healthy 66⅜. By the following week the deal had passed into Wall Street's equivalent of history, a tombstone advertisement in the papers and some data on a disk. Morgan Stanley had exercised its option to take the extra 1.6 million shares, so 17.6 million were finally issued: a bit more money for everyone. Tom Saunders and Anson Beard went round to talk to a major institution they suspected of behaving badly, selling stock into the bid on a large scale. 'He didn't do anything, as far as I could see, that was illegal,' said Saunders. 'Our point was that he wanted to have his cake and eat it. We said, "Don't think because your orders have come through five different brokers, we don't know it's you." And at the end of the session he admitted, "I was wrong."'

I said that if it wasn't a legal issue, it had to be a moral one. '*Yes,*' said Saunders, 'they were moral arguments.'

As an exercise in capital raising, it provided $1,143,120,000 for AT&T, after the $1.30 was deducted. Even this was not quite the final figure, since the company also had to pay certain printing expenses, the SEC's filing fee and other sundries, to a total of nearly half a million dollars; there are many outstretched hands. 'So,' said Tom Saunders after the weekend, 'you've seen this country's major corporation, raising over a billion dollars in an unstable market, in an unstable world.' He said it was this kind of business that had made Morgan Stanley great. I wanted to talk to Neal Garonzik, but he had gone to Japan. 'In the old days,' said Saunders, 'people used to sit around and savour a deal. An issue like this would have hung about for months. Now it's right on.'

I talked about it with other members of the syndicate. It was ancient history for them, too. 'Risk?' said Robert Towbin of L. F. Rothschild. 'Christ, what have they got to lose? The worst that can happen to

Telephone is that it goes down a little bit.' At Salomon Brothers, a co-manager to the issue, the chairman, John Gutfreund, a solemn figure, made it sound a little nobler. He said that $66\frac{1}{4}$ had been 'aggressive pricing'. It was gauged towards the interests of the Telephone Company rather than the purchasers. 'But Morgan,' he said, 'is a skilled practitioner of the art.'

On the following Friday I went to American Telephone at 195 Broadway. It would not be there much longer; a new headquarters in Madison Avenue, in midtown, was being built. Larry Prendergast was a serious young man in an office of ominous size. He said that when raising money the company chose its managers carefully; it was the largest private user of capital in the United States; the issue was, of course, a record. My footsteps echoed slightly as I left. A drinking fountain on the wall produced its creamy jet from a carved figure like a Buddha. In the entrance hall below were pillars, spaces, shadows, more echoes. Chandeliers and seats of marble seemed to wait for a ceremony. To one side, like a chapel, was a region of books and cubicles. The nation's phone directories hung in perfect order, like manuscripts on display, and behind them were the phone booths, immaculate, row upon row, each with a seat, a shelf and a folding glass door. No dust, no graffiti, no vandals, just empty phone booths in the twilight. It was almost grander than Morgan Stanley.

* * *

The titles people give themselves, or pick up, often confuse everyone else. Perhaps this is the idea; there is comfort in mystique. 'Investment banks' in the United States are not banks in the sense that most people understand the word, taking deposits and making loans. The same is true of Japan, with the complication that there they are more often called 'securities houses'. In Britain 'merchant banks' are not merchants, but at least they are banks.

This amorphous community is different in different countries by historical accident. In the United States, investment bankers didn't exist as such until the 1930s. J. P. Morgan offered what was regarded as a normal range of banking services: at one end handling customers' deposits, at the other issuing securities to raise capital for a select clientele. But in the wake of the Wall Street crash, the authorities decided that banks were dangerously involved in the securities business. The draconian Glass-Steagall Act of 1934 separated the functions. Banks had to decide whether to be in the 'commercial', deposit-taking and lending business, or whether they were to be investment houses, issuing and handling securities. The house of Morgan opted for banking, where it remains today as J. P. Morgan & Co., with many subsidiaries, principally a leading commercial bank, Morgan Guaranty Trust Co. of New York. The following year some of the partners, among them a Mr Stanley, resigned and set up their own firm to operate on the securities side of the fence. This was Morgan Stanley. All banks had to make the decision. Those that chose the non-banking side became the heart of a specialist business concerned with raising capital by issuing securities. Together with other services for large corporate clients, this 'underwriting' business enjoyed an air of special respectability, relying as it did on long connections and old friendships. That cosy world has gone. Raising capital is a rougher business, and it is no longer the chief source of revenue. Selling and trading in securities, once left to humble brokerage firms, the so-called 'wire houses', is now the engine of most investment banks. Many wire houses have done the opposite and plunged into the new-issue business, Merrill Lynch being the prime example, to become investment banks. What continues to distinguish them from commercial bankers is the absence of a core of deposits. Like hunger, this keeps them on the move, looking for business. They are meaner, sharper and funnier than their commercial colleagues; it is in the nature of what they do. But the community has now been invaded by American commercial banks outside the United States, where Glass-Steagall's writ doesn't run. Few US commercial banks with global pretensions lack an investment-banking subsidiary, which usually operates out of London. (Some Wall Street bankers have retaliated with tentative moves into commercial banking, in Europe and elsewhere.)

Other countries have their own variants. Japan had a version of the Glass-Steagall system wished upon it after the war as part of the American occupation. Since then the securities houses of Tokyo have become *de facto* investment banks, opening branches around the world. In mainland Europe, no one legislated banks into categories; they tended to be all things to all men, although the 'private banks' of Germany and Switzerland, and the French *banques d'affaires*, had specialist roles.

London did things on a grander scale because it was where banking dynasties first grew into one another to make a financial centre whose sum was greater than its parts. Names like Kleinwort, Samuel, Hambro, Rothschild, Schroder and Lazard belonged to foreign bankers and merchants, usually Jewish, always enterprising, who set up shop in the City through Victorian times and beyond. Like Pierpont Morgan, they were just bankers. But London's position as a trading centre, which was part of the attraction in the first place, gave them a special interest in trade finance. The original label of 'merchants and bankers' was replaced by 'merchant bankers'. Their names lent credibility to deals involving other people's money; the merchant banks took deposits of their own, but on a modest scale, and mainly from large customers. They didn't join the rush to serve the masses. They remained private and specialist, their vigour seemingly spent by the 1930s. There was no call to legislate them into two halves. The UK had no 1930s banking crisis as traumatic as America's; in any case, legalistic solutions are unpopular with the British. Merchant banks, too, have no securities business in the American sense. They raise capital, but unlike investment banks, they are not members of the local stock exchange. Thus they are less concerned with distributing the securities once they are issued; historically this function was left to stockbrokers. The merchant banks plodded along through World War 2, emerging rejuvenated in the 1950s both as bankers to industry, as it revived, and as middle-men to brusquer times, doing new versions of old tricks – lending, guaranteeing, arranging, advising. The clearing (commercial) banks could have done it themselves but somehow never did. The merchant banks found a new role and a sort of fame, backing into the limelight, attracting publicity by the very act of waving it away – enterprising, colourful and more artful than ever.

By 1984 they were being caught up in a fresh wave of changes that was likely to have a profound effect on the way they – and the City – worked. The London stockbrokers' monopoly (not to mention their beloved structure of fixed commissions) was disintegrating, following the threat of legal action by the Office of Fair Trading. Merchant and commercial banks were striking up alliances with Stock Exchange firms, positioning themselves to be more like their New York cousins – traders and distributors of securities. Unfortunately for them, their New York cousins, as well as a variety of British financial institutions, were also joining in the London free-for-all. The merchant banks are not very big alongside the giant investment banks. In 1983 Tokyo's Nomura Securities, a group of alarming ambition, had earnings (i.e. profits after tax) of $292 million. Wall Street's Merrill Lynch earned $230 million. Kleinwort Benson, the largest of London's merchant banks, disclosed earnings of $32 million, which means that its true profits were a bit higher; not high enough, though, to affect the argument. Disclosed earnings of N. M. Rothschild, the most famous name of all in merchant banking, were a little over $3.6 million. But size, they tell themselves in Cornhill and Bishopsgate, isn't everything, and hope that their famous flexibility, and perhaps a few judicious mergers, will yet secure their future.

Whatever their exact titles in different continents, people know them all after a fashion, by their caricatures. They are reputed to be clever, discreet and quick on their feet. They recur in gossip columns with beautiful women in tow (they are not supposed to be women them-selves, and although I know that women investment bankers hold senior positions, I didn't come across any). They are good value for romantic novels ('Stephen had grey eyes and a cool profile. He worked in a merchant bank'), even for the captions to photographs in men's magazines ('Ursula likes to go underwater swimming with her special friend, who's an investment banker'). They are young rather than old, daring rather than cautious. They live handsomely by the exercise of competitive skills, appropriate figures to admire in times when nothing seems more admirable than money. Often they are greyer and more ordinary than the caricature. But the caricature has enough truth in it to be valid. Dedicated to ensuring that the system works, expert in its nuances, they try hard to be in the right place to make the most of what's going. They are capitalism boiled down to its essentials.

2

DYNASTY: ROTHSCHILDS AND HAMBROS

Family affairs— Mr Evelyn and a matter of style —
Mr Jacob eats a sandwich and builds an empire— Baron Edmond and Baron Guy—
Nationalising the Rothschilds— Hamburg's Hambros— Venture capital —
Hambro Life, a good idea— Hilmar Reksten, not such a good idea —
Laughter from the Front Room—Sterner times

Merchant banking in London was a family affair, but few of the families remain. Four directors of Baring Brothers (of twenty-seven) are Barings, among them the chairman. Kleinwort Benson has a solitary Benson; there is a Kleinwort son-in-law, and the holding company has a solitary Kleinwort, but he lives abroad. J. Henry Schroder Wagg has one Schroder on a board of more than forty; another director is married to a Schroder daughter, and the family, it is true, has control through its shareholding.

A Montagu can be found in the City, but no longer at the former family house of Samuel Montagu, which is now jointly owned by a deposit bank around the corner and an insurance company in Hartford, Connecticut. Montagus faded out of the firm. It is a not uncommon City story. The family had founded the bank in the middle of the nineteenth century, later acquiring wealth and a peerage. When the third Lord Swaythling and another Montagu were there in the 1930s, in offices with thick ledgers and respectful clerks, it had shrunk to a banker's bank with fewer than a thousand accounts, dealing in bullion and foreign exchange. Lord Swaythling, still living in 1984, was a farmer at heart, and played little part in bank affairs. His son, the Honourable David Charles Samuel Montagu, was the last of them to make a living from the firm. He did it by climbing the ladder to the chairmanship, too late to be more than a gesture as far as the family was concerned. In his words, 'I realised the Montagus had let a jewel slip.'

The first Samuel Montagu wasn't short of sons, but later generations hadn't cared, or hadn't cared enough. According to David Montagu, 'Even my grandfather was never number one. My father had an office at the bank and went in three or four days a week to do his farm records, but he was miserable there. He'd go back to the country, put his gumboots on and be happy. He became a formidable expert on dairy cattle. I take my hat off to him. But he was financially able to do it and I wasn't. I had to make my living. I made up my mind I would either be chairman of the bank at forty or go off and do other things. The then management did everything they could to break my heart.' The bank had picked itself up since the war. David Montagu achieved his ambition a year or two after the deadline of forty, but when the Midland Bank took over the firm early in the 1970s, he declined an invitation to stay. The world had moved on again. There are no Montagus on the board, and Aetna Life & Casualty of Hartford, which owns forty per cent of it now, proudly displays the bank's golden logo in its publicity material, together with the front entrance of what might be Samuel Montagu but is really the Midland, a mild deception. A red London bus is passing, and a bronze figure of A Boy with a Goose looks on as if nothing had happened.

Exceptions to the rule survive. Operations at Hambros Bank, still powerful and idiosyncratic among the City's elite, are dominated by the family. Their initials pepper the internal telephone directory, an R.N., an R.A., J.O., J.D., C.E.A. and a C.E., Miss. I once telephoned Miss Hambro. A woman's voice answered. I asked if that was Clare Hambro. The voice said, 'No. I wish it was.' N. M. Rothschild, best known of them all, is still in the hands of the family and run by a Rothschild. To see either Hambros or N. M. Rothschild as dusty and old-fashioned would be misleading. In their different ways, both have chosen to retain traditions and styles in the English manner. Rothschild, like Hambros and all the senior merchant banks, is a member of the Accepting Houses Committee. To be an 'accepting house' is now of little practical import-ance, but the archaic title is still sought after.

All the accepting houses are debating their future. In N. M. Rothschild's case, some of that debate became public property in the 1970s when two of the family, Evelyn and Jacob, quarrelled and parted company. The Honourable Nathaniel Charles Jacob Rothschild, son of Lord Rothschild, left the bank. Evelyn Rothschild remained as chair-man. The day I met him he was smoking the end of a thick cigar from a lunch in the West End. I had been told a few things about him; the Rothschilds have been attracting gossip for two hundred years. One banker said that Evelyn was a patrician to his socks, a man who 'won't know what he's doing the next day. People like that don't *want* to know what they're doing next day.' Oddly enough, when I followed up a letter by telephoning his secretary for an appointment, she said that 'Mr Evelyn' was free to see me any time on Wednesday. 'Any time' is not a phrase often heard from bankers' secretaries, who prefer to say they might 'squeeze you in'.

The bank's building is modern, but occupies the site at New Court, down a lane barely wide enough for a car, that the Rothschilds went to long ago. The past bears down on the visitor. The story of the dynasty is well known: how Mayer Amschel Rothschild, a Jewish merchant in Frankfurt whose family name derived from an ancestor's house-sign, a red shield ('Rot Schild'), prospered in the latter part of the eighteenth century and sent his five sons abroad as merchants and bankers. Nathan Meyer (1777–1836) established himself in the City in time to catch the tide of London's fortune. The French Rothschilds seem to have been richer over the years, or at least more flamboyant, but Nathan Meyer and his descendants happened to be, or had artfully inserted themselves, in the first centre for world finance. Their popular history is about hard men making money with bold gestures. It is standard practice among Rothschilds now, even those of Evelyn's traditional cast, to dismiss the legends as nostalgia, unfitting for a modern bank to care about. But in the same breath they draw comfort from the fact that in the dimmest corners of businessdom, the name 'Rothschild' is respected and carries, still, a spark of magic. The legends, although much exaggerated – like the one about how Rothschilds alone enabled the British Government to buy the Suez Canal, by finding it a few millions – survive at the back of people's minds and create a commercial asset. N. M. Rothschild regards itself as a 'Jewish house', another nod to its past. It does this out of principle, putting up with the inconvenience of being blacklisted and boycotted by the Arabs, and no doubt benefiting as well, as it is entitled to, by being seen to take a stand. The Rothschilds once cancelled a loan they were organising for the Czar because the Russians began a pogrom as the deal was about to go through. In recent times N. M. Rothschild has refused to do business with a country because it was held to be anti-Semitic, a satisfying reversal of blacklists.

Evelyn Rothschild chose a small boardroom to talk in: anonymous ground, perhaps, depersonalised. The view included a greenish cupola and other firms' windows, one of them in a room with a dirty roller

29

towel. The corridors upstairs in the bank were silent after the entrance hall, which bustled with messengers against a background of pictures and busts, like a fine-arts gallery. I mentioned the silence to Rothschild. He looked reproving and said, 'We do a lot of work.' Lean and sunburnt, with gleaming eyes, he seemed years younger than fifty-two, despite the grey hair receding from the temples; but in profile he was older again, the features austere and not so English.

The family row was about size and style, in particular the style that inevitably attaches to a family bank. 'Are businesses more dynamic if you have one or two people who are actually in control?' asked Rothschild. 'If businesses are run by hired hands who feel that they're faceless, does the entrepreneurial spirit go away?' The question seemed to contain its own answer. But he said the firm was evolving all the time. He had opened it up, bringing in non-Rothschilds as managing directors. N. M. Rothschild was the last merchant-banking partnership in London, lasting until 1970. 'It's a pretty frightening thought,' he said, 'to be an unlimited partnership, trading as a bank, with everything down to your socks on the line. If you hire people, and they go off and do something [wrong], the liability is colossal. So first of all we had to change the firm into a corporate entity. What we've tried to do, and I think successfully, is run a private company as if it was a public company, with very strict rules. A lot of abuse has been levelled over the years at people running private fiefdoms and not respecting the degree of decorum there should be in how you pay yourself, in what benefits they get. We run it in a very disciplined manner.' As for non-Rothschilds, 'the top slots are available. Well, maybe not the chairmanship. But I'm not saying that won't happen. The proprietorial side is much less than when I came here. I think one has tried to be egalitarian – awful word. But making people feel they belong.'

There is no shortage of Rothschilds at the bank: the third Lord Rothschild is chairman of the controlling company, Rothschilds Continuation Holdings AG; Leopold is an executive director; also on the board of the bank is Leopold's elder brother, Edmund. All these are cousins of Evelyn Rothschild. Edmund's son Lionel is in the investment department. Eric from the French Rothschilds is on the board. But the four managing directors immediately under Evelyn Rothschild – in charge of banking, corporate finance, investment and overseas operations – are all from outside the family.

A former executive said that traces of resentment were to be found within the firm, 'though not from senior people', about the family and its position. This is a cross that anyone called Rothschild who runs a bank called Rothschild has to bear. Imagine, said the former executive, a deal that carried a fee of £300,000. 'Everyone knows that X per cent, whatever it is, goes straight to the man at the head of the table, Mr Evelyn Rothschild, because he owns the place. Some people find that hard to bear. That is the problem of working in a private bank. What makes it easier to bear is that if, for example, someone had to go into the executive committee next Tuesday and say, "By the way, such-and-such a job is at an end" – which might mean that Evelyn loses X hundred thousand pounds – he'd say, "That's life. You win some, you lose some."'

This is the stuff one expects from Rothschilds no less than from their employees. 'Anyone who joins the bank,' says one of its vice-chairmen, Sir Claus Moser (he used to be the British Government's Statistician), 'knows that control and ownership are firmly in the family hands.' In particular they are in Evelyn Rothschild's hands. Among N. M. Rothschild directors, his 524,000 shares in Rothschilds Continuation Holdings far exceed everyone else's put together. Runner-up is Leopold Rothschild with 133,000. Lord Rothschild has a nominal holding of one share.

The original Rothschilds Continuation was created by Evelyn's father, Anthony, early in World War 2, when the firm was a partnership with only two partners. Were either to be killed, the entity would survive. In the event, Anthony Rothschild ran the bank for years after the war. Counting the founder in Frankfurt, Mayer Amschel, as the first generation, he belonged to the fifth. The bank seemed to have fallen asleep. Old habits persisted. The door to the partners' room was not to be knocked upon. A clerk or assistant who sought entry had to stand by the glass pane and wait until admitted. A regular visitor remembers Anthony Rothschild closing up the room at lunchtime. Before locking the door he drew a curtain over the glass. In poor health for years, he died in 1961. His nephew Edmund succeeded him, first as senior partner, then, when the firm became a limited company, as chairman; change seeped into New Court.

During the 1960s and early 1970s two young men, Rothschild cousins, emerged as candidates for long-term tenure of the bank. Jacob, the son of Lord Rothschild, and a director of the bank from 1963, was an innovator. He had a decent private fortune, but only a modest holding in N. M. Rothschild itself. He made himself a reputation in the City, establishing the firm in the new business of 'Eurobond' issues,

31

enjoying himself with an offspring of the bank, Rothschild Investment Trust. This was publicly owned. Jacob ran it vigorously, moving in and out of stakes in property and industrial companies. People noticed Jacob. They remember him in New York at Morgan Stanley, where he worked briefly, learning the business; they say he had a knack of finding what he needed. The other candidate was Evelyn, also a director. He was the very rich Rothschild. His ideas were more traditional; he saw the past as the bedrock of the bank.

Evelyn belonged to the sixth generation, Jacob to the seventh, but only a few years separated them; the fecund Rothschilds are a genealogist's delight. The conflict that emerged was complicated by the fact that Jacob's father, a distinguished scientist, was chairman of the bank during a brief interregnum in the mid-1970s, and went on to become chairman of Rothschilds Continuation. Thus Lord Rothschild presided over his son's angry and well-publicised departure from the bank to begin a new career in the City. The interregnum, 1975–6, must have been when the bank was marking time before Evelyn was ready to assume control. The decision about Jacob had been taken by 1976. A cautious streak had prevailed. 'Jacob became non-executive when his father became chairman,' says Evelyn. 'He still sat here and things smouldered.' By 1980 Jacob Rothschild had gone, and Rothschild Investment Trust went with him. He rewrote his entry for *Who's Who*, deleting the opening words, 'Director, N. M. Rothschild & Sons Ltd, since 1963', and substituting 'Chairman, RIT Ltd (formerly Rothschild Investment Trust Ltd), since 1971'. This told the world that he was still in finance but had no connection with the bank of that name.

Evelyn Rothschild, who is chairman of the *Economist*, said he thought it wiser to talk about the row than not. 'Families do have problems,' he said. 'It is a chapter which unfortunately is on the record.' He praised Jacob's skills as an investment banker – 'imagination', 'drive', 'initiative', 'a very good financial brain' – drawing attention to his 'opportunistic view of things in trying to pick the place up'. He said 'opportunistic' twice, talking cryptically about a person having to choose how aggressive he should be. It was all history now, he said, but the problem for each generation was how big a firm ought to be. Theories had arisen that merchant banks must amass capital and keep growing to survive. He had disagreed. 'My philosophy,' he said, 'is very simple. We have here an ingredient which is second to none. I'm not being pompous. There are only two great names in banking in the world. One is Morgan. The other is Rothschild. They are the two which have stood the test of time.'

After 1976 Jacob Rothschild built up the investment trust (in which the bank was only one of the shareholders). Eventually bank and trust went their own ways. He found himself at the head of a firm that called itself 'RIT'. In 1982 it merged with another investment trust, Great Northern, to become 'RIT and Northern' – RITN. These lacklustre titles had to be used because the family name became an issue between Evelyn and Jacob. When the articles of association were originally drawn up for the Rothschild Investment Trust, some prudent person inserted a clause that denied it use of the name Rothschild if trust and bank had no directors in common. That situation had come about, so 'Rothschild' was reduced to an initial. However, there was nothing to stop associated companies in the RIT group carrying Jacob's name. He was a Rothschild and entitled to do business as one. The cover of RITN's report to shareholders (1982) had 'RITN' in large letters at the top and 'Management Company: J. Rothschild & Co. Ltd' in small letters at the bottom. J. Rothschild Investment Management Ltd was also associated with the group. Perhaps to emphasise his separate identity, Jacob Rothschild had offices a hundred yards from RITN's headquarters. On legal advice the switchboard operators there were instructed to answer 'J. Rothschild', not 'Rothschild'.

Among RITN's senior directors was the David Montagu who had been chairman of Samuel Montagu, another exile from a family bank. RITN began to take on the outline of a 'financial services' group, buying interests in leasing, life insurance and, significantly, London stockbroking, whose monopoly of securities trading was just beginning to crumble.

A week after meeting Evelyn, I went to see Jacob. His offices, in the West End, were being converted from a couple of houses in a quiet street. Reached via staircases with bits of plaster on them, he sat in an L-shaped room eating a late lunch of sandwiches. He said he hoped I didn't mind and went on eating, looking doubtfully at my tape-recorder, which I didn't switch on. It was hard to think of Evelyn Rothschild discussing the bank through mouthfuls of ham sandwich. Wearing a dark suit, sitting with his back to the light as he unwrapped a bar of chocolate, the Hon. Jacob Rothschild looked older than forty-six. He might have been making a virtue of being a plain man, as perhaps Evelyn Rothschild made a virtue of being patrician. His face was more complicated than Evelyn's, his sentences vaguer, his manner more

33

guarded. He had a subtle air. Someone had called him 'Jake the Trader' to me. That seemed appropriate.

He said RITN was 'not really a merchant bank – you shouldn't be talking to me. We don't directly lend money or take deposits. But we have a range of financial services.' I said something about 'taking RIT with you' when he left the bank. He said, 'That sounds as if I took it away from N. M. Rothschild. I didn't. It was owned by its share-holders, of whom N. M. Rothschild was one. But I suppose it was regarded as my show, for want of a better word.' He came reluctantly to the quarrel, saying that he saw 'formidable difficulties' in a bank being owned and run by a family if it wanted to stay in the first division. He had no doubt about the advantages of being a 'democratic' company with access to outside capital. 'After all,' he said innocently, 'the virtues of democracy over absolute monarchy in the latter half of the twentieth century are generally accepted.'

But within that 'democratic' framework, he seemed to see himself as a figure in an older tradition. Having denied half-heartedly that the firm was 'really' a merchant bank, he kept walking around the question of what merchant bankers were or should be today. He said that perhaps he could be called a merchant banker after all, sounding as if he wanted to be one quite badly. At a cocktail party he had overheard his daughter telling someone that he was 'in insurance'. 'I feel sometimes I have no sense of identity,' he said cheerfully. 'What am I?'

By the time I saw him again, at the end of 1983, he was answering the question. In the middle of that year RITN looked towards Wall Street, paying, in stages, $63 million for a half-share in the investment bank of L. F. Rothschild, Unterberg, Towbin. There was no discernible con-nection between the Louis F. Rothschild who founded his firm, in 1899, to advise friends on investing their private capital, and the European Rothschilds. This didn't stop people making bitchy jokes over City lunch-tables about Jacob doing the L. F. Rothschild deal to annoy Evelyn, a suggestion of course denied by all concerned. Robert Towbin, who had known Jacob for years, says it was he, Towbin, who proposed the arrangement, over dinner in London, as a means of injecting capital into his firm. Jacob Rothschild expressed interest, and the deal stemmed from the conversation – 'there was no grand strategy'. Towbin adds, though, that 'Jacob had this peculiar "name" thing – obviously it could be eventually not "LF" but "Jacob" Rothschild, and all that that signified.' It wouldn't be surprising if the thought crossed Jacob's mind. It probably crossed their minds at New Court, where callers from newspapers were told firmly that Louis Rothschild was no relation. But as it turned out, Jacob Rothschild soon found a way nearer home to write his family name across the scene.

A few months after the L. F. Rothschild agreement, RITN made the most spectacular of the new deals that were breaking out in the City, merging with the Charterhouse group to form a financial conglomerate with capital and reserves of £350 million. This made it comparable in size to a large Wall Street investment bank. Charterhouse had industrial holdings and owned a merchant bank, Charterhouse Japhet, a member of the Accepting Houses Committee. J. Rothschild was back at the heart of the City, a merchant banker again, if he chose to call himself one. In the new City, where the trading and selling of securities is likely to dominate financial markets, two Rothschilds will be at work. I asked Jacob Rothschild if the Accepting Houses Committee mattered any more. 'Well,' he said, 'it's a good franchise to trade off. It's a snobbish world.' He looked less casual than on my first visit; there were no ham sandwiches or bars of chocolate. The building works had been completed. The L-shaped room was panelled in pale wood, lined with books and pictures. On the sofa was a red and black cushion embroidered with the five Rothschild arrows, one for each son. Rothschild said he hadn't wanted to exercise the right to use his name prominently until he was sure it was 'in good hands'. The new firm would be called Charterhouse J. Rothschild, the 'J' carefully retained. 'It is our strategic objective,' he said, 'to become an important international investment bank.' When I left, he showed me to his private lift, which deposited me in a hallway lined with pictures. It wasn't the way I had come in. Voices murmured behind a door. I went out to the street, the door locking behind me, and had to ring the bell at the original front door, to be readmitted by the receptionist and collect my umbrella. A nice defence mechanism.

Upstairs in that discreet isolation, Jacob Rothschild continued to work out his private conviction or obsession. Only size, it seemed, was a guarantee of success at the level where he hoped to operate. No doubt the Rothschilds of the nineteenth century had similar ideas. Their reputation was still in the making; muscle was important; they were the Morgan Stanleys or Merrill Lynchs of the day. Soon 'Mr Jacob' was on the move again. He and Mark Weinberg of the Hambro Life insurance group, whose story is told later in the chapter, became interested in one another. Hambros Bank sold its remaining share of Hambro Life to Charterhouse J. Rothschild, and there was much talk of Hambro Life becoming linked with the investment-banking, financial-services empire that had taken shape around Jacob Rothschild – although it was one thing to talk about these complex deals, and another to make them happen quickly. Still, it showed the temper of Jacob Rothschild's thinking. If he had, indeed, set out to prove something to the world or to his cousins at N. M. Rothschild, he was doing it in style.

At New Court, Evelyn Rothschild presides over a bank of modest size, with its earnings (in the British fashion not all disclosed) of £2.5 million, and share capital and reserves of £70 million. (Hambros, one of the larger accepting houses, had capital and reserves of £110 million in 1983, and disclosed earnings of £9.9 million.) In London the bank is prominent in raising capital and advising companies, in selling off nationalised industries for Conservative governments, in bullion dealing, in managing portfolios of securities, in foreign exchange and currency swapping. It has done one of the new deals, buying a stake in a large Stock Exchange firm. Outside Europe it has operations in Latin America, Africa and the Far East. Hong Kong is a full-scale banking operation. In Singapore the firm is an investment adviser to the Government. The deputy Prime Minister of Singapore, Dr Goh Keng Swee, was once a pupil of Sir Claus Moser when the latter taught at the London School of Economics. Dr Goh remembered his guru, and Rothschild was invited to bid for the contract. In the end it was appointed for strictly commercial reasons. But old friendships help, and bankers make the most of them.

N. M. Rothschild is no longer owned in Britain. The holding company was moved to Switzerland, to become Rothschilds Continuation Holdings AG, in 1982. Ownership of the group, covering its operations around the world, now resides in the obliging canton of Zug. Evelyn Rothschild says the move was designed to 'commercialise our opportunities and bring the family closer together'. There was already a private bank in Zurich, Rothschild AG, run jointly with the French Rothschilds. Anyone who transfers control of a financial operation to Switzerland is liable to have it construed as a safety measure. Perhaps the Rothschilds saw straws in the wind. When France elected François Mitterrand President in 1981, the French Rothschilds were caught in the socialist net and had their bank nationalised. In the City there were intermittent fears that a left-wing British government might be in the offing, until the socialist débâcle in the 1983 election reassured the bankers that all was well for another five years.

Apart from Evelyn and Jacob, the chief 'financial' Rothschilds in Europe are David, in Paris, and Edmond, in Paris and Geneva.

Edmond de Rothschild, who has the honorary title of 'Baron', is a thick-set Frenchman with a heavy moustache, in his late fifties, who inherited a fortune from his father, and operates both as a private banker and an entrepreneur with fingers in many pies, among them communications and leisure. He belongs to the fifth generation, and may be the richest Rothschild in the world. In Geneva, where he spends part of his time, he runs the Banque Privée. This does some commercial business with international companies, and manages investments for wealthy clients. It is not worth the bank's while to handle an individual portfolio worth less than about $200,000. In general neither the clients nor their investments are physically located in Switzerland. 'Some of the clients are very rich,' says Rothschild. 'They give you two or three million dollars to invest. For them it's not the largest part of their fortune. They say, "Try to do whatever you can. I would like you to take some risks and increase the capital." Other people may have only half a million dollars, their sole fortune. They want it managed in a conservative way.' The holding company that controls all Edmond Rothschild's interests is in Geneva, too.

In Paris he has the Compagnie Financière (he also has a bank in Israel and an interest in another in California), behind a sedate façade decorated with wrought ironwork; it is in the same street as the Palace of the Elysée, the official residence of the President, where police with automatic weapons stand around on the pavements as if war had just been declared. A courtyard (with a man on guard) and a reception desk lead to a tiny unattended lift, which ascends to a waiting-room on the top floor, carpeted in blue, furnished with a worn leather sofa and a model of a yacht, the *Gitana VI*. Windows overlook a private garden. Rothschild's office nearby, carpeted in the same blue, is a sitting-room with a desk at one end. Long windows overlook a balcony with boxes containing a handful of white flowers. The day I was there, the winter sun was low enough to be dazzling. Rothschild fiddled with a panel in the wall behind him. He pressed a switch and a hooded awning swung down over the balcony, too far. He pressed again and it went up, too high. Windows opened and closed, not doing what he wanted them to. 'It is my daily exercise,' he said placidly.

In France the nearest thing to a merchant or investment bank is the *banque d'affaires*, its special function to invest in industry and services. This is what Edmond Rothschild has done, though as an individual rather than a banker. The Compagnie Financière does commercial banking for corporate clients, and manages investments, for individuals and in trusts, in the same fashion as the Banque Privée. 'I would define myself, if I had to, as an international financier,' he said, 'trying to keep my place in the western financial establishment, for myself, for my son and for future generations.' He is on good terms with the other banking Rothschilds, and he and Evelyn have interests in one another's firms.

Edmond's cousin, Guy de Rothschild, who is also a Baron, is the best known member of the French family. This is partly because he denounced Mitterrand's Government for nationalising his bank and went to live in New York; partly because he then wrote his memoirs, *Contre Bonne Fortune*, which conjured up the luxurious life-styles of the family and became a bestseller in socialist France. His son, David (sixth generation), has remained in Paris, where he runs a modest finance company, in which the Rothschilds hope their name as bankers will be born again. His desk-top, like Jacob's cushion, is inlaid with the five arrows. The French Rothschilds date from the Napoleonic wars, their former premises in the rue Laffitte from soon after. In the years before it was nationalised, Banque Rothschild went into retail banking, with mixed results, while making its industrial investments through a holding group, the Compagnie de Nord, once a Rothschild railway company. In 1978 the investment group was merged with the bank. Had it been left separate, the banking side would have escaped nationalisation, since the criterion was the size of a bank's deposits. As it was, the Government set a figure small enough to catch the Rothschilds, large enough to allow other private banks, such as Lazard, to escape. 'It is quite known,' says Pierre Haas, a senior figure at Paribas, the largest *banque d'affaires*, which was itself taken over. 'The Government wanted Rothschild, the mythological name. It didn't want Lazard, so it set the line between the two. A typically Gallic way.'

Baron Guy, seventy-two when the bank was nationalised, now spends part of his time with Rothschild Inc. in New York, where he is the non-executive chairman. I saw him there, in a skyscraper at Rockefeller Plaza, a dapper man, not taking himself too seriously. 'I wrote an article in *Le Monde*,' he said, 'to explain that I was fed up. Twice in my lifetime the Rothschilds were the target of the French Government. Under Pétain and the Vichy Government [during the German occupation of France], my father and uncles had their assets seized on untenable grounds. We had to rebuild from scratch after the war. Twice in a lifetime is too much.' The article was reprinted in many countries. 'For Pétain I was a Jew,' wrote Rothschild, 'for Mitterrand I am a pariah.' Two years later he had stopped sounding bitter. 'I decided I was on strike and wouldn't co-operate any more. I thought, I will go to America.' He sounded as if he had had an emigrant ship from Bremen or Liverpool in mind. 'I decided to try and maintain the international credibility of my branch of the family – not to let it be parochialised, and leave only the English Rothschilds with an open window on the world.'

Rothschild was accompanied by a small dog that he said was danger-ous to strangers: not 'could be' but 'was'. He and the dog sat at ease in what looked like somebody else's office, while he opened mail and talked about the slow progress of the Rothschilds in the New World since the first of them reached its shores in 1849. Their agent in New York for much of the nineteenth century was a clever German called August Schönberg who translated his name into French and became 'Belmont', a sort of *homme fatal*. He went there in 1837 and achieved fame and riches through the Rothschild connection. But the first family member to arrive, according to Rothschild, was his grandfather, who was sent over after the revolution of 1848 to avoid military service. 'Not very brave,' said Rothschild, 'but there was no war on, so it didn't matter.' He wrote to say that Belmont was unreliable and the Americans seemed an enterprising nation, and suggested the family open a branch in New York. 'We have no record of the reply,' said Rothschild. 'Presumably they told him to shut up and come home.' Other Rothschilds (like Louis) popped up in New York's high society. Stephen Birmingham in his book *Our Crowd* refers to them as 'the Brooklyn branch'. The real Rothschilds stayed in Europe as far as banking was concerned. It was not until 1940 and the war that actual bankers, the Baron's father and his uncle, went to New York, and then only as a place of refuge. Some assets were transferred from Holland, including a million dollars' worth of gold, and after the war a modest firm called New Court Securities was founded, with French and British Rothschilds as equal partners. The title suggested the family, without using its name. The Baron said it would have been unthinkable to call it 'Rothschild' when they merely owned it from three thousand miles away. By the end of the 1970s it was a busy firm, but not run to the family's taste. They began to interfere, brought in a Wall Street lawyer, Robert Pirie, as chief executive, and changed the name to Rothschild Inc. It was coincidental that Banque Rothschild was nationalised soon after. 'I hadn't thought of changing my life,' said Baron Guy. Another French Rothschild, Nathaniel, arrived not long after as a director.

In Paris the new proprietors of Banque Rothschild tried to have the best of both worlds, claiming that although it had been nationalised, everything except the name was unchanged at 21 rue Laffitte. An international advertisement said: 'L'EUROPEENNE DE BANQUE: A NEW NAME FOR BANQUE ROTHSCHILD. L'EUROPEENNE DE BAN-QUE: BANKING EXPERTISE SINCE 1817.' Piling insult on injury, the text declared that 'Banque Rothschild will from now on be known as l'Européenne de Banque. But it is only the name that has changed. The staff is the same, and so is the banking expertise that dates back to 1817.' 'L'Européenne de Banque' was a name the Rothschilds used for a subsidiary, and they had agreed the Government could have it. Resenting the way it was being exploited, they hit back, though feebly, with full pages that displayed the famous arrows, a headline that read like an unfinished sentence, 'THE FRENCH ROTHSCHILD'S [*sic*] FINANCIAL TRADITION AND EXPERTISE SINCE 1817', and a list of services still offered: 'Money management. International advisory services. Corporate finance.' These services continued to be legally available from the family's new non-banking entity, Paris-Orleans, whose name, however, didn't appear in the advertisement, thus muddling the reader still more.

Had they been able to get away with it, the French Government managers would probably have gone on calling the nationalised firm 'Banque Rothschild'. But the family had been ready to sue. Once again the name was sacred, arousing the Baron in Paris as it was arousing cousin Evelyn in London at about the same time. 'We negotiated with the Government to remove the name without a legal fight,' said Rothschild. '*A l'amiable*, as we say. Otherwise the English and the other Rothschilds would all have helped us. We were told the Bank of England would give us their support. It's a family name. The name can't be squandered as long as the family exists. You could say it is against the rights of man.'

The dog was eyeing me, and my hour was up. Rothschild said unsmilingly, 'He mightn't let you leave.' He, dog and I now occupied the three points of a triangle. 'He sits very quiet,' said Rothschild. 'And then, when someone leaves, he tries to kill that person.'

The eyes followed me. But nothing happened.

*   *   *

The Hambros don't have banking cousins in other countries. There is an important branch of the family in Scandinavia, but it produces professors and lawyers. Hambros Bank has a very English air. It is not exactly unpretentious, but it is inclined to mock the pretensions, though without quite giving them up. If merchant banks were tourist attractions, like Stratford-on-Avon and the Tower of London, visitors in search of local colour would flock to Hambros and feel they were getting value for money.

A potted history has the usual ingredients, immigrants making good and becoming more English than the English. The family reached London from northern Germany via Denmark. 'Hambro' should have been 'Hamburg', when a Jewish immigrant to Copenhagen used the city he had left as a surname. Someone's handwriting or speech modified the word, and the family tree began with a C. J. Hambro, granted a work permit in 1779. He traded in clothes, later in wools and silks. The Hambros progressed to banking. A grandson had started a bank in London by 1839. By the 1880s the Everard Hambro who would reign over it until 1925 was already in place, his personal income £150,000 a year; the figure is in the official history, so large in today's terms that it is almost incalculable, £5 million, £10 million, free of tax – it hardly matters.

As a family they like the countryside and gentlemen's pursuits. Some of them own racehorses. They shoot with others of their class and affluence. Jocelyn Hambro, now in semi-retirement from the bank and its holding company, Hambros PLC, told me how three Hambros, all chairmen of the bank, had died in quick succession early in the 1960s – Olaf in 1961, then Olaf's nephew Sir Charles, then Charles's second-cousin Jack. 'Charles died in 1963 so Jack took over,' he said. 'Two years later Jack was shooting with Kim Cobbold, who used to be Governor of the Bank of England, in December. He shot a very high pheasant and had a heart attack on the spot.' Olaf's son Jocelyn became chairman, the sixth. A tank commander in World War 2, he had won the Military Cross in Normandy, and shortly afterwards had been wounded and lost a leg. This happened on 12 August, when grouse-shooting starts in Britain. Major Hambro is reported to have said, 'What a day to be shot!' Forty years later he was spending short weeks in the City and long weekends a hundred miles away, 'looking', as he put it, 'over a gate in Gloucestershire at a horse's arse'. In 1983 his eldest son Rupert became eighth chairman of the bank, succeeding another Charles, a second-cousin (as at N. M. Rothschild, you need a family tree to keep track), at the age of forty. Charles in turn became chairman of the holding company, succeeding Jocelyn. Rupert was the youngest Hambro to head the bank since his great-grandfather, Everard. He wanted to get Hambros moving again. I happened to be in the same room at the bank when a visiting business associate suggested they go shooting the following Monday. Rupert Hambro gave him a sharp look and said, 'I only shoot on Saturdays. Mondays to Fridays I work at the bank.'

Hambros does all the bread-and-butter things that merchant banks do, lending money, raising capital, advising companies and managing investments for clients. It has subsidiaries in the Far East and the United States. One of its specialties has been investing its own money in companies, like a small-scale *banque d'affaires*. Merchant banks have always done a certain amount of this. In Wall Street the idea of risk investment in carefully chosen companies and individuals has begun to appeal to investment bankers. It is a good hedge against inflation, and, when successful, makes the investor feel he is behaving as capitalists should. Americans, being more positive, call it 'venture capital'. Hambros, more than most in the City, has gone in for long shots. The result is a bizarre portfolio that now and then can be satisfyingly profitable.

Bespak, a company making specialised valves for aerosol sprays, began in a small way years ago, borrowing £40,000 from Hambros. A condition of the loan was that when it was repaid, the bank would have the right to buy a third of the shares in the private company. It did this in 1967, paying rather less than £20,000. Time passed and the company prospered. Hambros owned thirty per cent of it. One morning in 1982, the bank held a press conference to publicise the fact that Bespak was being launched as a public company on the Unlisted Securities Market. Hambros was selling shares that represented just under half its holding to investors. Some directors of Bespak and their families, who owned the remainder of the company, were selling a smaller slice of their interest. Five directors, one stockbroker, one Hambros man and nine City journalists gathered in the boardroom at the bank. Most of the journalists carried drinks handed out in an ante-room. 'G and T please, not much G,' said a woman with a thin nose. The shares, 2,750,000 of them, were being 'placed' via a firm of stockbrokers, which had already done the deal with the buyers. The journalists were just there to give Bespak a good send-off on its public life. Before they arrived, the others had been having a rehearsal behind closed doors, equipped with a list of questions they might be asked. 'Do you suffer from cyclical trading?' was one. Another began, 'Your growth is largely attributable to increased sales of two products. . . .' They were only precautions; no one was out to savage them. The Bespak directors sat along one side of the table, under an oil painting of a castle. The managing director still owned twenty-one per cent of the company after selling half a million of his own shares for a third of a million pounds. He looked happy. He produced products containing the firm's valves from a cardboard box. There was a famous cologne spray and a famous bronchodilator. Bespak was the market leader in valves for cologne sprays. 'We do a self-defence device,' he said, groping in the box. 'All it is is a can with gas inside and a perfume valve. It gives a whistle. It comes in useful for young ladies who are being chased by journalists.' It shrieked as he pressed it. Two lady journalists gave a dutiful jump. Next morning the financial columns reported more or less favourably. The placing price was seventy-five pence a share. If Bespak was pleased, so was the bank. Hambros had sold shares worth more than £1,100,000, and retained a holding of nearly £1,300,000. Its investment of under £20,000 had increased nearly a hundred-fold. (Nine months later, when Bespak obtained a full Stock Exchange quotation, the shares were worth more than four times as much again, and Hambros had cashed in most of its holding.)

Bespaks don't happen every day of the week. Peter Hill-Wood, one of seven departmental directors who work together in the 'Front Room', ran through some of the long shots. Hill-Wood has Hambro blood via his mother, whose maternal grandfather was Everard. The company that owns most of the long shots is called Merchandise and Investment Trust. Technically it is separate from the bank, both bank and MIT being owned (as are other entities within the group) by Hambros PLC: a public company, 49.98 per cent of whose votes are controlled by the Hambro Trust (there would be tax disadvantages in controlling more), which in turn is controlled by some of the Hambros directors, their families and family trusts. This concentrates the voting power in safe hands.

Hill-Wood said that venture capital was a dangerous business, and the bank's enthusiasm for it rose or fell, depending how well companies were doing. He produced a book with floppy covers. Here was a company that dealt in horticultural seeds, here was one trying to develop a gold mine in South Africa. He shook his head over another page. 'Here,' he said, 'is one that will probably fall flat on its face.' He came to Dolphin Cable, already extinct. 'It was set up to rescue submarine cables in the North Sea,' he said. 'You take out the steel, the copper and the gutta percha. Unfortunately it didn't work.' There were investments in several publishers, one of them in Milwaukee, on the principle that 'we're more inclined to understand books than things like gas turbines, which is probably wrong'; in a company making a heart machine; in a communications business that was in a bad way; in a cigar-importing firm that was waiting for the day when Havana cigars would once more be imported into the United States; in an everlasting electric lightbulb. *An everlasting lightbulb?* I said that my father, who was an electrical engineer, used to talk about the perpetual filament that had been invented long ago, but suppressed by vested interests. 'He may have been right,' said Hill-Wood. 'I believe people have been leaned on. I don't quite know how this one is supposed to work.' As a rule, he said, they heard about opportunities for risk investment through people they knew. They had tried advertising in the *Financial Times*, but 'we got a lot of letters of the *Dear Sir, I've had a wonderful idea* variety. It was all rubbish'. There was a company owning vineyards that didn't seem to produce much money, and a company he knew absolutely nothing about because it was run by a cousin of another Hambros director. Towplan Securities owned the bank's apartment in Wilton Place. Another South African company owned platinum mining rights; there seemed to be some platinum, but it was a long way down. Qatar Fertilizer, on the other hand, had been an instant success. It made urea out of natural gas that had been burning away into the Middle Eastern sky until Hambros suggested they build a plant. The bank raised the money and took ten per cent of the shares for itself. 'All you do,' said Hill-Wood, 'is pipe the gas in, treat it in some way, and out comes the stuff in a bag at the other end.' He added that you then threw it on a field and it made the corn grow, or something. He might have been telling a fairy story about the Pirate Coast of Arabia, where air was turned into money. But that was only his style. MIT had just sold its shareholding to the Government of Qatar at a large profit. He hoped all this gave me an idea of the range. The list of investments went on and on. Hambros had bought a three-quarter share of an advertising agency in 1979 for less than half a million pounds, and sold it back to the agency four years later for nearly two million. 'Basically we'll sell anything,' said Hill-Wood as I was going. 'It's our nature.'

Some of the big investments are more permanent, like diamond broking and merchanting; there are close Hambro connections, personal and commercial, with De Beers Consolidated Mines and the diamond cartel. The best investment the bank ever made was in a company called Hambro Life. This has been worth nearly £200 million, at a time when Hambros suffered alarming losses through its involvement with the moribund tanker fleet of a Norwegian tycoon, now dead, called Hilmar Reksten. No other merchant bank has had a Reksten in recent years; but none has had a Hambro Life, either. In the popular version, a man went to the bank at 41 Bishopsgate and asked for a million pounds to start an insurance company. He was promised it within half an hour, and never looked back. What happened is more complicated, twisting in and out of City offices, one association sprouting another: as if, in the end, everyone in finance was linked to everyone else by a golden chain.

The man who wanted the million (in 1970) was Mark Weinberg, a young South African, who had begun to offer life insurance in Britain in 1962. Life insurance can be very profitable, but is not an easy commodity to sell, an expensive reminder of the grave. Weinberg had started his own company, Abbey Life – its name chosen to suggest solidity – with £60,000, most of it borrowed from friends. He made fashionable (though he didn't invent) the concept of life insurance linked to stock market or other investments whose value, when the policy matures, dictates the size of the bonus. At first the firm grew slowly. To raise capital he sold it in 1964 to two American firms, Georgia International Life and International Telephone and Telegraph, half each. Weinberg stayed on with his salesmen to run the firm. A proud as well as a resourceful man, he decided it was time to give Abbey some standing in the City, where the idea of 'selling' had not yet caught on (it has still not caught on entirely), and people were inclined to smirk at the stock figure of the life-insurance salesman with his foot in the door. All he wanted was for a merchant bank to put a director on the board and endorse Abbey Life by his presence. But he knew no merchant banks. S. G. Warburg had acted for ITT, but now said No, fearing a conflict of interest because of its connection with another insurance group. ITT had a connection with the Rothschilds through Paris, but N. M. Rothschild didn't seem interested (Evelyn Rothschild says it was 'our mistake not to have been quicker on the draw'). A stockbroker introduced Weinberg to Hambros. He met Jocelyn, not long chairman, and Charles. They agreed to nominate a director, but saw to it that he wasn't a Hambro: although the literature could say 'Representing Hambros Bank', people would see that the family had withheld one of its own members.

This, however, was the important contact. Weinberg noticed an absence of the 'stiffness and bureaucracy' that he had come to expect from City elders. His new concept was to link insurance policies with investment in unit trusts. At that first meeting in the Front Room, where the brass desk-lamps with green shades are on for most of the day, he couldn't decide whether Jocelyn and Charles were as knowledgeable about the novel business of unit-linked assurance as they appeared. One minute Jocelyn would make a throwaway remark about having been on the board of Phoenix Assurance for years, but still being in the dark about insurance. The next, he would say something that suggested he was quite at home with it. Weinberg didn't know whether this was bluff or double-bluff. 'To this day,' he says, 'I'm not sure if their incisive statements were shots in the dark.' He liked their style. Unlike banks that demanded a series of meetings and much paperwork, Hambros proceeded by intuition – 'Their style was very much, *That sounds interesting, Charles, what do you feel, we've got nothing to lose,* sort of thing, and that was it.' Hambros took to Weinberg, who is lean and composed, with an intellectual edge to his manner. In his early days he wrote a textbook called *Takeovers and Mergers.* Its fourth edition remains in print, very expensive.

Abbey Life prospered as Weinberg's salesmen took business from under the noses of their slower competitors. The price the Americans had paid for the company, £110,000, already seemed cheap. Each of the owners, ITT and Georgia, was anxious to buy out the other. Weinberg says they bickered for years. Hambros, aware of the profitable door it had its toe in, agreed to finance the deal if Georgia won. But in 1970 ITT bought out Georgia at a cost of nearly £16 million. Weinberg, having seen his company make so much for others, washed his hands of Abbey Life. Most of his senior colleagues went with him. He started all over again.

It was now that Weinberg went to Hambros and asked for a million. His account over the years is consistent: 'I walked into Jocelyn Hambro's office, and literally as I walked in, he said, "How much money do you want to start our insurance company?"' He observes now that it was 'a pretty good deal' for Hambros, who would have spent far more in financing the buy-out of ITT. It would have been a pretty good deal for anyone, and as soon as it was known that Weinberg was pulling out of Abbey Life, he was propositioned by several merchant banks. They had changed their minds about the newcomer. But he stuck to his friends at Hambros. For their million, they were told that Weinberg, besides wanting a stake in the equity for himself and others, insisted that the management be independent and that the company be allowed to go public as soon as possible. These conditions were met. So was Weinberg's insistence that the company should be called Hambro Life. 'They thought they could soften the name by calling it "Allied Hambro", but I fought very hard,' says Weinberg. Some of the Hambro board, though not the Hambros themselves, were less than keen. The matter came to a head at a bank lunch for Weinberg and his aides. 'Jocelyn,' he says, 'had this habit of not subtly preparing. He'd rush into a thing and horrify his colleagues. He announced, quite simply, that their name was behind the company, and if things went wrong they would have to take responsibility. So the sensible thing was to give it the best possible chance of things going right, and lend it the name of Hambro. Not fiddle around with Allied.' Those of the board who had been saying that Hambros (like every merchant bank) was a wholesale operation, that it was unwise to let its sacred name be dragged into retail services, found it difficult to argue in front of Weinberg and his team. Hambro Life was launched in the spring of 1971, and did all that was expected of it.

Thus Hambros, perhaps without fully realising it, became an early subscriber to what was taking shape across the Atlantic, an industry of financial-service supermarkets, breaking out of the old categories. But it remained an onlooker in someone else's revolution. The bank took a handsome income from its holding, like a landlord taking a rent. Hambro Life grew, went public and developed a life of its own, with Weinberg moving towards other mass-market financial services, banking among them. When Hambro Life became a public company, the bank owned sixty per cent of the shares. Over the years it sold slices of Hambro Life when it needed cash. By the beginning of 1984 it owned only 24.8 per cent. Soon after that it owned nothing at all. Jacob Rothschild's ambitions coincided with Weinberg's, and Charterhouse J. Rothschild acquired Hambros' remaining interest in Hambro Life, paying £126 million and looking ahead to co-operation between the two. On its original investment of £1 million, Hambros had received in all a return of £195 million.

I first visited the bank in 1959, when I was writing a book about the City. Hambros was embarking on a profitable decade. Margins in bank-lending were as yet unclipped by competition; new lines were opening up; lending to corporate clients for longish periods, years instead of months, was a business that many of the merchant banks plunged into, going where the clearing banks feared to tread. A professional publicist told me what an amusing crowd they were at Hambros, but it was not until long afterwards that I realised why the bank had become public-relations-minded. It had recently been on the losing side in a takeover battle for British Aluminium, defending it (with Lazard) against a joint bid by the American Reynolds Metals and the British

47

Tube Investments. Siegmund Warburg, still regarded as an upstart in the City, advised the predators. His aggressive buying of British Aluminium stock in the market helped it to win; so did the way he used the press to publicise his clients' case to shareholders. When it was over, Olaf Hambro decided that the time to court Fleet Street had come, and the bank appointed a publicist. He was the one who dropped its name into our conversation. (After the Aluminium War, Olaf Hambro and Siegmund Warburg were estranged for a while. Then Warburg, aged fifty-six to Hambro's seventy-four, went round to make his peace. They embraced in the Front Room. 'Siegmund,' said Olaf, 'haven't we been awful fools?')

In 1959 Hambros talked much about the 'flexibility' of which merchant banks were proud. They had plenty of scope for it in the next ten or fifteen years. 'There was a more relaxed attitude to lending in the sixties,' says James Hambro – now a director, but still at school in 1959. 'People didn't lose money. Very lucrative business. We expanded vastly into Eurodollars. We were coining it in those days.'

Perhaps being too relaxed is a bankers' disease. The big commercial banks were to be relaxed about their lending in Latin America; they were coining it too. Hambros came to grief over Hilmar Reksten's oil tankers. Reksten, an autocrat with a touch of the pirate, was a friend of the Hambro family. Loans to finance a fleet of tankers he was building went sour in the mid-1970s, when the oil market collapsed. Hambros' losses were compounded by the fact that Reksten, later bankrupt, was suspected of illegally salting away a fortune in overseas havens. The bank emerged with its reputation intact. But one way and another, the affair had cost it more than £70 million by 1984.

Hilmar Reksten had not been the best of entrepreneurs to back. He was a wartime friend of Sir Charles Hambro, later fourth chairman of the bank, who interrupted his career to serve in the Special Operations Executive. Reksten, an ambitious shipowner who had brought some of his vessels to Britain, was recruited into cloak-and-dagger work. The relationship created under those conditions haunted the bank later. Reksten was an adventurer, charming and bullying in turn, who came to see himself as a Scandinavian hero with a mission to build a maritime empire. A British businessman, Sir Alexander Glen, who also served with the cloak-and-dagger brigade and was a friend of Reksten until he died in 1980, thinks him 'the incarnation of an eighth-century pirate', who 'forged golden spectacles for Sir Charles to see him with'. Hambros, with its strong Scandinavian connections, was a natural banker for

Reksten as he developed his complicated group of companies after the war. By the time Sir Charles Hambro died in 1963, the connection had been woven into the bank's thinking. The ships that caused most of the trouble were a dozen or so large tankers, built for the Reksten fleet after 1969. Hambros made loans to finance most of them, secured against mortgages. With the mid-seventies oil crisis, the end of cheap fuel and the start of world recession, tankers were the worst kind of ship to own. Their value fell sharply. In any case, Hambros was involved in rescue attempts with the Norwegian Government to try to save Reksten, and didn't foreclose on mortgages as it might have done. In retrospect its loans left it dangerously exposed.

At the same time, the authorities in Norway already suspected that Reksten was guilty of exchange-control and income-tax fraud. He was convicted only once, at Bergen, in 1979, when he was eighty-two years old and dying of cancer. The court found that he had failed to declare a profit of 13 million Kroner (about $1.7 million) on the sale of a tanker. The original charges had accused him of evading tax on $55 million. People gave him flowers in the street afterwards. He was a folk hero. To Hambros he became a trial. For several years, income from Hambro Life was used to pay the dividend to Hambros PLC's shareholders. 'Those bloody ships' came to be hated around the offices. Every so often one of the ageing hulls laid up in a Norwegian fjord would be towed away to a breakers' yard in Korea or Taiwan, to fetch a few million dollars against the ten or fifteen million that Hambros had lent to build it in the first place. Besides its financial loss, the bank found itself accused in Norway of condoning Reksten's alleged wrongdoings, on the grounds that it must have known what was going on with the string of companies through which he manipulated his affairs, and which Hambros had helped set up. Hambros insisted that it never had evidence that Reksten was the 'beneficial owner' of the companies, and that it had behaved with propriety. An official commission of inquiry was set up in Norway. Hambros told it that 'the bank does not and did not know whether Mr Hilmar Reksten owned a foreign fortune. If he did, that fortune was not and is not under the control of the bank.' When the Commission reported at the end of 1982, Hambros, along with various other parties, was exonerated. This didn't stop lawyers from continuing to pursue Reksten assets, or politicians from complaining that things were far from over.

The bank hoped it had heard the last of the affair. By 1984 the talk was of 'controls' and 'safety nets' and 'sieves' to ensure that nothing like

Reksten ever happened again. One still heard that favourite remark of merchant bankers of the old school, that by having them work in the same big room, instant communication is guaranteed. This is the partnership principle. 'The idea,' said Jocelyn Hambro, 'is that you can put your hand over the phone and shout, "Do you know anything about Jones?" And if a chap shouts, "Christ, I know all about him!", you say, "I'll ring you back."' But since the senior directors had been sitting in the Front Room since time immemorial, the system was hardly relevant to what happened over Reksten. 'Reksten concentrated the mind,' says Charles Hambro. When Mark Weinberg was praising the family for their style, with its absence of 'stiffness and bureaucracy', he added, 'I think it's fair comment that *that* must have been the way they got into the Reksten affair.'

Hambros thus found itself hoping to retain a tradition, while cultivating the methods taught in business schools. Phrases like 'management by objective' were heard around the old place. Rupert Hambro, the new chairman, said the Reksten affair had been destructive, and the bank had stagnated while others pulled ahead. 'The answer is,' he said, 'we've not been managed, and we've been bad at communication. Trying to run a business in the old partnership form in the 1980s is out of date. We put too much money into too few things.' Oil and gas investments in the United States ran into trouble and produced more losses.

James, who is Rupert's youngest brother (in between them comes a third brother, Richard, also a director), said, 'Had we employed our present systems with Mr Reksten, we probably wouldn't have lent him as much as we did. But if one becomes philosophical, we *are* a family business. The family are running it, make or break. At Kleinwort and Schroder, the name on the door is no longer the person sitting behind the chief executive's desk. But that's still the case here. Whether it's right or wrong is another matter. Over the years we've made a number of mistakes. Before the First World War, one of my ancestors tried to extract oil from coal, and nearly bust the organisation as a result. I think more than any other merchant bank, our philosophy is to back entrepreneurs. We've had failures, we've had successes. Hambro Life is a success. Reksten is a failure. In the long run, one probably balances the other.'

This civilised approach, so unAmerican, so unJapanese for that matter, is only one of many threads in a complex embroidery. A new dealing room, opened in 1982, was briefly the most modern in Europe (the title passes as fast as banks open dealing rooms). Above, attendants in dark clothes still glide along the corridors like butlers, speaking in low voices. A men's hairdresser still visits the bank, Wednesdays and Thursdays, to give subsidised haircuts. Rooms have sliding peepholes, worked from the outside. The washroom opposite the Front Room has the deep basins of some Hotel Splendide, polished pipework and piles of clean, rough towels that actually dry the hands, unlike thin cloths or air from nozzles.

But sterner times have come. A director points to a wastepaper basket, not far from the Front Room, and remarks that the space it occupies is costed at £70 a year. Is that a joke? No, the premises are valued piecemeal. Mundane areas without mahogany and the brass lamps come cheaper (and the computer and clerks are out in Essex). So the posh quarter, where a clock chimes and a visitor hears laughter coming from the Front Room, works out at £70 per square foot per year, the size of a wastepaper basket. 'To think,' says Rupert Hambro, 'that a ship cost thirty-five million dollars to build, would cost eighty million to replace, and its scrap value is two or three million – that's pretty dramatic.' He is not too disheartened. A deal with a London stockbroker (Strauss Turnbull), and a further link between both and a French commercial bank (the state-owned Société Générale) to form an international securities business, raised morale in 1984. The family was staking its claim to a piece of the new markets. Rupert Hambro produces a complicated English-style analogy between a bank and a football team, something about all kicking in the same direction. 'Every dog has his day,' he says.

3
WORLD LANDSCAPE WITH FIGURES

Global markets — What the tombstones are saying — Arab customs —
Swiss role — Brokers to the rich — Rivals of East and West — Passing the book —
Early birds — Mitsubishi's bonds — Morgan Guaranty's conjuring trick —
A little leak — Noughts for your comfort

Investment bankers have a keen sense of the money they can make by operating across the world in 'global markets'. In this they are like the multinationals of industry. The advantage for the investment banker is that his presence can be established, if not cheaply, at least on a modest scale, merely by opening an office and equipping it with telephones and data screens. There may be political objections; Japan can be particularly difficult. Otherwise the banker who satisfies local regulations is in business. Communication is becoming so good, in any case, that a deal being done in one country can be monitored from another. Few investment bankers would see this as a reason for not meeting people in the flesh as often as possible. But it makes life easier when computer graphics or the contents of research analyses can be hurled from a terminal in New York to a terminal in Tokyo within seconds.

The outsider doesn't quite grasp the scale of progress. Someone was talking to me in New York about the 'teleport' then being built on Staten Island, across the bay from Manhattan, where dishes send and receive signals via satellite. Wall Street will be its biggest user, paying a fortune for the privilege. 'The user gets speed like never before,' said my informant. I said I had just come from an office where they could call branches in Europe or Asia via a special circuit by punching three digits on a telephone. That seemed quick to me. She shook her head. 'That's not *speed*,' she said, 'that's a direct connection. Speed is the ability to have a computer in New York talk to a computer somewhere else at the speed of a computer. The teleport is for computers to talk to computers, or for video conferencing – big, big pieces of communication.'

The 'global market-place' for financial services, of which one is constantly told, would be impossible without good communications backed by efficient air travel. As a market-place, it still has a long way to go. It is a concept that appeals to financial giants, smacking their lips at the thought of selling the same products and services in dozens of countries at once; exactly what it means in practice is less clear.

One way to see one face of it in action is through the advertising that appears in financial newspapers, or in the financial sections of the press in general. These are well upholstered with advertisements, a joy to newspaper managements, who add financial pages whenever they can. Banks want to show themselves to the world, and have no hesitation in buying a full page in the *Wall Street Journal* for $60,000 or in the London *Financial Times* for a bargain £16,500. Sometimes they merely announce their presence, a dignified trumpet to say they are there. Often the firm's name is connected with a specific piece of business. This is a favourite with investment banks. The 'tombstone' advertisement commemorates an issue of shares or bonds. It may be a purely domestic occasion, or it may be a deal in the Euromarket, outside any one national jurisdiction, and firmly in the 'global market-place' category. Tombstones, domestic or international, invariably add, in small type, that 'All these securities having been sold, this announcement appears as a matter of record only.' The tombstone is a technicality; the real reason it appears is that if a bank or broker doesn't see its name in print it feels neglected. An important tombstone may give a tiny mention to more than a hundred banks and brokerage houses, with a dozen countries represented. Most investment banks think this desirable. 'Chairmen like it,' says James Hambro. 'It gives them a nice warm feeling when they open a newspaper.' Vulgar squabbles break out if banks feel they have been deprived of their rightful place in the complicated 'brackets' into which a tombstone may be broken down. Top left, where the lead manager sits, is the prime position. The firms at the bottom are there more as a gesture. They will not have underwritten many of the bonds, but who knows when they may be needed, or when they may be in a position of power themselves?

The important thing is that they *want* to be there. A banker is judged by the company he keeps. A Eurobond tombstone, he hopes, will air his name in many countries. A few firms still think this is not the way that gentlemen behave; should they be part of a syndicate, they remain anonymous. Brown Brothers Harriman & Co. of New York, an idiosyncratic partnership that for historical reasons manages to be both a commercial bank and a brokerage house, will not go near a tombstone. It has one advertisement which appears once a year, a meagre statement of its financial condition, accompanied by a tiny worn-out drawing of a man clutching what looks like a candle to light him to bed; it turns out to be a quill pen. Lazard Brothers, the London merchant bank, is another stranger to tombstones, though it will make an exception if a client begs it to. Non-appearance has a sly commercial value of its own. But for most investment banks, the question doesn't arise. Expensive monthly magazines for the trade like *Institutional Investor* and *Euromoney*, weighing several pounds between them, carry up to forty pages each of nothing but tombstones. Financial advertising in itself is nothing new. But there is more of it now, aggressively displayed for an international audience. The ads catch the glamour of bigness and newness. There are more participants, with more money to play with, willing to go to greater lengths to beat their opponents.

Potentially there is a global application for every financial service ever invented. Since raising capital for clients is the traditional activity of investment banks at home, the same is true of them abroad: thus the Eurobond tombstones, as borrowers tap the dollars and other currencies that float around the world, owned outside the countries where they originated. But the investment banker's related business, of trading and selling securities that have already been issued, is even more important. It is how the large American and Japanese investment banks make most of their money inside their own countries. If there is going to be a global market-place, the logical next step is to sell securities to investors everywhere. The Americans offer IBM and Texaco and US Treasury bonds; they may also offer shares in unknown electronics companies in California, but investors far away in other continents need strong nerves or faith in the salesman before they are likely to buy. There is much debate about how quickly this cross-country traffic in securities will develop. In theory there is no limit. Once local regulations are complied with, attractive securities issued in any country can find investors in any other, as long as there is no exchange control to stop people sending their money abroad (as there was in the United Kingdom until 1979). But outside the ranks of professionals, the idea takes some getting used to.

The Americans have been best at selling their securities to investors of other nations. Merrill Lynch, the largest US investment bank, with extensive retail business, has more branches in more countries than anyone else. In Hong Kong, its Z. T. Wong reports happily that rich Chinese there and in neighbouring countries are jolly good customers. 'Merrill Lynch very sound, never go bankrupt,' he says, beaming. In Tokyo, Milton C. Beard Jr said they did a brisk trade selling US shares to Japanese institutions. I asked why it was that the leading Japanese securities firm, Nomura, had been a member of the New York Stock Exchange since 1981, but Merrill Lynch couldn't be a member of Tokyo's. He said that in theory it could, but the fee would probably be five million dollars, and (apart from the cost) 'you have to ask yourself, what does this do to your relationships with the Japanese securities companies?'

New York's Salomon Brothers, which is not a retail firm, but was anxious to have a branch in Tokyo, spent two years obtaining a licence from the Japanese Ministry of Finance, a citadel packed with bureaucrats of which Kafka-esque tales are told. The mistake was to be a little presumptuous and to assume that when Salomon decided to move its Asian branch from Hong Kong to Japan, the Ministry would be only too pleased. The firm found itself with a mere 'representative office', able to channel business but not initiate it. Some confident remarks to the press had not been well received; nor had the fact that Salomon was thought to have overreached itself by acquiring eight thousand square feet of space. A period of humility, from 1980 to 1982, was necessary before branch status was granted.

Everywhere investment banks probe the hosts' defences discreetly. In London, where the City is receptive to most overseas firms as long as they are respectable, hungry newcomers have been biding their time, waiting for the day when the Stock Exchange is reformed, and they too can be local stockbrokers, dealing in British shares. Foreigners who in private have derided the London Exchange for living in the past have kept quiet in public, anxious not to offend. In any case, the situation suited them in one way. The same outmoded circumstances that kept Americans out of the Stock Exchange kept British stockbrokers out of new international business. There are some exceptions, but until recently they were not significant.

'You're sitting in an unregulated part of the City right now,' I was told at a US investment bank in 1983 (it was not Merrill Lynch). 'In a London stockbroker's office you would be in a very regulated part of the City. They spent a hundred and fifty years building up rules, with huge walls to keep invaders out. But they got caught by the same rules. At first they couldn't go out and compete with foreign houses coming into the UK to develop the Eurobond business. They can now, but they're vastly undercapitalised beside Wall Street.' This was said by a former London broker who had joined the Americans. Since he talked to me, the changes have begun, with mergers designed to produce stronger City groupings. But the invading firms, based on domestic economies larger and wealthier than Britain's – the American, the Japanese – have sent a chill down City spines.

Finding new sources of money and cultivating old ones is the investment bankers' single most important task. Finding it outside their own national territory is the best game of all. It is why Hambros sends a roving director off to the Gulf, and Salomon Brothers in New York pays court to central banks in Asia. Oil money, gushing from the Middle East, tends to be channelled into investments by the governments of the countries themselves, because the local banking system is not yet highly developed. And there is no private ownership of oil: it all belongs to the state. A visiting banker without the right credentials may sweat for days in an hotel on the edge of the desert, waiting for a message from the Kuwait Investment Office that never comes. The contacts that matter are personal rather than corporate. The 'private banker' who brings with him the close, discreet atmosphere of a banking house in a cobbled street with a brass plate on the wall has had an advantage in the past over wealthier but brasher competitors, and perhaps still has. This has helped some London merchant banks, modest in size but rich in subtlety, to gain the confidence of Arabs with money or access to it. Baring Brothers of London has important connections, never admitted to or discussed, with the Saudi Arabian Monetary Agency. Founded in 1763, and so the oldest merchant bank of all, Barings has English roots; it is not a bank started by immigrants, like most of its kind. The fact is irrelevant in a British context, but one reason Barings originally appealed to the Arabs may well have been that nothing could be further in origin from a 'Jewish house'.

Arabs still like the British, anyway, even if they feel a bit sorry for them at times. Wealthy Arabs, so a Lebanese investment banker who knows about these things explained, enjoy the niceties of trading, the distinction between the 'yes' that means yes and the 'yes' that doesn't; they like secrecy for its own sake. To enter a building and be received by half a dozen people makes them uneasy. One is better, as long as they trust him. It is the James Bond end of investment banking. Such customers, said the Lebanese, were demanding. If they were able to talk in the same breath about money, ships, trade, industry – the

56

Renaissance men of finance – they expected their advisers to be equally catholic. The banker who hoped to handle Arab money should remember that it was not always money that the client wanted to discuss. It might be nothing, a social call, a polite appraisal. They believed in people, not institutions. 'A client,' he said, 'wants to feel that if he calls me in London from Saudi, from Kuwait, from the Lebanon, he will recognise my voice on the telephone. That he can talk to me about whether he should be moving fifty million dollars into yen, or selling IBM shares and buying Mitsubishi, at the same time as he is saying, "My son is at university, can you send him some money?" Or, "I'm coming over, would you mind calling my housekeeper?" Or, "I am interested in buying Islamic art or selling Persian carpets." He wants a *private* banker.'

The Japanese and the Swiss are on the investment banker's itinerary because they, too, have constant supplies of cash to invest. Japan is prosperous and turns a lot of income into savings. Switzerland remains a haven for the world's money. These days it happens to be caught between the need to appear as a good world citizen that doesn't knowingly harbour criminal funds, and the need to go on offering the traditional goodies, the numbered account, the blind eye, the minimal income tax. But it remains unshakeably a major source of investment funds. Swiss private bankers, often seemingly insulated from the culture of a changing world, manage investments of the rich and famous. Visiting investment bankers, anxious to distribute their wares among these super-managers of portfolios, cultivate them socially, waiting on them as they wait on the Arabs, perhaps with no more sympathy for their unreformed little ways than they feel for life in Saudi Arabia. A Canadian, not noted for his feminist sympathies, asked the Swiss private banker he was dining with how long it might be before women reached senior positions at the bank. The Swiss frowned in silence, working out the answer. After a long pause he got it. 'Never,' he said.

Investors, always at risk when bank or broker has a vested interest in marketing securities, face additional dangers in appraising stocks and bonds from faraway places. This works to the advantage of famous names that investors can trust, and has made the Eurobond market a favourite borrowing place for big US corporations; investors take their bonds without thinking, as the shopper takes a familiar brand from the supermarket shelf. Even so, the never-ending pressure to pump out securities and get them sold in order to make way for the next means that investors must be wary. An American investment banker who lives and sleeps Eurobonds said to me that 'if you put enough juice in a primary transaction, the hapless investor is going to own the bonds whether he likes it or not – either through a portfolio that somebody is managing on his behalf, or because he'll be directly encouraged and pressured to buy them.' 'Juice' means 'selling concession', a powerful incentive to salesmen. The investment banker's need to find the funds, to buy the securities, to please the issuers, to get some more, creates a kind of merciless imperative. At one extreme of the investing spectrum it is the 'Belgian dentist' – a mythical figure unkindly conceived to stand for the individual collecting his Eurobond interest without deduction of tax, and not declaring it to his government. At the other end it is the commercial banks, pension funds, insurance companies and investment trusts, bureaucracies from roof to basement, as knowledgeable about securities as are the investment banks that are selling them. The institutions are solicited all the time, their restless policies studied by every major investment bank.

In all this international scrambling for other people's money, it is usually assumed that institutions have more of it lying around than individuals. But this is a murky area, edged with disinformation. Many of the securities that institutions buy from the issuing banks (usually at cut-price rates) are later resold at a profit to individuals, who become the end-investors. * In any case, it is the rich individual investor that we all want to know about, the wily customer with the low profile and the handmade shoes. All bankers, investment and otherwise, are on the look-out for him. 'Wily' may be overstating it. He is wealthy and wants to move discreetly; who can blame him?

The City agent of a Swiss private bank told me of an American citizen, on a visit to London, who went to him with a personal introduction and passed thirty thousand US dollars across the desk, in cash. It was money he had acquired outside the United States; he didn't want to take it home and pay tax on it. 'We opened an account in Switzerland,' said the agent. 'Next day he talked to his lawyer in the States and came back to see me. He was nervous because he was afraid the CIA would find out. I said that wouldn't be easy – only two or three people in the bank could match up his account number and name. Anyway, he withdrew his dollars. I told him a lot of Americans invested in Panamanian bearer bonds, which they think are safe. I don't know if that's what he did. He

* See Chapter 8, 'Belgian Dentists'.

58

probably spent it at Harrods.' But a nervous American with only thirty thousand dollars is not important.

Bankers and brokers in Hong Kong, another excellent centre for not asking more questions than necessary, receive regular sums from investors in neighbouring countries who use imaginative methods to avoid exchange control. No one seems to mind talking about it. As the Swiss always say, there is nothing illegal about it at *their* end. But the Swiss, and most Anglo-Saxons, soon change the subject. They don't want to be seen benefiting from fiddles, even fiddles that legally take place elsewhere. This doesn't worry them much in South-east Asia, where they have a tolerant approach, like the Latins of Italy and South America. 'I have customers in Taiwan,' said one broker. 'They have exchange regulations there. They have the threat of Communist China. So they secretly smuggle money out, convert it into dollars and buy American shares through Hong Kong. It is all legitimate.' How did they smuggle the money? 'There are black market dealers in Taiwan who charge two or three per cent. The customer hands over a bundle of Taiwan notes. Two days later we get a dollar cheque drawn on somewhere respectable like Chase Manhattan in New York. The Taiwan Government keeps its eyes closed. Or people use double-invoicing – they hide illegal transfers inside legal trading.'

The same happens with fugitive money from the Philippines and Malaysia. You begin to see why Hong Kong has so many brokers offering Japanese and American securities. This is not to say that New York investment banks like Prudential-Bache (just 'Bache' in Hong Kong) and Merrill Lynch make their living only from these shadowy investors. Among the 5.3 million inhabitants of Hong Kong, ninety-seven per cent of them Chinese, a few tens of thousands are wealthy enough to be of interest to Wall Street. They are much sought-after. John Wei, the Bache manager, says that regular customers sit in the branch all evening, watching the gold and stock market prices in London, but really saving themselves for midnight, when trading is under way in New York. Z. T. Wong at Merrill Lynch says a good customer will have two or three hundred thousand US dollars to invest in a year. Negotiated commissions are around one and a half or two per cent. It is Merrill's most profitable branch in Asia.

London is another catchment area for the elusive rich of many lands. Mr A is a senior official of a Wall Street bank whose job is to find and service them. If he uses unusual methods, they were not disclosed; he advertises, and hopes that satisfied customers will recommend his firm to their friends. From time to time stories surface in newspapers of marauding securities salesmen who do unethical things. Mr A says his team wouldn't dream of it. 'I deal with the rich,' he declares, as if that in itself is a pretty moral thing to do. 'People from whatever country of the world, who happen to have a place in London. Maybe he high-tailed it to Paris originally from Beirut or Iran. The atmosphere in Europe is fine. People can eat the right food – it's very civilised. I deal with the wealthy South American who maybe doesn't live in London but has a home here and uses it as a base. For years now I've been dealing with Indians, Arabs, Chileans, Peruvians, Italians. I've got authors! I've got movie stars! I've got ex-ambassadors! I've got politicians! I deal with anyone who has money that he's legitimately investing, but we really are going after clients with a million dollars net worth and more. There's no mystique. We have no team of marauding salesmen. Our books are open to everybody, though one thing to remember is that we don't carry customers' accounts in this office. All accounts are carried in New York. What's the significance of that? It's self-evident. A lot of people who have assets today trust very few places. I would suggest that Switzerland and the United States would be everyone's favourite place. London, too. But the United Kingdom is a country that has had exchange controls, and may have them again. Customers like to deal with London, where the expertise is. But physically they like to have the securities held in Switzerland or New York.' He took a swipe in passing at the Swiss, declaring that some of the world's rich were 'beginning to feel fed up with the investment advice they get from Swiss banks', and were turning to firms like Mr A's. (The Swiss are used to being denigrated behind their backs.) For customers who find securities alone too constricting, Mr A has other avenues for the investor. There are commodities for those who understand the risks. For the very wealthy there is even the foreign-exchange market, the worldwide network of banks through which currencies are bought and sold, both for the purposes of trade and as speculation. In recent times this market has become hyper-active. Political unrest, the size of oil revenues, the instability of interest rates, alarm at the millstone debts of poor countries, and in general a certain wobbliness about the financial system, keep money switching from one currency to another. Prudence and fear explain some of it; greed and the banker's sporting nature the rest. World turnover each day in yen, marks, francs, pounds, dollars and the rest is problematic, but thought to be well in excess of one hundred billion dollars. This, in turn, far exceeds the amount of money needed to finance trade. Commercial banks are the leading participants, but anyone can join in, and investment banks do their share. Mr A said that a colleague at his firm had a client who has 'done a million dollars with us this year, just trading currencies'. I said, fancy one man buying and selling a million dollars' worth in a year. Mr A shook his head. 'A million dollars in *commissions*,' he said. 'I am telling you that this client generated *commissions* of a million dollars by trading currencies.' He was a corporation with worldwide needs, not a person. Even so. I asked what kind of a turnover in pounds, dollars and yen was needed to produce a round million for the firm. 'Huge,' said Mr A.

The Japanese are as anxious as the Americans to be investment bankers to the world. Their big securities firms, in the form they have taken since World War 2, are constructed on American lines. They lead issues in the Eurobond market, where everyone is nice to them because they can dispose of so many bonds inside Japan. They have never-ending sales drives to convince foreign investors, especially American, of the virtues of Japanese securities. As a rule their branches have been run and mainly staffed by Japanese nationals. This is the opposite of what happens in Tokyo, where foreign financial firms are expected to use local staff wherever possible, and need to, given the pitfalls of language and culture. Mr Shigeru Uemura, chairman of Daiwa Securities in New York (one of sixteen offices outside Japan), said apologetically that most of the senior staff in New York were posted there from Daiwa's head office in Tokyo. 'The salesman has to give information on Japan,' he said. 'The original is always in Japanese.' Every day financial articles came from Tokyo through the facsimile machines. American salesmen couldn't read them. 'I think we will have to change,' he said. Philosophy is another obstacle. Yamaichi Securities has nineteen overseas offices. In 1983 its managing director in the City, Hitoshi Tanaka, who is a graduate of the London School of Economics, spoke to me about 'the Japanese way'. Gradualism was its essence: easier to learn the language than to reach an understanding of the importance of consensus within a firm. Since Yamaichi's strength in Europe derived from its strength in Japan, he said, how could his branch flourish without the understanding of its parent? I asked if this didn't make life difficult in the Eurobond market, where chaos breaks out as issues are announced and fought for, and he who hesitates will not make a profit. He said Yes, it did. Sometimes he had to act without the support of head office. It was painful. It was Europe. Tanaka spoke of the absence of any system, as yet, for training Western recruits in

61

Yamaichi's ways. But by 1984, a year after that hint, the firm was changing direction. Eight British graduates had been recruited from universities and were destined for a spell of 'orientation' at head office in Tokyo. Tanaka's face smiled out of full-page advertisements that spoke of 'Merging Japanese and British Talent – The One of Us Concept'.

Japanese investment houses possess sharp claws and boundless ambition. At their head is Nomura Securities Co., a firm that meant little to bankers in the West twenty years ago. Now they regard it with respect or irritation, usually both. Nomura sees itself as the Merrill Lynch of the East; its roots are in the retail brokerage business, but it is now a major investment banker and wholesaler of securities as well. Merrill is the firm it wants to beat. Its English-language publicity material devotes pages to charts that show it chasing the American firm in various categories of income, capital and type of business, and sometimes overtaking it. American comparisons in general are import-ant in Japan, as though, for all their commercial success, some echo of military defeat still haunts them. Japanese securities firms hold quan-tities of customers' stocks and bonds for safekeeping. A Nomura official in Tokyo said that while the comparison might not be strictly relevant, I would undoubtedly like to know that his firm held customers' securities to a value of seventeen trillion yen, and customers' cash deposits with the Bank of America, the commercial-banking giant of California, were the equivalent of only three trillion yen more. (A trillion is a million million. One of the minor problems of Japanese finance is that one yen is so confusingly small. It is as if the British currency had no pounds or pennies, and everything was expressed in the ancient farthing. Where trillions of them are involved, the noughts seem to go on for ever, and totals are easily misread.) Nomura earns more than a fifth of its profits overseas; in 1983 this meant $60 or $70 million of $292 million. It operates in some thirty locations in Europe, the Americas, the Middle East and Asia. Merrill Lynch is not amused at Nomura's declared intention of earning half its profits outside Japan by the end of the 1980s. The Nomura house magazine, published in English for the overseas branches, emphasises teamwork, energy and the family atmosphere; its slogan is 'Together around the world'; the firm says there will soon be more non-Japanese in senior posts. News from newly-weds in Singapore ('I call her Sunshine for the day and Moon-light before going to bed') appears alongside an account of a day in the life of a young American who is training in Tokyo to be a Nomura securities analyst ('Throughout the company's bachelor dormitory, gentle music begins to play'). In London they describe themselves watching cricket and eating fish and chips, determined to understand the British. Lengthy interviews and discussions explore the company ethos. 'Our work has no borders between countries!' declares a headline. Mr Yoshimi, Honolulu office, concludes his column with an appropriate message. 'Nomura is People,' it says, 'Selling is Stamina.'

A mythology has grown up about the Japanese broker or banker overseas: pushy, dedicated, ingenious and willing to cut his margins to the bone to get the business. When Nomura opened new premises in Hong Kong, it bought four pages in the *Asian Wall Street Journal* to celebrate the occasion and remind readers that 'Day after day, Nomura works to make a positive contribution on your behalf.' At the same time a team flew in from Japan and did the rounds of banks and brokerage firms. A British merchant banker who was on their list was dismayed to find half a dozen Nomura executives in his office, their briefcases full of graphs and statistics. They gave senior staff a presentation about the future of South-east Asia in general and the rosy prospects for Japanese securities in particular. They were still talking when the time came for him to go to a cocktail party. Next day a colleague told him that before they left, the Nomura team tried to sell him some shares for himself. The more people repeat such anecdotes, the more they do Nomura's work. Teams of Nomura analysts are well known for their 'missions' to north America, visiting twenty or thirty institutions in a week. It is said that mutual funds (comparable to the British unit trusts) and pension funds in the United States have between two and three trillion dollars invested in one form or another; this ungraspable sum is no more than a good guess, but the figure, whatever it is, is very large, and attracts investment bankers of many nationalities. Nomura's analysts and salesmen carry detailed information to convince fund managers that no one in his right mind could refuse Japanese shares coupled with the firm's knowledge of the Tokyo stock market. According to one of Nomura's staff in New York, the funds had about 0.5 per cent of their money invested overseas, mainly in Canada and Europe, but were beginning to diversify. He thought that Japanese investment banks – in general, he was not being greedy – should be able to get one per cent for themselves. That would be twenty or thirty billion dollars; or, in yen, say five or six trillion. It is not unknown for western brokers to do what they can to injure the Japanese by alleging behind their backs that their advice is not to be trusted: specifically, that they always give positive advice, to buy a security, but will never give negative advice, to sell it.

Oddly, the Japanese will admit this. 'There is a psychological element,' said a Nomura manager in Tokyo. 'We hesitate to send out a printed recommendation to sell. After all, we have long-standing relationships with the companies that have issued the shares. But of course we often give the advice verbally. And even in America, we have found that large brokers publish "sell" recommendations less often than we thought.'

Whatever their nationality, investment bankers expect nowadays to work in concert with other people's time-zones. Tokyo and Hong Kong share the financial leadership of the East, neatly placed between the two key time-zones of the financial West, one containing London, the other New York. Providence has fitted the geography to the economics. The fit is imperfect, and to make the trading day at one centre flow into that of the next means an invasion of the trader's private life. Firms like Merrill Lynch and Nomura can now claim that they trade around the clock; a desk with the necessary powers is always open somewhere, carrying a 'book' of securities. 'The book' is the term for the positions that the firm holds in all the securities it handles, together with the strategy being followed. Embodied in computer print-outs and telex messages, its content passes around the world east to west, following the sun – New York to the Far East, back to Europe, on again to New York, every twenty-four hours. When the book leaves New York in the early evening, it is breakfast time next day in Tokyo; branch offices in different time-zones across the United States may also be involved. When Tokyo passes the book back to the West at the end of its after-noon, the morning's work has just begun in London. London has the book to itself until 3 pm, give or take an hour for daylight-saving, when Wall Street begins to trade. It is then 10 am New York time. Until London closes, the two trade side by side; late afternoon is not the best time to try to see an American investment banker in the City.

Twenty years ago, before investment banks were trading-minded, they knew where to draw the line. A banker who had been with Morgan in Paris in the 1960s said that occasionally he used to have trouble with colleagues who rang him from Wall Street in the evening. 'I cut them off sharp at midnight,' he said, 'by pointing out to the partners in New York that I had their home numbers, and ten in the morning in Paris, when they were still asleep, would be a very convenient time for *me* to call.'

The mould is sterner now. Even the senior person on holiday in a far country isn't safe. A few months after I met Richard Fisher at Morgan Stanley and sat in on the Day of the Telephone, he was on holiday with his wife in West Wales to explore Dylan Thomas country. Travelling via France and Scotland, they reached a small seaside hotel to find the phone ringing with business from the syndicate desk. This is no more, perhaps, than the way people with duller lives expect investment bankers to live. But the bankers notice a change in their own routines. Peter O'Brien is corporate syndicate manager at Merrill Lynch, in charge of the desk that distributes shares underwritten by the firm. 'The time-scale of deals gets shorter,' he said. 'The working day gets longer.' Stock and bond markets are more volatile; fund managers, less inclined nowadays to buy securities and forget about them, trade them more often; foreign buyers in countries where it is later or earlier pay more attention when salesmen call them from New York.

'It's not unusual to spend twelve hours in the office,' said O'Brien, 'and on top of that maybe commute an hour and a half or two hours each way, and then get phone calls at home. Right now I typically get up at 4.45 in the morning, catch a train from Connecticut at 5.30, and am in the office by 6.45. You can't have a breakfast meeting that accomplishes anything later than eight o'clock because then it starts to get too busy. In the syndicate business five or ten years ago, there used to be more personal relationships with friends who worked for competitors. It was normal to go out to lunch. You know, it's very admirable to go out to lunch. Now I either skip it entirely or have a sandwich at my desk.' I asked if there was a Mrs O'Brien. Yes, also two small O'Briens, aged three and a half and seven. There might be three phone calls waiting for him when he got home. 'It changes your life,' he said. None of this seemed to upset him. He worked for a service industry, so 'if the client calls, you don't tell him you're too busy.' I said I hoped investment banks paid well for long hours, betraying a European misconception of the way things work in the land of sticks and carrots. 'You're not paid on the basis of time put in or how hard you work,' O'Brien said patiently, 'but on the profitability of what you do.' He probably earns more than any chairman of a public company in Britain. He said he had a device called a voice mailbox to make life easier. One could argue it made life harder. 'During the course of the day,' he said, 'or certainly if you're travelling, you can call in to your mailbox and listen.' He demonstrated from his office, feeding the call through a loudspeaker. Four musical notes sounded as he touched the buttons. 'Hello,' said a woman in metallic tones. 'This is Voice Messages.' She was only a recording. 'Please dial your ID number,' she said. He punched out six more notes. It took a second and a half for the machine to give an electronic squeak

65

and report that he had no messages after all. He could erase messages or save them or transfer them to other people. Travelling in Scandinavia, he reaches the Grand Hotel in Stockholm at midnight. He can call his voice mailbox. I said that was marvellous, but didn't it mean that instead of going to sleep, he started working again in the middle of the night? 'That's right,' he said. 'I'm in a service industry.' He glanced at my pencil. 'Don't tell me the printing presses aren't running tonight.'

I began to collect examples of investment bankers who worked long days, but soon gave up; the category was too broad. The working breakfast, so often called 'uncivilised' in London, is eaten regularly in Wall Street. Some of those breakfasting call it uncivilised, too, but the habit is ingrained. Breakfast or no, senior officers, to chief executive level, drift up from subways or chauffeur-driven cars on winter days at an hour when the raw mist blowing in from the river, along what are said to be the coldest streets in the city, is barely tinged with daylight. I visited the president (as he then was) of Lehman Brothers (as it then was), Lewis L. Glucksman, a New Yorker who looks like the captain of a destroyer in a film about Pearl Harbor, at ten o'clock on a Monday morning. Lehman had been a famous investment bank with dignified traditions that fell on difficult times before it purged itself and rethought its role. Glucksman kept a ship's telegraph in his office, which looked on to the sales-and-trading floor through plate glass. The brasswork shone and the maker's name was visible: 'Chadburns, London and Liverpool'. Glucksman, now aged fifty-eight, lives up to his well-worn features. He was in submarine chasers, 'the last guy at the top of a major Wall Street firm who was in World War 2. My wife calls this office Starship Command.' He said he had been there since 5.30 that morning. 'I like to properly read the newspapers,' he said, 'the *New York Times*, the London *Financial Times* and the *Wall Street Journal*. By the time I've done that and made a cup of coffee, it's seven-thirty. As a matter of fact I don't usually get in till a quarter of six; I was early today. By six-thirty our chief administrative officer was in, and so was our head of bond trading.' He began to reel off the names of managing directors he had seen. 'Shel Gordon was in by seven, Roger Altman wanted to talk to me about something at ten after seven. . . .' He recalled an old saying, that loyalty begat loyalty; he expected employees to be loyal to their officers. It sounded vaguely Japanese, the kind of thing one reads in the Nomura magazine. But he said they used to say it in the Navy.

*　　*　　*

The simplest way to see investment bankers in action on an international scale is, once again, when they are raising capital. We are back to the tombstone business, this time in the Eurodollar market. The market has no physical location; there are no marble pillars and trading floors. This doesn't help the outsider to understand it. Nor does the fact that there is no such thing, legally or physically, as a Eurodollar. Eurodollars are US dollar credits owned and circulating outside the United States. They are the nearest thing the world has to international money, replacing the more modest function that sterling used to have. Eurodollars are just dollars, ultimate claims against the United States monetary system, which is why they are popular; if that system goes, everything goes. They began to accumulate in noticeable quantity about 1960, in the form of deposits in European banks. This led to the prefix 'Euro', disliked by financial purists for years. Now there is no special connection with Europe except that much Eurodollar business is handled there, particularly in London, as well as in New York and the Far East.

The world's money market for bank borrowing and lending is, in effect, the Eurodollar market. Commercial banks are the real players. Investment banks, not having the deposits to be borrowers and lenders, confine themselves to organising some of the big syndicated loans; certain City merchant banks have done nicely at this, on the old principle of 'your money, my brains'. The piece of the Euromarket that investment banks have made their own is where borrowers who don't want straight bank loans issue interest-bearing bonds to investors, and borrow their Eurodollars that way. The banks that make up the core of this bond market are part of the City scene. But every Eurobond issue is also a small global event, a drawing-together of threads. It fires the veins of the banks that act as managers, big business with complicated features writ large across continents. They are the ones who find it glamorous.

Mitsubishi Corporation of Japan raised a hundred million US dollars in April 1983, or rather, ninety-eight million by the time the bankers took their share. Morgan Guaranty Ltd of London (MGL) clinched the deal in Tokyo and managed the issue through the City, working closely with its commercial-bank parent in New York, Morgan Guaranty Trust Co. When it was over, and the money had been raised, MGL held a formal signing ceremony in London. One representative apiece came from each of the twelve co-managing banks, two Mitsubishi directors came from Tokyo, and so did MGL's man there. No doubt the visitors who hadn't seen them before were directed to the photographs and models of J. P. Morgan's famous steam yachts, all named *Corsair*, in the big dining-room. They had champagne and lunch, and Mitsubishi was given a silver cigarette box to take home. A few days before the issue, when I happened to be at Morgan Guaranty Ltd in the City, they had asked me if I wanted to see it happen. Later on, in Tokyo, I talked to Morgan's man there and pieced together a picture. By then it was water under the bridge. They were on to new schemes.

Morgan Guaranty Trust Co., the parent, opted for the commercial-banking side of the business at the time of the Glass-Steagall Act; it left investment banking to the breakaway firm of Morgan Stanley, which thus has a distant familial relationship with MGL. But in daily business relations in the City, MGL and Morgan Stanley International show each other no favours. Morgan Guaranty Trust Co. – 'The Morgan Bank' in its advertising, and plain 'Morgan' among bankers – owns MGL via another subsidiary based in Miami. MGL has an office in Tokyo as well. This isn't licensed to do banking business. But Morgan Guaranty Trust has a branch nearby in Tokyo which is. These weblike structures baffle outsiders who don't know the legal, political and historical ingredients. The object of MGL is to do those things in the world at large which its parent can't do in the United States until the day when some future Congress repeals Glass-Steagall. In particular, it exists to raise finance in the Eurobond market. MGL has been more successful at this than have the other US commercial banks with subsidiaries in London, probably because Morgan is a 'wholesale' bank, with no retail customers, and a longer tradition of providing services outside the mainstream of commercial banking. 'Morgan avoids the mundane,' says one of its officers. Whether true or not, that is how it likes to perceive itself, in its sumptuous headquarters at 23 Wall Street. MGL feeds on this self-assurance.

The Mitsubishi deal went to Morgan because it offered interesting technical features that were more interesting than anyone else's. This bald explanation sounds disappointing, especially since the interesting features boil down to something called an interest-rate swap. But it is typical of the new investment banking. Historic or social connections are a wasting asset; long-standing alliances or happy hours shared on the golf course are forgotten; a quarter per cent here, a technical feature there, will win the mandate, as the phrase is. The proposal that Mitsubishi raise a hundred million with an associated interest-rate swap is said to have come from MGL in the first place. I heard slightly conflicting stories. Did MGL respond to a rumour that Mitsubishi was thinking of making a big issue of bonds, or was it taking a shot in the dark? What definitely happened was that MGL made a proposal, and Mitsubishi brought other firms into the discussion. Nikko Securities, a leading investment house in Japan, has a 'relationship' with the company. Nikko gave advice; was probably itself a candidate. Merrill Lynch, which had had dealings with the company, was asked to make its own proposals. At some later stage, Morgan Stanley, the Morgan Bank's distant relative, was involved. Morgan Stanley has had a close relationship with Mitsubishi; if loyalty had been a factor, it probably had the best claim of all to manage the issue. 'They were asleep,' says a rival banker. Asleep or awake, they didn't get the mandate.

MGL's man on the spot in Tokyo was its chief representative there, Ian M. Clark. Clark is an Australian who spends much of his time travelling around South-east Asia or making expensive telephone calls; the annual phone bill at his apartment is around twenty-five thousand dollars a year. He did the marketing with Mitsubishi, selling them the concept that MGL in London, working with Morgan bankers in New York, had produced. Inside the company, consensus was doubtless at work. As the decision took shape, the rate of Clark's meetings with Mitsubishi accelerated. By the middle of March he was discussing fine details with officials every day. In the third week of the month came the decision that Morgan Guaranty Ltd would be lead manager to the issue. Soon after that, Richard Sharp, a young manager in MGL's corporate finance department, flew from London to Tokyo with a lawyer, to help draw up the 'offering circular', the standard descriptive document that accompanies Eurobond issues. The circulars are complicated, though not as complicated as the full prospectus that is needed to borrow in the New York market. This one ran to forty-eight pages, with columns of figures and a few sentences of history – 'Mitsubishi Corporation is the largest trading company in Japan and is a descendant of the pre-war Mitsubishi "Zaibatsu", or industrial conglomerate, which was formed from a shipping and trading company established by Yataro Iwasaki in 1870. . . .' As negotiations came to a head, drafts were being sent between Tokyo and London. Without word-processors at either end, making it possible to rewrite and agree amendments at speed between the two centres, couriers would have had to make the sixteen-hour journey by plane.

When I asked Clark why MGL had won the mandate, he said it was because 'we were able to offer a firmer commitment and tell them the all-in cost of the swap'. The swap was crucial. As the day of the issue (which was going to be some time in April) approached, managing the swap was the hinge of the exercise. A conjuring trick was about to be performed. Behind the scenes, Morgan Guaranty would issue the bonds through the familiar machinery of the Euromarket. But it would immediately relieve Mitsubishi of the need to pay the fixed rate of interest at which Mitsubishi was borrowing the dollars, replacing it with a fluctuating rate which the company, for reasons of its own, would prefer. A 'counter-party', some other borrower of a similar amount from a bank, who would normally be saddled with a fluctuating rate, but wanted it to be fixed for reasons of *his* own, would take on an obligation to pay a fixed rate. This exchange of obligations would take place through M G L, acting as intermediary. The 'swap' consisted of Morgan in the middle, reconciling different needs. It is a complicated process, appealing to all concerned for that reason. For the bankers who perform the trick, it is a satisfying piece of mystique. For the issuing company, the ingenuity of its bankers is a kind of flattery.

The interest-rate swap is one of the devices thought up by investment bankers to widen their appeal. The difficulty lies in finding counter-parties. In this case, who could be matched with Mitsubishi? A few banks will take a chance and arrange a swap regardless of whether it can be matched neatly on both sides. If it can't all be done in time, the bank goes ahead and takes on the burden of the unswappable portion, passing it on later when it finds a taker. This is how M G L operates, using its parent bank's resources. It was what Clark meant when he spoke about being able to offer a 'firmer commitment'. From the start, Mitsubishi, though still responsible for paying the fixed rate of $10\frac{1}{2}$ per cent interest at which the \$100 million of bonds were issued, knew it would receive the money to make those payments from Morgan Guaranty, and in return would pay Morgan Guaranty a floating rate of interest. In fact the bank had matched only \$25 million worth of bonds when the time came to make the issue, but the shortfall wasn't allowed to hinder the deal. The Morgan men who cultivate this aggressive approach are torn between pride in their work, which leads them to talk about it, and anxiety lest too much publicity leads to others imitating them. But everyone in the City knows that Morgan goes in for open-ended interest-rate swaps.

The company that M G L found to cover the first \$25 million was Redland PLC, a British-based building materials group. Redland and its associated companies have an annual turnover of more than a billion pounds. It had no trouble obtaining bank loans. But in the elitist Eurobond market, it couldn't borrow at such a favourable rate as a name like Mitsubishi, if at all. So Redland borrowed from banks, paying the going rate for interest as it rose or fell. When trying to plan ahead, interest rates are an unknown quantity. In 1983, when Redland already had about $100 million of fluctuating-rate debt, it fancied having a fixed-rate loan of $25 million. This is what made it a suitable counter-party for Mitsubishi. Someone at Morgan made the connection; the bank is always seeking candidates for swaps. Morgan sat in the middle and conducted an arithmetical exercise. The operation had four parts. First, using Morgan commercial-banking facilities in New York, M GL would arrange for $25 million to be borrowed in the 'interbank' market (very cheap for banks, because it is 'wholesale' money) and lent to Redland. Second, it would charge Redland a fixed rate of interest – it was 11.8 per cent. That would make Redland happy. Third, Morgan would pay Mitsubishi the fixed interest that Mitsubishi had to pay the bondholders ($10\frac{1}{2}$ per cent, except that it worked out a little higher, 10.9 per cent, because what Mitsubishi raised was only $98 million, after its bankers' costs were met). Finally, Mitsubishi would pay Morgan a fluctuating rate of interest, related to but actually below the cheapest interbank rate. If the interbank rate fell, Mitsubishi would hand over less; but in that case, Morgan would be paying less for the interbank money it had borrowed to lend on to Redland. What the outsider might regard as a dog's breakfast of figures had been neatly worked out to send everyone away grateful. Morgan had taken a shrewd view of the relative strengths and needs of the two companies. It had also, as a Morgan banker put it, ensured that there was 'a little something in the pot'. The little something he had in mind was around $40,000 a year for the seven years that the loans would last. This was the profit shaved off as the four sets of payments moved in different directions, all of them passing through Morgan in the middle, the guarantor of the scheme.

That was the theory. The practice was that the swap covered only the first $25 million. On that basis, M GL prepared to go ahead. The formal decision to issue the bonds was taken in Tokyo by the Mitsubishi board on a Monday afternoon, 11 April. Morgan was authorised to act at any time it thought fit during the next three weeks. One reason for the time-limit was the Japanese Ministry of Finance's desire to have issues follow an orderly pattern, and so avoid congestion. In fact M G L had no intention of waiting at all, unless some political or economic crisis upset interest rates and thus the Eurobond market.

The previous Thursday, when I visited M GL for the first time, a street and an alley away from the Bank of England, I was told that an issue for 'a major Japanese company' would almost certainly be made early the following week. On Monday evening, David Craig, M GL's deputy managing director, telephoned me from his home to say it was set for the next day; 10 am or even 10.30 would be early enough. At that point I didn't know the company was Mitsubishi. The sequence of events, as I pieced them together later, began on Monday with a message to head office from Ian Clark early in the morning, London time, that Mitsubishi had given its formal approval. During the day M GL conferred with Morgan in New York, and the decision was taken to go ahead immediately. By the time Craig telephoned me, around 7 pm, he and his colleagues had begun coping with the unswapped $75 million of the deal. They had to protect the bank against a shift in interest rates. In a perfect world the $75 million would already have found another Redland as the counter-party. Morgan would have borrowed $75 million of interbank money, loaned it to Company X, and agreed the fixed rate of interest that Company X would pay Morgan for the next seven years. Since no Company X had yet been identified, Morgan borrowed the $75 million anyway, and locked it to the interest rates prevailing at that moment by investing it in US Treasury bonds. This constituted a 'hedge', a protection. It might take M GL a month to find a counter-party. During that month world interest rates might fall. In that case, if M GL had to unload an unhedged $75 million, the counter-party that borrowed it would expect to pay less interest. Morgan's delicate calculations, based on one set of interest rates, would fall apart with this introduction of an alien rate. Instead of finding a little something in the pot, the bank might find that managing the swap was going to cost money. This would never do. Owning $75 million of US Treasuries was a simple but efficient hedge against empty pots. The price of bonds varies with interest rates, to keep the underlying 'yield' constant. When interest rates fall, the price of bonds rises, and vice versa. So if Morgan found itself with a counter-party that was paying less interest than the pot required, the increased value of the bonds themselves, when liquidated into cash, would be a rough-and-ready compensation. The exercise turned on small percentages that, applied to sums like $75 million, could have substantial outcomes. The loss of one half of one per cent interest on that amount, over a period of seven years, would be about two and a half million dollars.

On Monday evening three Morgan men assembled to see the hedge

72

set up: John A. Mayer, MGL's managing director, Leonard Gayler, the syndicate manager, and David Craig.* They were in Craig's house, south of the Thames, because he has two telephone lines. Gayler spent much of the evening using one of them to talk to Morgan's chief Government bond trader, George Kegler, in New York, where it was still the afternoon. The first purchase of Treasury bonds, $25 million worth, was made around 7.15 pm London time. This may have been when Craig rang me; the operation was now under way. In the next few hours Gayler talked to New York about fifteen times, buying as and when it was possible to obtain the best price. US Treasury bonds constitute the biggest securities market in the world; it is how the American Government borrows week by week, a vast pool of obligations, secured against the state. There is so much US Government paper in circulation that it provides instant liquidity: it can always be bought and sold, in amounts that would cause chaos in the trading of most securities. The quantity of US debt outstanding has risen above a trillion dollars; Morgan's purchases that Monday amounted, perhaps, to a trifling one fourteen-thousandth of the whole. It was all over before midnight. A phone call to Tokyo, where it was already Tuesday, woke Ian Clark and told him that today was the day. Then they went to bed in London, to wait for Tuesday to begin in Europe.

When I arrived, at 10 am, David Craig, a youngish Englishman with long legs and a crisp manner, dressed in a pinstripe suit, was sitting in his position at the head of the syndicate desk, talking softly into his telephone. 'Today,' he was saying, 'Morgan Guaranty will lead-manage an issue for Mitsubishi Corporation. You know who Mitsubishi Corporation is?' That was a joke. 'It's rated triple A by Standard and Poor,' he said. 'The issue is a hundred million dollars. . . .' He was inviting one of the co-managers, a Japanese bank in Europe, to join the underwriting syndicate, and take five and a half million dollars' worth of bonds. The desk was busy. The L-shaped trading-room rang to electric bells and voices. They seemed to have started promptly at ten. A lighted wall-map of the world with clocks showed it was 10.01 in London, 11.01 in Paris, 2.01 in the afternoon in Kuwait. In Tokyo it was 6.01 in the evening. In New York it was 4.01 am, too early even for Lewis Glucksman in Starship Command. Craig talked quietly and smoothly. A faded newspaper headline pasted up by his telephone read, 'Our debt to Craig'; it wasn't about him. Next to him was Len Gayler, with his jacket

---

* Craig and Gayler left MGL in 1984 to set up their own company.

off. For some of his conversations he squatted at his position, head below the level of the lighted dealing board, his mouth almost touching the desk. 'OK, Peter,' he was saying, 'five hundred we sell you.' He meant five hundred bonds at one thousand dollars each.

It turned out they had started at 9.15. News of the issue had leaked out to the market. 'I just walked in through the door,' said Craig, who was off the phone for a moment, 'and seven people telephoned to ask how the issue was going.' By 8 am, calls had been pouring in from Europe, from the Middle East and from Asia, asking at what price the bonds were available. This was good news for the issue because it showed people were interested, but irritating news in the short term for MGL, who didn't want to be upstaged by their co-managers – who were only now being officially invited to take part – unloading their allocation of bonds in a mad scramble. 'It's much cleaner to have a fait accompli,' said one of the salesmen, 'rather than have it floating around for hours, and everybody getting bored. We had people ringing up first thing and saying, "We've been offered bonds in three places now. We *know* you're the lead manager. We *want* to deal with you. But for Christ's sake get your finger out."'

It seemed to be the Japanese who sprang the leak. There were two schools of thought about this. One school was led by Shiu Tomioka, an MGL manager in London, himself a Japanese. He wore a sad expression and shook his head when he heard it suggested that Mitsubishi, proud of such a deal from their bankers, had let their excitement get the better of them. 'That's all right,' someone explained, 'he doesn't want to prejudice Mitsubishi in your book. It was a bit naughty of them. But some people feel a sense of pride. They start with something fixed and end up with something floating, very cheaply. They like to talk about it.' Tomioka rather spoiled his case by producing, about eleven o'clock, an English translation of a report that had appeared in a Japanese financial newspaper that morning. Headed 'Interest Rate Swap by Mitsubishi', it spilled the beans in a few paragraphs. The paper was on sale in Tokyo by noon; from the Japanese point of view, the deal was being done on Tuesday, and Tuesday was already half over. A facsimile of the page had arrived at Morgan Guaranty, but long before that, the phone calls to Europe had started. That was how the market had been alerted, before the sun was up.

Pink strips of telex paper hanging on walls fluttered as people scurried past. Salesmen and women crouched or stood, telephones in hands. Each telephone had a white button on the receiver. This had to be pressed when speaking, or the microphone cut out, and the party at the other end couldn't hear. Some of the calls were about the Mitsubishi bonds, some not. An American at one position was saying 'Nein sprechen Sie Deutsche. Is Herr Kessler there ...? Nein sprechen Sie Deutsche. OK. Fine.' He let go of his button and called, 'Help!' 'Hang up,' yelled another salesman. 'Have you given them your name?' 'Nope,' said the American. His colleague said, 'If you're in real trouble, hang up. Better not to be involved.' The American hung up. In a lull, Len Gayler said that Morgan itself had already sold more than ten million dollars' worth of the bonds. The buyers, all of them institutional, included banks in Kuwait and Switzerland buying for their customers' investment portfolios, banks in Finland and Bahrain buying for themselves, a London merchant bank, a London stockbroker, and insurance companies in Canada and Sweden. Despite the hiccup over Herr Kessler, the room had an easy cosmopolitan air. Holding on for a connection at a French bank, a man yawned and speculated about the music they were playing down the wire. 'It sounds like the Last Waltz,' he said. 'They are abysmal at answering their telephones in Paris. A-bysmal.' Someone waggled a small Union Jack in the air for no apparent reason. Traders often have flags on their desks. Len Gayler said there were fewer salespeople on duty than usual because four were away on business in Brussels and the Middle East.

David Craig was finishing off his calls to the co-managers. 'Good morning, this is an invitation to the Deutsche Bank to co-manage a deal for Mitsubishi Corporation, which is the flagship company in the Mitsubishi group....' The Deutsche Bank wouldn't have liked the idea of being called last instead of first. But there had been problems getting through to Frankfurt. It was going to be a lucrative issue for Morgan, which was itself selling seventeen million dollars' worth of the bonds; it would earn in excess of a third of a million dollars, beside the little something in the interest-swap pot, which at $40,000 a year for seven years almost doubled the managing-and-selling profit. The tombstone would duly appear ('This announcement appears as a matter of record only') with thirteen names on it: Morgan Guaranty Ltd in the prime position, top left, followed by three co-lead managers, all of whom had been candidates to manage the issue, Merrill Lynch International, Morgan Stanley International and Nikko Securities (Europe). Then, in alphabetical order, the nine co-managers, one French, one German, three Japanese, two Swiss, one British and one hybrid, Credit Suisse First Boston. Various other banks seem to have been included in an unofficial selling group that was given no publicity. Some of them would have been friends of Mitsubishi. I heard a Eurobond salesman at another firm say he was fed up with offering Japanese bonds to banks as favours. But the borrowers insisted. The Japanese were great believers in the old pals' act. The old school tie was regarded as peculiarly British, but don't you believe it, said the salesman. The club was universal.

By the end of the morning the issue was successfully launched, and I had more or less grasped the outline of an interest-rate swap. David Craig drew diagrams in my notebook, and I studied them later, like homework. He showed me relics of earlier swaps, chalked up on a board, with code-words for the clients; Shogun, Kamikaze, Kiwis. The board showed if positions in earlier deals were still unmatched, waiting for counter-parties to be found. He said that under certain conditions, he would deliberately do a swap without seeking a counter-party at all. It depended on the relationship between various figures. He went into detail but I lost him. In a lucid moment I heard him say, 'I am a bit of a buccaneer in that sense.'

One or two people went out to lunch. Someone said he was going to Switzerland. 'You can't!' said Gayler. 'You have more holidays than the rest of us put together.' The man said it was business. 'Ee-e-ech!' said Gayler, waving a finger at him. All this was in a lull, while he was explaining to me about the US Treasury market. It was Gayler who told me that more than a trillion dollars of US debt was in circulation. The latest figure he had was 1.1 trillion. 'That's one, one oh oh, oh oh oh, oh oh oh, oh oh oh,' he said.

A woman with her button off called across the desk to ask if Mitsubishi was rated by the Moody's agency. No, said Gayler, Standard and Poor's, triple A. He paused to take a call of his own. He told someone he would keep him in mind.

When he turned back to me, he said, 'That's a million million. But they're telephone numbers. It's more dollars than the weight of the world, or something. Actually – it's a very interesting fact – the weight of the world in tons is twenty-two numbers, so that's more. I got it out of a boys' book of facts many years ago. It's a thing I've never forgotten.' Somehow the analogy was a comfort.

4
WALL STREET: THE MONEY MACHINES

Upper crusts — 'A cottage industry' — Jews and gentiles —
Judge Medina and the Club of Seventeen — Rise and fall of Lehman Brothers —
Fall and rise of First Boston — Joe Perella's banana hour — The traders' dogma —
Taking risks at Salomon Brothers — 2023 AD — John Gutfreund and the Truth —
The Goldman Sachs syndrome — Morgan Stanley says No —
Brains, blood and money — Mr Merrill and Mr Lynch —
From birth to grave — Hard dollars, soft dollars

In alphabetical order, the six most prominent investment banks in the United States are First Boston, Goldman Sachs, Merrill Lynch, Morgan Stanley, Salomon Brothers and Shearson Lehman/American Express. The six have their headquarters in New York City. There is intense rivalry between them, and some resentment of them from outside their charmed circle. Like all leaders, they attract publicity to the detriment of others who are less visible but might be just as good.

Their special status is not entirely a matter of size; in two cases (First Boston and Morgan Stanley) the firms, although enormous beside British merchant banks, are not among the Wall Street giants. History and reputation are important. But all are part of a Wall Street melting pot that makes everything uncertain. For years firms there have been going out of business or merging with stronger partners. Those who remain at the top have either fought their way up or have resisted attempts to drag them down. They can be sure of nothing. When I first visited Wall Street in 1983, the inner circle consisted of five firms, not six. There was a firm called Lehman Brothers, modest in size though high in prestige, that almost qualified, but not quite. Shearson Lehman/American Express didn't exist.

In 1983 the five firms constituted what was called the 'special bracket' of underwriting firms, a concept that arose about thirty years ago on the basis of might is right. 'Special bracket' refers to the top group of names on a tombstone, after the managers of the issue. It is sometimes called 'the Bulge', because of its typographical shape. Its members are the 'Bulge firms'. The category is less exclusive than it sounds: many New York issues are led by humbler firms, and the special-bracket firms will take a lower position if a non-special-bracket bank invites them to join a syndicate it is managing. The term itself is a throwback to the old days of Wall Street, when important underwriting was the preserve of an upper crust. Three of the special-bracket firms (Goldman, Merrill, Salomon) are comparative newcomers to what is now a very different sort of crust; they have their origins in broking and trading, which still provide most of their business. The other two are in the old upper-crust tradition, but would not have survived as leaders had they not become sellers and traders. In 1984 the 'special bracket' changed again – and perhaps the concept expired – when Lehman Brothers was bought by Shearson/Express. Overnight the new firm became the second largest in Wall Street, after Merrill Lynch. But for those who still fancied 'upper-crust' ideas of investment banking, the Lehman slice of the firm was something to cling to.

Europeans often expect Americans to be free of snobbery, a mistake. There was plenty of it in the old investment banking. As late as the 1960s, the special bracket consisted of firms that regarded themselves as superior, because of the nature of their business, to traders like Salomon or brokerage houses like Merrill Lynch. Around the end of that decade there were four special-bracket firms, First Boston and Morgan Stanley (the two which have remained at the top), Kuhn Loeb and Dillon Read. Kuhn Loeb later merged (with Lehman Brothers) and disappeared. Dillon Read decided that small was beautiful, or perhaps adopted that philosophy in retrospect to explain its failure to keep up with the leaders. Twenty years ago the function of investment banks like these was to raise capital for companies on the basis of long associations and old friendships. It had little to do with the distributing and trading of securities. Martin Mayer's book *Wall Street*, published in 1955, had one chapter on 'The Brokers' and another on 'The Underwriters'. They were different worlds. A banker at Morgan Stanley can still say today that Pierpont Morgan would 'die at the thought' that it was now really a trading-and-commission house. But that was the case, he said, with its business as brokers and traders producing well over half the revenue.

The Wall Street community has never been large when measured by the size of its firms. Between them, in 1983, four of the five Bulge firms (the exception was Merrill Lynch, a special case) employed barely

12,000 people. Citibank, the largest commercial bank in New York (or the world), had five times that number on the payroll. The capital and reserves of the investment-banking and broking business is about eleven billion dollars, no more than that of any two or three big commercial banks put together. 'A cottage industry,' Wall Street will say, self-deprecatingly, not really meaning it. The capital-and-reserves figure is enormous beside the resources of London merchant banks and stock-brokers. The number of Wall Street employees may be comparatively small, but that is only because a high percentage of them are bankers and traders, personally responsible for major deals. There is no army of tellers and clerks to deal with a retail public (the reason Merrill Lynch employs more staff is that it still has a big retail brokerage business). The return on capital is high by banking standards, perhaps twenty per cent for Wall Street as a whole, more for the large investment banks. This concentrated profitability gives Wall Street its flavour, and encourages the visitor who wanders along its nondescript pavements to fancy that steam comes out of the gratings in the shape of dollar signs; the place is a cliché, founded on a fact.

In more exclusive times, power was still more concentrated. The 'special bracket' twenty years ago existed because the four firms were in a position to say that they would not underwrite issues unless issuers granted them special status: a laughable proposition today, with com-panies more inclined to let investment banks bid for the privilege of raising their capital. Firms were smaller then; a dozen partners was a good complement. They were more concerned with contacts than with technicalities. 'When I came here in 1958,' said another Morgan Stanley banker, 'Perry Hall, who was our managing partner, used to say within the confines of the firm that we could easily hire all the people we wanted to write prospectuses. He said, "I'm interested in the man who can bring the business in. Leave the rest to the business school students. Once you do the deal, put on your hat and go home."' Everyone knew everyone else. It was a club of sorts, run largely though not exclusively by East Coast Protestants. Morgan Stanley and First Boston were part of that tradition. So to a lesser extent was Dillon Read (Birmingham's *Our Crowd* notes that the original Mr Dillon changed his name from Lapowski). Kuhn Loeb was a Jewish house. The Jewish/gentile dis-tinction has ceased to be of more than historical interest as far as Wall Street's daily round of business is concerned. Yet there are still half-truths in casual exaggerations like that of the English banker in Wall Street who remarked that 'you might find one senior director at

Salomon who isn't Jewish, and you might find one senior partner at Morgan Stanley who is'.

Gentile or Jew, there is no doubt that years ago, the kings of Wall Street were sharply aware of their status. Raising capital was altogether grander than trading in shares. It rested on fewer, larger events. It sounded important. 'Financial engineering' is a phrase sometimes heard to describe the deal-making end of the business. At Lazard in New York, an investment bank that has ignored the trading-and-distribution side, and clings to the old ways, it is hard to get through a five-minute conversation without hearing about 'financial engineering'. The phrase itself is more recent, but the concept is the old one. A major deal was something to be savoured for weeks or months afterwards. Trading and commission business, on the other hand, came and went every day. It was a business for young men with quick wits and strong constitutions. It was also faintly vulgar. Now that investment banks have come to rely on it for a high percentage of their income, few still look down their noses at the traders. As it happens, the best of these are often Jews, who dominate many trading floors in the West with their quick cleverness, as expatriate Chinese do in the East.

The severest charge levelled against Wall Street's inner circle in the past was that it operated as a cartel against the public interest. The theory that a small group of investment bankers carved up the underwriting of securities among themselves, at the cost of competition, had obvious attractions for anyone in search of financial conspiracies. A small group of bankers plainly existed and flourished. Not long after World War 2, the United States Government charged seventeen firms, Morgan Stanley being the ringleader, with entering into 'a combination, conspiracy and agreement' to monopolise the securities business. The original complaint was filed in October 1947. It has been said that the real motive was that Harry S. Truman, the Democratic President, thought it would be politically useful if he were seen to be mounting an attack on Wall Street. The case came before a circuit judge, Harold R. Medina, who lived with it for the next seven years. The Government's case rested on circumstantial evidence. Since the circumstances went back at least to 1915 when the prosecution supposed (erroneously) that the syndicate system had been invented – it went back another twenty years – the amount of evidence was formidable. Ten thousand documents, and 1,700 pages of transcripts from preliminary hearings, had been assembled by November 1950 when the trial finally got under way. This ended two and a half years later (by which time Eisenhower was President and the Korean War was nearly over), and produced twenty-four thousand pages of transcript. The total number of words spoken and written, before Medina delivered his judgement in 1953, must have been twenty million or more, the equivalent of two hundred substantial books; his own judgement makes a good-size volume. It is unlikely that any branch of the financial industry anywhere has ever been subjected to such detailed, painstaking and tedious analysis.

The result of this enormous labour was a small, very dead mouse. Far from finding a mosaic of conspiracy, Medina saw only 'a constantly changing panorama of competition among the seventeen defendant firms'. The Government had claimed that an improper reciprocity could be detected in the way investment banks exchanged favours by inviting one another into syndicates. Medina shrugged his shoulders and found that the banks, 'motivated by various considerations of a purely business character', were simply following the way of the world, where 'it is a natural and normal thing for those in the same industry occasionally to seek business on the basis of business given'. Among the innumerable threads that ran through this 'hodge-podge' (Medina's words) was the relationship between Morgan Stanley and AT&T, dating back to the bank's earliest days, and an issue of stock worth $43 million in 1935. American Telephone had been a client of the house of Morgan. When the Glass-Steagall Act drove commercial banks out of capital-raising in 1934, investment bankers queued up to solicit custom from AT&T. But as soon as Telephone's president heard that some of the Morgan partners were breaking away to form their own investment bank, he declared, 'That solves my problems', and gave them the business, which has helped nourish Morgan Stanley ever since. Why should there have been any impropriety? asked the judge. Surely it was more reasonable to look at the Morgan reputation for integrity and success. Accompanied by many such sanguine observations from Judge Medina, the US Government's case collapsed into a few tons of waste paper. There was no conspiracy and no monopoly. Business for the 'Club of Seventeen', as the trial led people to call it, went on as before. It was only after another twenty or thirty years, as commercial pressures began to break up the structure of Wall Street, that a certain justification for the original prosecution becomes apparent. In the legal sense there had been no conspiracy. But the case had surely sprung, in part at least, from a perception that the investment bankers were having a fine old time inside their protected world, and that 'competition' was a

81

relative term. Lewis L. Glucksman of Lehman Brothers – a prominent member of the 'Club of Seventeen', and until 1984 one of the most powerful firms in Wall Street – remarked in passing that 'The Medina case may have been bad law – the truth is that the industry was not as competitive as the defendants liked to allege.'

The scene that Medina brooded on has changed irrevocably, not least in the style of its practitioners. The recent history of Lehman is worth a glance, by way of introduction to that scene. Its full title was Lehman Brothers Kuhn Loeb; the weaker firm was absorbed in 1977. Although not one of the Bulge firms, it felt it deserved to be. The firm traced itself back to the 1850s. Commodity broker in the nineteenth century, it moved into investment banking in the twentieth, solidifying into a partnership built around the Lehman of the day. The final incumbent was Robert, whose heavy-looking bust stared at visitors in the board-room, forty-five floors up in a modern tower near the Battery. The banker who was showing me around in 1983 said that Bobby was suspicious of journalists, which one might have guessed from the implacable look of the bust. The view from these high office blocks, where many investment banks have moved from older premises, is spectacular, across the crinkled Upper Bay, busy with craft, to the Statue of Liberty and Staten Island. But new premises give physical shape to a break with the past. In Lehman's case, the move pained some of its older partners (they became 'managing directors' when the firm ceased to be a partnership, but the old title lingered). Their previous home was a wedge-shaped building, eleven storeys high, at 1 William Street. There the imperious Bobby Lehman presided over a firm that failed to change quickly enough to stay in the front rank. Presumably it could have been content with a smaller excellence, like Lazard and Dillon Read. This may have been what some of the partners wanted. But Lehman's death in 1969 left a vacuum and lack of leadership that combined with falling profits and insufficient capital to undermine the firm. It was not until 1973, with the appointment as chairman of a businessman-politician, Peter G. Peterson, that the bank began its rough ride back to prosperity. Peterson, an American of Greek descent, had been Nixon's Secretary of Commerce in 1972, leaving the Administration before the Watergate scandal. He reorganised the management and gave Lewis Glucksman, who had been with the firm for ten years, his freedom to develop trading and distribution.

Lehman Brothers came back to life and power, which now meant size as well as quality; within a few years of Peterson's arrival, the number of partners had doubled to above eighty. In 1973 the firm's capital was less than $13 million, nothing like enough to enable a busy trading house to 'take positions' in stock and bonds, where the underlying bedrock of capital must be of a certain size to support the superstructure of borrowing what is needed to finance those trading positions. Investment banks may also need large sums at short notice to buy new securities from a company. This is the novel and more dangerous kind of underwriting, the 'bought deal', where a company sells off an entire issue of stock or bonds to the investment bank that pays the best price. There may be no time to form a syndicate. Under a new regulation, introduced (to sharpen competition) in 1982 by the Securities and Exchange Commission – Rule 415 – a company can register the deal and then leave the securities 'on the shelf', ready to issue when it thinks the time is right. Instead of an investment bank that acts as an old friend, discussing the deal at leisure and on an equal footing with the client, there may be a string of banks bidding hastily against one another for a piece of business. The winner buys the deal outright. This makes investment banking a kind of block trading. The method is neither as profitable nor as dignified as the other. A bought deal doesn't have to be a '415' offering. The technique was already in use before the rule was introduced, especially by Salomon Brothers, whose aggressive skills thrived on it. Rule 415 began as an experiment and was confirmed the following year. Almost two-fifths of the $97 billion underwritten by Wall Street firms in 1983 was in '415' offerings. They crystallise the shift to a 'trading' mentality, stripping the arcane capital-raising business of its trimmings, reducing it to a simple sale of a block of securities to whichever bank or banks will pay the most. This is the mentality to which everyone had to adjust. To the outsider, once he has had the technicalities explained, it seems simple enough. But it has no emotional content for him. To the insider it marks the destruction of landmarks and habits. This is why Richard Fisher became president of Morgan Stanley and Lewis Glucksman chairman of Lehman Brothers, because they had always been on the 'trading' side of their firms, and could make the adjustment. Lehman, slow to appreciate what was happening, eventually moved before it was too late. In the ten years from 1974, the firm's capital rose to $300 million, enough for it to be taken seriously in the trading age. Having outgrown William Street, Lehman moved in stages to the new building at 55 Water Street, where it occupied six floors; the last part to go was the investment-banking department, which didn't leave its panelled den until 1980.

The new Wall Street grates with some, reflecting one generation's view of the next. Among its critics is Stanislas Yassukovich, the son of a Wall Street banker, himself now a well-known banker in London. He says that the old-style partners, often prosperous in their own right, not needing to rely on the firm's profits year by year, have been 'replaced by people who are possibly harder working, probably cleverer, certainly more ambitious. They start with no money and are out to make it quickly, which produces a different ethical approach.' A New York banker, the survivor of a family broking firm that was swallowed by a bigger fish a few years ago, and who now works for the predator, said that 'Wall Street will adjust to any technical changes if people pay them enough to do it. We will do anything for money.' I said, 'Anything?' 'Anything, if you pay us enough. It's one of the problems of Wall Street. Basically there is a strong ethic and morality that runs through the place. But the dominating theme is the making of money. The possibilities of making enormous amounts of money attract a certain percentage of people who become indifferent to any kind of ethical standards.' It wasn't clear whether he meant today or always. But under the surface of what he was saying lay the bitterness of someone who felt that a dishonourable system had wronged him. A distaste for the new Wall Street can even appear in a novel, treading where reporters can't. The novelist Michael M. Thomas once worked for Lehman Brothers. His father, the late Joseph A. Thomas, was a partner there in its imperial days. An author's note to *Green Monday* (1980) says that his father is the principal source of 'whatever is insightful about investment banking' in the book. The novel, about high finance, nicely catches the feeling of lost worlds in its opening pages. Michael Thomas makes a banker of the old school say that 'the Street' is changing, that 'there are awful people coming into the business: shoe salesmen disguised as brokers'. Another character mourns the end of discretion. 'Today,' he says, 'the partners in firms fight with each other and boast and publicise their "conquests" like motion picture starlets displaying their underpants.'

Such comments, however heartfelt, are no more than marginal notes to a process that grinds ahead. The investment bank is dead: long live the investment bank. Lehman Brothers, in the shape of Peter Peterson and Lewis Glucksman, invited me to hear about the firm from them at nine o'clock one morning. The meeting was in a private dining-room. Breakfast was served; I had already eaten, thinking that breakfast meetings began earlier. Peterson's title was chairman, Glucksman's president. From other accounts it seemed standard practice that they be

84

interviewed together, to stress that they ran Lehman jointly. Peterson had a lined face and made impeccable simplifications for me in a flat, cool manner. Glucksman was pinker and plumper, and said less with more warmth. Peterson remarked that there was often a lag between the true state of a firm and the outsider's perception. After Bobby Lehman died, there was a positive lag: outsiders thought it was still the firm it had been in his day. Now they had a negative lag: the world had caught up with the post-Bobby Lehman situation, but wasn't always aware that that, in turn, had been superseded by a series of 'profound' improvements. 'Lew and I are the closest of friends,' he said, and Lew nodded. 'We consult several times a day. We can finish each other's paragraphs. We share a common vision of what we are trying to do with the business.' Years ago they had sat down together to visualise the future of the industry and Lehman's place in it. They agreed on the need to be strong in trading and distribution, and the symbolic importance of the move out of William Street. 'A large body of opinion on the investment-banking side thought it was a serious mistake,' said Peterson. 'They said that the mystique, the elegance, the legacy, the history, whatever words you want to use to describe the essence of this business, would be lost. He and I were arguing something different: that in this more competitive, sophisticated financial world, the distinction between trading-and-distribution and underwriting would get blurred. It was essential to integrate them, physically and psychologically. Today if you go down to the trading floor, we have fifteen investment bankers working there. I think Lew would have been laughed at for that concept a few years ago.'

'I *was* laughed at,' said Glucksman.

They talked about how underwriting by itself was no longer a firm's bread and butter. Clients, more knowledgeable now, raised capital wherever it was cheapest; margins of profit had shrunk. 'I believe there is no firm now that derives as much as half its revenue from investment banking,' said Glucksman. They wouldn't say what the figure was. I asked if it wouldn't be logical to abandon investment banking altogether and concentrate on trading in securities, if that was where the money came from. You couldn't, they said. Trading was capital-intensive and carried higher risks. Its profits might be high, but they were also volatile, because securities markets were volatile. In a sense the trading side was out of one's control. Despite all the changes, the investment-banking business was steadier. Apart from underwriting, there were activities that didn't involve committing large amounts of capital, such as restructuring companies or arranging mergers and acquisitions, both of which gave a good return.

Peterson said the bank had a clear management structure now. He talked about lines of responsibility, budgets and discipline. When he went to Lehman Brothers in 1973, people made decisions fuzzily, by consensus. 'When you have fifteen people voting endlessly on things, it isn't likely you will have a sharp cutting edge,' he said. He spoke of Bobby Lehman. 'I'm one of the few people in the world who didn't know him,' he said. 'He must have been a marvellous human being, a unique person and a unique talent.' (Peterson seemed to have it off by heart. Two years earlier he told the magazine *Euromoney*, 'I'm one of the few people in the world that didn't know Bobby, but he must have been a really remarkable human being and person.') He said Lehman had been a Toscanini who could orchestrate groups of people. 'There were separate string quartets, each playing,' he said, and sawed at an imaginary violin. 'Somehow the entire ensemble sounded good. That structure, I think, Lew, worked fine as long as Bobby was here. It was built around a series of strong personalities. One of the things that as Lew knows troubled me when I came here was that many of them referred to clients as *"my* clients". Groups were withholding information. Very bluntly, some of these people felt free to talk to the press and express their views about colleagues in less than flattering terms.'

All this had been swept away. But it was interesting that Peterson, one of Wall Street's most efficient new brooms, represented, in the style of his conversation and his background, the traditional type of investment-bank partner. The firm still included some copper-bottomed former politicians, as in the past. When Peterson joined it, apparently he had no intention of running the firm. He was just another distinguished recruit, the difference being that he arrived at a climacteric in Lehman Brothers' history, and saw the need for drastic action. His status enabled him to attack the problem from within an elite group into which, in calmer times, he might have been absorbed. In so doing, he saved the firm and changed its face, even if the salvation turned out to be short-lived. As breakfast came and went that winter morning early in 1983, when perhaps Lehman Brothers thought that another hundred and thirty years of independence lay ahead, Peterson and Glucksman talked about the reawakening of the firm. It was impossible not to notice the contrast in styles. The chairman was precise, haughty, impatient, severe. He was the king or general. Glucksman was the field commander. He was earthier and seemed less at ease than he did when we talked

86

later, on his beloved sales-and-trading floor, with the ship's telegraph by his desk, or in his private sitting-room nearby with a US Navy chronometer on the wall, and a bookcase with a soft hat on top. Before we left the breakfast-table, there was a poignant incident. The chairs we were sitting in were light-framed, in some antique style. After an exchange of views, the heavily built Glucksman leaned back and the chair broke, almost throwing him to the floor. 'I hope you didn't hurt yourself,' Peterson said in the detached voice of a thin man under whom chairs don't collapse. 'No,' muttered Glucksman, inspecting the damage, 'this one's been broken before.' We might have left it at that. But Peterson pursued the subject. 'In the old days,' he said, 'I could have attributed it to your weight. But now. . . .' He turned to me. 'Mr Glucksman, as he's grown in intellectual and psychic power and so forth, he's lost about sixty or seventy pounds.'

Mr Glucksman gave no sign of resenting this. Presently he took me down to sales and trading, and we sat in his glassed-off quarters. Enormous sums of money drifted through the conversation. 'Half a billion dollars is a number that doesn't bother me,' he said. 'Depending on the way the market seems to be going, I wouldn't mind owning a billion dollars or more at risk.' That is, the firm might own that quantity of securities without initially having a buyer. Two weeks before, he said, they had bought an issue of $550 million floating-rate bonds from a client. The deal was done over a Thursday and Friday – the worst time, because it left the firm holding the bonds over a weekend, two days without trading, ample time for a crisis to erupt somewhere in the world and affect Monday's prices. 'But this,' said Glucksman, 'is a game for the bold and imaginative who are willing to take risks. We seem to have learned how to do that quite well. Look at their age on the floor. These are young people.' Desks, TV screens and chairs with red upholstery stretched in two directions. Glucksman asked me if I noticed anything special about the room. I didn't. He said there were no windows, or rather there was one window remaining, but that was going soon. 'Trading is its own environment,' he said placidly. 'I'm blocking them all off. Windows are one of my fixations. It doesn't mean I'm right. But I've decided the focus should be on the room. I really think windows are wrong.'

What seemed, from the outside, the idiosyncrasies of a colourful man, may have had a different meaning for some of Lehman's principals. The conflicts of style between 'traders' and 'bankers', latent in many Wall Street houses, were nearer the surface at Lehman Brothers.

In retrospect, Peterson's prepared phrases about Bobby Lehman betray a nervousness about the balance between the old and the new. Glucksman was less tactful than he might have been about the old guard. He may have harboured resentments of his own. What is certain is that in mid-1983, Lehman Brothers Kuhn Loeb announced that Peter Peterson was leaving to start a venture-capital business, that Lewis Glucksman would progressively assume complete control, and that on the first day of 1984 he would formally be named sole chairman of the firm. It was the new Wall Street at work. The field commander seems to have confronted the king and told him there had just been a change of government. Peterson was bewildered. He confided in a friend that he hardly knew what happened, the move was so sudden and violent. He planned to retire in two or three years, in any case. Rather than deepen conflicts within the firm, he went quietly. Rumours of bloodshed were discounted. When the London *Economist* wrote that Peterson had received 'a polite but firm shove out of the door', one of Lehman's bankers, the former politician George W. Ball, hurried into print to affirm that there had been merely 'an amicable transfer of power'.

But the resentments were there. They increased later in the year when some 'bankers' felt that 'traders' were being favoured with bonus payments. At the same time, securities trading struck a bad patch. The same was happening at other firms. But at Lehman it may have helped erode Glucksman's authority, despite his high standing as a trader. Under the circumstances, this was as inevitable as it was unfair. The emphasis may have shifted too far and too fast from 'banking' to 'trading', and not only at Lehman Brothers. Rumours circulated that the firm was up for sale. Its capital was said to be insufficient for the role it wanted. In April 1984 the directors sold Lehman Brothers for $360 million to one of the new Wall Street conglomerates, Shearson/American Express. The old Lehman ceased to exist. It became part of a financial-services, investment-banking corporation, itself (see Chapter 5) a cauldron of change. It was thought that Lewis Glucksman, to be retained as a 'consultant', would collect about $13 million for his personal shareholding in the firm. It may not have been victory, but it was quite a comfortable way of losing.

*   *   *

First Boston, like Morgan Stanley, has its headquarters in mid-town Manhattan. It occupies ten floors in a glass tower of which it's a part-owner. The address is Park Avenue Plaza, a mild deception, since between the tower and Park Avenue stand the select premises of the Racquet and Tennis Club. The way in to Park Avenue Plaza is from 52nd Street. The plaza itself is the spacious air-conditioned hall that occupies the ground floor. A café, open to its surroundings, suggests that you are outdoors and not under a roof. On the wall, water flows down a sheet of some darkly glowing mineral, the size of a cinema screen. The usual security men prowl about. To reach the offices above, you travel up an escalator to a mezzanine level. Here a bare floor that clacks underfoot leads to what looks from a distance like a breast-high wall or barricade. It is made of some gritty, marbled substance, sloping inwards from its base. Men and women stand behind it with telephones and lists. His destination checked, the visitor is directed to a bank of lifts. A sign warns: 'Elevators under video surveillance.' Each car has a lens in the roof. Someone is watching the top of my head as I go up forty-three floors to the First Boston reception.

Even more than in Lehman Brothers' case, the building has symbolic importance. For a period in the 1970s, First Boston was moribund. Both its distribution and investment-banking capacities were inadequate. As in the case of Lehman, a stranger was needed to force a change of heart. The board chose the president of Merrill Lynch, George Shinn, a taciturn man of Scots descent who plays the bagpipes. As president, he was No. 2 in Merrill Lynch's large and complicated hierarchy. His arrival at First Boston in 1975 displeased the old guard, who, on familiar old-guard lines, caricatured Merrill Lynch as a conglomeration of salesmen, performing their mundane task of serving retail clients through offices all over America. Shinn hired and fired remorselessly, 'and some of the people that I left on their own,' he says, 'I *wish* I had fired.' The firm's worst year, darkness before the dawn, was 1978. Profits had all but vanished. Behind First Boston's back, some of its rivals were whispering to clients that the firm was about to collapse. Shinn's changes, which included a bigger staff and a stronger trading department, were still working their way through the system. But one weekend that year, he signed the deal with European partners that produced the investment bank of Credit Suisse First Boston, a profitable associate. In the same year he signed the lease for Park Avenue Plaza, 'because I decided our previous location wasn't good enough. We didn't go to Sixth Avenue, where some of our friends are [he meant Morgan Stanley]. *This* is the international banking centre, between the PanAm building and Fifty-ninth Street.' Shinn's good deed still reverberates in the firm's spacious premises. 'We were living in a rabbit warren downtown in Exchange Place,' says one of his fans, 'and that's a kind expression. He signed the lease in the worst year financially in the firm's history. And now look at these quarters. They're the envy of the Street! Nobody's got offices like these!'

A Wall Street insider might guess that a man who speaks with built-in exclamation marks at First Boston is going to be the engaging Joseph R. Perella. Perella, born 1941, is the joint chief (with Bruce Wasserstein, born 1947) of the firm's M&A, its mergers-and-acquisitions department. Each probably earns millions of dollars a year. Perella is one of the most publicised investment bankers in New York, his dome of hairless head and thick piratical beard a familiar sight alongside articles about the drama of the takeover. One or two senior people at First Boston groaned when I said I was hoping to see Joe Perella. They don't deny that Perella, Wasserstein and the rest of the smoking-hot M&A department are doing a magnificent job, etc., but please would people remember that First Boston does a few other things as well. 'What you ought to be doing,' snapped an executive on the sales-and-trading side, 'is dealing with the financials – how profitable is this firm, from whence is it making its money? Then if you want to embellish it with colourful stories about Joe Perella and stuff like that, OK.' The financials he was keen on showed that in the previous year, 1982, First Boston had revenues of $500 million. Among the Bulge firms, this almost certainly made it larger than Morgan Stanley and much smaller than either Goldman Sachs or Salomon Brothers. The uncertainty is because two of these three rivals are privately owned and don't disclose revenue or earnings, and the third, Salomon, is part of a larger corporation, in which its own figures can sink conveniently from sight. First Boston is a public company (as is Merrill Lynch, the biggest of them all), so its figures are in the annual report. Of the $500 million of revenue, almost half came from trading in securities. A fifth was in commissions from clients (First Boston acting as a stockbroker) and in interest on dividends and loans. That left $150 million, thirty per cent of the total, being generated by 'investment banking', most of it underwriting and mergers-and-acquisitions. After the costs of running the firm and the payment of taxes, First Boston's earnings for the year were $93 million dollars.* (This is fifty times what they were in 1978.) The sales-and-

---

* The 1983 figures had a different emphasis. Of $515 million in revenue, trading provided only thirty-four per cent, commissions thirteen per cent. Investment banking was now the largest item, thirty-eight per cent, confirming what the old hands say, that because trading is so volatile, it is not entirely to be trusted.

trading man who was directing my attention to the figures got carried away when he showed me investment banking's thirty per cent and cried, 'It's a peanuts business.' Furthermore, he said, their operating costs were higher. Investment banking generated thirty per cent of revenue but not thirty per cent of earnings. Study the numbers, he kept saying, study the numbers.

Whatever M&A's contribution to the profits, its contribution to the revenue is $50 million or more. It says something for the bravado of big Wall Street firms that anyone can say that generating $50 million is peanuts. In 1984, when Texaco absorbed Getty Oil in the biggest corporate takeover until then, worth $10 billion, First Boston, brought in at the last minute as intermediary, was paid $10 million for seventy-nine hours' work, a bit more than $2,000 a minute. Goldman Sachs, hired earlier to advise the Getty management, was said to be getting $18 million. All investment banks resent the idea that their M&A work is done on the basis of time spent. The value of the deal, the quality of the advice, are what matter. A First Boston apologist says it's like complaining that 'you went to the best brain surgeon in the world, and he only took two hours to remove the tumour'. This doesn't stop outsiders continuing to shake their heads at such figures. There is a kind of madness in them. Sometimes it seems to be a game where it is impossible to lose. When Texaco was pursuing Getty, apparently it decided at first to hire Morgan Stanley. At almost the same moment that Texaco called one part of the firm, another of the leading oil companies, Standard Oil of California (Socal), was calling another part, to retain Morgan Stanley in any possible takeover bid; the oil business was in turmoil just then. The Socal commission was accepted a few minutes before the Texaco news was circulated. Morgan had to turn down Texaco. First Boston got the job and earned a fortune. However, Morgan Stanley, not being involved, was able to speculate on the outcome of the Texaco–Getty deal, and made $11 million in securities dealing. A couple of months later, Socal decided to swallow Gulf Oil. This, in turn, became the biggest takeover in US history, worth more than $13 billion. Morgan's fee for this was around $20 million. A Morgan banker said that, to be honest, there was a lot of luck in it. 'You have,' he said, 'to be standing on the right street corner when the bus comes through.'

Waiting on the forty-third floor to meet Perella, I passed the time with a package of material sent out by his department. It came in a handsome bronze-coloured folder containing thirty-four exhibits; most of these were offprints from newspapers and magazines. Presently I heard voices from a gallery or half-floor above, that was linked with the waiting area by an open staircase. A man said, 'Did you take care of that one over there?' I looked up expectantly. A woman said, 'There's too much sun.' The speakers weren't visible. Then a young woman in jeans carrying a white urn and a feather duster came down the staircase. It was like an episode in a dream, until the urn changed into a watering can. She bore down on a straggly plant by a window that framed the East River, dusting and sprinkling it. Then Perella came to collect me.

He wanted to know everything, what the book was about, how much tape I had in the tape-recorder, why I didn't think it important to drink salt-free mineral water; he kept a supply in his desk. Who had I been to see? When I reeled off names, he snorted and rolled his eyes in sympathy. Soon he came round to my side of the desk and sat with his knees touching mine, talking fiercely into my face, as though about to butt me with the fine parchment-coloured dome of his head. His office was separated by glass from the big room outside, and passers-by received a wave and occasionally a shout. Once he leapt to his feet, clicked his heels and gave a Nazi salute. 'He's a German,' he explained. After a while Perella declared, 'There's a banana hour in every work environment. Here it's usually around four to six o'clock. Banana hour is now over.' Even so, the conversation would suddenly take an unexpected turn. Discussing the creativity of investment bankers, he said dismissively that 'any profession has a high proportion of cookie-cutters'. I asked what a cookie-cutter was. It was a man who had nothing better to do than cut out cookies, he said. This began another train of thought. He produced a mail-order catalogue for kitchen equipment, and showed me what fabulous things one could buy for Italian cooking, like pizza bricks to soak up the greasiness that ruined pizzas cooked on a metal surface. After each aside he would seize the recorder and insist on winding it back a few minutes, 'to save your tape'.

His point about the creative banker was serious enough; so were all his points; no doubt the style was part of the armoury. All he did was exploit the conservative idiom of his trade by being its anti-matter. Investment bankers paid lip service to 'creativity', he said, and came to believe their own rhetoric. But most of them were implementors, not creators. The policy in First Boston's M & A department was to position creative people so that information could flow over them. Perella duly talked about technical innovation in the construction of bids for companies, but much of what he said came back to low, or perhaps high, cunning in the service of clients. For example, he said, when a banker was defending a company, it was useful to create doubts in the mind of the market about the raiding company. 'Because all that's operating here is greed,' he said. 'So you couple fear and greed, which are the two greatest forces at work in the market. If you get 'em greedy, the shareholders are going to be looking for a buck. But if you create the fear that the guy they've got their stock parked at may never pay them, you have an explosion in the emotional element of the deal. And on this matter I would have to say we have no equal. The path is littered with other firms who have tried to tangle with us.' He was full of praise for his firm, for George Shinn who told him, 'Joe, go out and hire people', for the 'backbone and fibre' of the place. Newspapers said First Boston was aggressive? 'We were the firm that was criticised for being sleepy, white-Anglo-Saxon Protestant, white shoe, whatever you want to say. OK, now we're making money, we're aggressive. What's wrong with that? Pretty soon we're going to be *too* aggressive, I'm sure.' First Boston, he insisted, was also 'an island of civilisation, and I'm speaking as a person who has done a lot of things. I've driven taxis, I've sold encyclopaedias, I've worked in bottling plants. I was an accountant, a CPA, what you call a chartered accountant in your country. That was about the highest level of work I did before I came here' (in 1972).

For the critics (there are many) of M&A activity, who see it as a black art practised by investment banks to line their own pockets regardless of the consequences, Perella had the pragmatist's scorn. A firm hired a bank to expedite a merger or fight off a predator, that was all. He had read an article about clients being goaded. 'What's the implication of *goad*? That people running businesses are weak-kneed individuals without minds of their own, and investment bankers come on the scene and start telling them what to do? Nothing could be further from the truth. These are people who have made up their minds. They've said, "Look, Turkey", or "Look, Sam", depending on what your name is and how they perceive you, "I've hired you guys and I'm paying you big money because you're supposed to be good. Now tell me how to get it done." OK? When you get a reputation as a group that gets tough deals done, people seek you out. But they don't sit there like blubber on a rock, saying, "Mr Wall Street Investment Bank, push me, shove me, any shape you want me."'

Among the handful of banks that practise M&A on a large scale, business is much sought after. Once a comparative sideline as far as Wall Street was concerned, it blossomed in the United States after about 1974. The stock market was depressed, companies were thus undervalued, and in inflationary times it was cheap to borrow to finance a takeover. The particular significance of 1974 is that until then the hostile takeover by a blue-chip company was regarded as unethical in Wall Street. The convention was already wearing thin when Morgan Stanley, having refused to act for several would-be predators, concluded that the taboo would be broken sooner or later, so why not by it? In at least one instance the bank had already told a target company that unless it agreed to a merger, it would be attacked. The company surrendered and the threat was never made public. Now Morgan Stanley advised International Nickel Co. of Canada in a hostile bid for a firm in Philadelphia. The bid failed but the point was made. Thus legitimised, raids on companies became standard practice.

At the same time, the old stable relationships between investment banks and their clients were breaking down. A sense that banks would one day be hired guns, selling their services (whether for underwriting or for M&A) one deal at a time, to clients who felt entitled to pick and choose, was creeping into Wall Street. As for fees, enormous capital values could be involved in a merger, and investment bankers were able to play their usual game of relating rewards to the largest figure in sight. Boards of directors and chief officers of companies threatened with unwelcome takeover were often willing to throw money (the shareholders' money) at any bank that could save them, typically by producing an acceptable 'white knight' who would take them over instead. Takeover battles are attractive in other ways. They suggest a landscape of heroic figures, battling for power and glory. Perella has a particular brand of flamboyance, but there is no shortage of personality. Morgan Stanley's Robert F. Greenhill has a thrusting, macho approach. The client is likely to be a powerful man in his own right, at a crisis in his life. 'His neck is on the line,' said Greenhill. 'If he's the target of a takeover, he can find himself at the short end of the stick, without a job.' I asked if chief executives ever wept on his shoulder or wanted to hit him. 'Sure,' said Greenhill, 'all of the above. It's important to know about a chief executive, whether he has the stomach for a fight. You see people with the veneer stripped away, in their elemental form.'

The amounts of money and the drama ensure newspaper publicity, agreeable in itself and also as a means of attracting more business from companies, which, it is hoped, will remember what they read about X's feats in the field when their own troubles come. From time to time there are spasms of self-advertisement. First Boston will buy full pages to crow, 'Leadership in Mergers and Acquisitions: Number 1', with a list of transactions and the flat statement, 'First Boston is regarded as the leading M&A advisor'. Lehman Brothers, before 1984 a contender for the title, would counter with 'Mergers. Acquisitions. Divestitures. And who *really* leads,' concluding of course that Lehman Brothers did. 'We can all prove it, based on our own definitions,' someone said at First Boston. Goldman Sachs is very active. Merrill and Salomon handle M&A business and would like to handle more.

I asked Joe Perella if Salomon Brothers was in the front rank. 'Well,' he said, unsmiling, 'Ira Harris [its M&A man] was on the cover of *Business Week*.' Rather like a show-business star, Perella is ambiguous about the media, which he sees as friend and enemy together. He described how a magazine had telephoned to say they wanted him and another firm's M&A man on the cover with champagne being poured over them, dripping on their suits. 'I said to them, "Wait a minute, it's not that I wear English suits and pay a lot of money for them" – They say, "Don't worry about it, our artist can draw it." I say, "You don't understand, I'm a professional person. I get paid good money. It's sort of demeaning to be on the cover of a magazine with booze being poured all over you." So then they decide to call my bluff. This other guy's an egomaniac, like half the people who work on Wall Street, and he can't *resist* being on the cover. So the magazine calls me up and says, "We've talked to our art director and he says the only way he'll do it is on his terms," and I say, "Well, I guess I'll just have to tell my kids I *could* have been on the cover. Goodbye." Boom! As a result they did the cover with faceless people down in the right-hand corner. There was a picture portfolio of people inside. *I* wasn't in it of course, because I'd been asked to be on the cover and had declined. My partner Wasserstein was in it instead.'

Even the language of M&A is larded with terms that sound as if they had been invented with the object of attracting attention. Among the Crown Jewels, the Big Rube, the Legs-Up Option, the Double-Barrelled Two-step, the Bear Hug and the Shark Repellent, some of them probably were. This is not to decry the technical skills that go into them. The best strategies demand an understanding of the law (Bruce Wasserstein is a lawyer) and of company structure, as well as of the shareholders' psychology. Not infrequently the courts are invoked by a losing company in an attempt, sometimes successful, to block an enemy strategy. Legal costs help to eat into the earnings of M&A departments. Nor does the handful of sensational takeovers fairly represent the daily round of business, which is full of expensive false starts and dead ends. Also in the M&A hierarchy at First Boston is the 'creative director', Bill Lambert, whose job it is to seek out promising situations. Lambert (born 1947) has a beard that rivals Perella's and wears corduroys and coloured shirts, unless he is visiting companies, when he puts on a suit. His title and appearance provoke banter on the lines of 'I thought First Boston was a bank, not an advertising agency'. *Institutional Investor* quoted an anonymous rival at another firm as saying that 'the concept of having a bearded guy in an attic thinking up ideas all the time is baloney'. Lambert is unperturbed. Before he joined First Boston he was a research analyst, studying companies and assessing their potential for investors. Much of his time now is spent doing what he did then, making visits and asking questions, though for different ends. His starting point is the '*Fortune* 500', the list of leading industrial corporations, but his interest extends lower down the scale. He is continually shuffling his information, looking for connections between possible buyers and possible sellers. The information itself is raw material, in theory available to anyone. But relationships have to be built up so that, when the day comes, his ideas will be listened to. Even in his time with First Boston, which he joined in 1978, he has found firms that aren't used to having bankers call on them: the old order of things was the other way round.

Lambert says his method is 'persistence', that 'you never know till you ask', that 'as Bruce says, there's money in the Street'. When he talks to a company, he has the outsider's privilege of being able to speak freely. 'The chief executive might have his junior assistant with him who'll be grimacing at me, like, *Don't say that*. Then the CEO will say, "You're right! I've got to do something about it, but I don't know what."' I asked Lambert if that made his heart leap up. 'No,' he said flatly, 'it just means there's potential.' As for those who criticised his approach, 'I figure, screw 'em. What can I tell you? Everybody does business in his own way. But it's funny, several banks recently have tried to do what we're doing. One guy called up a client and said, "I'm the Bill Lambert of my firm." He found it amusing. I don't find it amusing because I don't find competition amusing.' I said that flattery was all right. 'I like flattery,' he said. 'However, I prefer there to be no competition.' He got into his stride, an authentic Wall Street heart beating under his check shirt and jazzy pullover. 'Every time someone does a deal and I'm not in it,' he said, 'they're taking money away from me. As Morgan feels every time *we* do a deal. As Goldman feels. As

Lazard feels. These people will look at someone else's deal, as I do, and say, "How can we break it up?" Quite simply, "How – can – we – break – it – up?"'

I asked if there was an element of spite in that, but he said I had missed the point. Other banks merely wanted to get the business for one of their own clients. It was a transaction. It was nothing personal.

When a contested takeover is in progress, professional speculators, including those at investment banks, seek to make money by guessing the outcome – buying or selling stock in the companies involved, in the hope that the new value of the securities at the end of the affair will leave them with a profit. This is how Morgan Stanley made its $11 million in the Texaco–Getty deal. It is a pure trading function, an 'arbitrage' between prices under two sets of circumstances. Some specialist firms do nothing else. Investment banks all do it, unless they are acting for one of the companies involved, in which case the rules against insider trading forbid them to take a position. Arguments can arise inside a bank about whether it will make more money by declining to act for a company, and letting its arbitrageurs get to work, or by agreeing to act, and freezing all trading activity in that area. The profits (and losses) in this gambling on takeovers can be enormous; in mergers and acquisitions, as in most activities on Wall Street, the trading floor is never far away. When George Shinn announced his retirement from First Boston in 1983 – he had decided to go back to his old college, Amherst, and take a master's degree in English – his successor, promoted within the firm, was another banker with a trading background, Peter T. Buchanan. Buchanan says that 'the trading community has only recently emerged as a force unto itself', that 'the trading markets have exploded', and 'the opportunity for growth in revenues has outstripped the opportunity in corporate finance'.

After we had had two meetings, Joe Perella decided it was time I was introduced to the First Boston trading room. For our second conversation he had taken me to what he said was his favourite Italian restaurant, where he talked to the proprietor about vintage Ferraris, a car he was thinking of buying, and to me about deals, money, greed and other banks, tapping my tape machine significantly when he came to a bit he didn't want recorded for posterity. From some angles he looked like Lenin. As we walked back to the office, up Park Lane, a wild-eyed woman approached us waving a handful of dollar bills. 'Sir,' she said, 'can you help me? I've got to catch a train.' 'I can't help you,' said Perella, looking her up and down, not sliding past with averted eye in the British manner. At the bank, by the entrance to the trading floor, a woman at the security desk challenged him. 'I work here,' he said.

Hundreds work on the trading floor, which First Boston claims is 'the largest private trading facility in the world'. It covers not far short of an acre. Most of Perella's guided tour was incomprehensible. He pointed out a woman in a red sweater who used to work for him as a secretary and was now a professional. He pointed out Richard T. Curvin, then the managing director in charge of sales and trading, member of the executive committee and the board (he has since left First Boston). 'He's made us profitable in all markets, good or bad,' said Perella, and left me with him. Curvin had no time to talk then. He moved about the floor like a mission controller among the telephones and video screens, waiting for a launch. When I returned later he said he hoped I hadn't been seduced by the glamour of the investment-banking departments. The firm, he said kindly, was much bigger than Joe Perella and Bruce Wasserstein. The errors of Wall Street watchers seemed to weigh on his mind. He was lean with piercing eyes, his smile on the brink of a snarl. Take the new-issue business, he said. It was very expensive, with high overheads; it could be quite risky; there was a limit to how much any issue could earn – 'it has a cap on it in terms of upside potential', was the phrase he used. 'When you bring in a new issue,' he said, 'you can't mark it up in price, but you sure can mark it down.' I asked if the potential for loss as an underwriter was often realised. 'Oh God, yes,' he said. 'We lost four million dollars on one new issue last year. We've lost more than a million on several this year already. But if you're lucky and smart and do things right, you're going to have three or four successes for every failure. And not all your failures will be monumental.' (Some traders dismiss underwriting altogether, saying that it actually loses money nowadays, because of the heavy overheads incurred in getting and doing the business. Are such remarks a sign of the traders' new power going to their heads? Their banker colleagues say it's nonsense – underwriting generates trading opportunities that wouldn't exist otherwise.)

Curvin said he was in charge of everything in the firm except corporate finance (dealing with the investment-banking clients) and the back office (clerks and computers). 'All the trading reports to me, all the sales, all research, all underwriting,' he said. 'When you're looking at First Boston or at firms like us, the glamorous part shows, but underneath is the part that drives the ship – the engine. The bulk of our income,' and I was beginning to know the dogma by heart, 'is made by using our capital, and lesser numbers of people, to make markets, and sell and trade securities.' Curvin was as courteous as everyone else at First Boston. He passed me on to a colleague, asking him to spend some time with me. 'But not a *lot* of time, David,' he said, 'because we're here to make money.'

*   *   *

It is not surprising that bankers like Joe Perella are better publicised than traders like Dick Curvin. The business of trading and distributing securities is the rock on which Wall Street now stands, but the parts that constitute the whole are transient and shadowy. At the core of an investment bank is a flux of transactions, each sale and purchase separate yet all subsumed into constant activity. Few of the transactions are memorable in the sense of a banking deal. It is merely something that happens across a telephone. There is no obvious bonus to be gained from publicity; on the contrary, customers doing securities business with a firm might not like it, and the firm itself may prefer to keep quiet about details of its trading capability. The securities inventory of a large investment bank at any given moment may be so large that the numbers seem unreal outside Wall Street. Salomon Brothers often finds itself holding ten or fifteen billion dollars' worth of securities. The total figure reveals only that Salomon does a lot of trading, which its rivals knew anyway. But to know how the inventory was made up of particular bonds (Salomon's specialty) and stocks might be useful to a competitor, who would see for a moment behind the inscrutable face. 'There's an old aphorism in the United States,' remarked a trader at Merrill Lynch, on hearing of some reticence I had encountered at Salomon, 'that says the two things you should never see being made are laws and sausages. Maybe we should add a third: bond dealing.'

Nor is the fine web of relationships within the sales-and-trading department of an investment bank a matter that it will regard as anything but private. Yet it is these relationships which have much to do with a firm's performance. A tension always exists between the salesmen and women, who deal with customers, and the traders, who supply the sales force with securities. This division of labour is sharper in Wall Street than it is in Europe. Salesmen are busy running down the firm's stocks of securities by selling them over the phone to regular customers, as quickly as the dealers are running up stocks of fresh securities. 'Customers', at the top end of the business, means institutions such as pension funds, insurance companies and central banks.

Four of the Bulge firms deal only with institutions; the exception, Merrill Lynch, has a wide retail base, with more than four million customers, but serves many institutional investors as well. Whether the end-investors are fund managers in Connecticut or widows in Sun City, the 'distribution' of securities by a forceful sales staff is the act that matters. Salomon has four hundred salesmen covering the institutions. They are supposed to know the customer's every need, whether as buyer or seller. Competitors breathe down their necks; margins of profit may need to be cut and cut again; favours must be returned. But while the salesmen are trying to give their customers the best possible deal in the interests of the relationship and what happens tomorrow, the traders – who, together with the new-issue desk, have to find the securities to be sold, or are willing to take those being bought – must view the firm's position as a whole. This is where tension arises. According to a Morgan Stanley trader, 'Most American firms believe in creating a divided loyalty. Somebody has to look after the interests of the customer and make sure the trader doesn't gouge him. But then, somebody has to look after the interests of the firm and see that salesmen don't do every piece of business that comes along. We feel we need that conflict.' According to a Salomon managing director, 'It's a two-way street. Bond traders have positions which they're trying to manage to make money for the firm. Salesmen have clients who want to buy and sell securities. Either side can trigger a trade. The fact that a bond trader is long of securities might trigger a salesman to take that long position and sell it to a customer. Or a customer who wants to sell securities might trigger the trader into buying them. There's a constant tension between traders and salesmen. But we tend to be driven by our trading desk more than our sales force.'

'Good communications' is always cited as the most important thing on a sales-and-trading floor. It usually means people in the same group of specialists being within easy shouting distance of one another. The firm's salesmen in other cities or countries are in touch through electronic displays and word-processors, but the most effective method when speed matters, as it does nearly all the time, is the telephone with a direct wire that buzzes the branch office or other location when picked up. Linked systems of speaker boxes, into which those concerned can feed news of trades pending or executed, bring voices squawking out of the air. Stories are told of how some unlucky salesman in a branch office doesn't realise that an institutional customer of his has come into the market with a bid or offer that the firm would like to have heard of first.

The trading desk gets wind of it, and from a dozen loudspeakers howls the voice of a managing director, 'Find who it is and sack him.' On the Salomon trading floors (there are two), the setting for some of these apocryphal stories, the nearest I heard to rage was a man on the telephone who cried out, 'I've said it three times. I'm sorry, but there's nine million people screaming in this place.' Behind him a voice shouted, 'Hey, and they're all looking for you.' But the need for information to flow in to traders throughout the working day is no joke. The Salomon managing director said that suppose a trader in Utilities, who was long of ten million Telephone seven-and-a-halfs, decided that they looked cheap and that he would hang on to them until the price went up. If the Harris Bank in Chicago was thinking of selling a block of the same securities, thereby depressing the price still further, the firm (and in the long run the trader) was going to lose money unless he heard about it pretty damn quick. 'Going to lose money' are serious words. Anyone in search of the quintessential trader, hard-boiled, unrelenting and aged about thirty, will find him or her at Salomon.

The traders, together with the bankers who now work alongside them doing 'bought deals' to acquire big blocks of new shares, are the risk-takers. They 'commit the firm's capital', another of those Wall Street phrases that is spoken with due emphasis, as though the act, besides being practical, has a trace of the symbolic as well. The trading game can be played between professionals, a Morgan Stanley trader against a Merrill trader, often with a firm of specialist brokers interposed. But as a rule, the margin for profit when one professional plays another is small. Where possible the trader will marry his deals in the market-place with the customer business that his salespersons are generating. The content and balance of his 'book' of securities is changing continually as he services the sales staff, at the same time creating and exploiting favourable trading positions. The resulting revenue is the item that shows up in First Boston's accounts as 'principal transactions', in 1983 $176 million out of a revenue total of $515 million. Salomon's accounts are partially concealed within those of the conglomerate to which it now belongs, but its income from 'principal transactions' will be far greater. (Its overall earnings before tax, the only earnings figure available in 1983, were $415 million. This is $20 million or so more than the comparable figure for Merrill Lynch, a much bigger firm.)

Large trading income can be generated only by traders who are bold and swift as well as clever and well-informed. When Salomon says in its annual review that 'the Firm's daily net securities inventory averaged

$7.9 billion' it is boasting in a restrained sort of way about its willingness to 'commit capital'. Money is perpetually at risk on the dealers' books, night and day, in the sense that the bonds and stocks owned by the firm can all change in value. These shifts are likely to be only marginal, a fact that sometimes leads merchant bankers in London to talk derisively of the big Wall Street firms as 'paper-pushers', processing securities in a mundane, almost riskless manner, the clerks of investment banking. Perhaps there is a grain of truth as well as a grain of envy in the charge. But it is not the picture as it appears inside the trading-rooms, where they all know that mistakes in position-taking have contributed to the disappearance of more than one firm.

The danger lies in the size of the inventory that an investment bank is holding. Salomon's average inventory of almost eight billion dollars, rising at times to double that figure, dwarfs its capital and reserves. Nobody in Wall Street has eight billion dollars of his own to buy the securities that make up the trading book. It is borrowed, in a never-ending series of short-term contracts, using the securities that are bought with the loans as collateral. This financing of the inventory is a small world in itself. The procedures are technical and complex. Little discussed outside Wall Street, they are the key to successful trading and, in turn, to the profits of investment banks. It is the way financial industries work, exploiting the difference between cheap and expensive money. It would not be realistic to borrow continually from commercial banks; even if they were willing to accommodate the borrowers, the interest rates would be too high. A difference of one per cent on eight billion dollars over a year means a difference in interest payments of eighty million dollars. So the investment firms borrow, wherever possible, in the form of 'repurchase agreements'.

The first I heard of these was in conversation with Gedale B. Horowitz of Salomon, member of the executive committee, a genial man ('I am an unreconstructed New Yorker') with glass walls between him and the bond-trading floor, smoking a thick cigar (John Gutfreund, the chairman, who passed me on to him, was armed with a similar weapon. 'By the way,' said Horowitz, 'not all partners of Salomon Brothers smoke cigars.'). Horowitz mentioned in passing that a key element in trading was financing the securities. 'We carry them on our bank lines and repurchase agreements,' he said, and then was reluctant to say more. 'I'm not going to help you much,' he said, 'because this is almost a trade thing. But there are other ways to get money than by borrowing it from a bank, let's put it that way.' Eventually he gave me a brief account, and so did others. The principle is no great secret. Under a repurchase agreement, or 'repo', an investment bank will sell a block of securities to a lender (an industrial corporation, say, or a pension fund) which has surplus cash that it wants to invest for a couple of days; at the same time, the bank contracts to buy back the securities at the end of the brief period, at a price that amounts to an interest rate for the lender. The securities involved are often US Government bills and bonds, which make up a high proportion of all the securities being traded in the US, or other high-quality paper. There is also a 'reverse repo', where the investment bank buys securities, again for a brief period, typically from another investment firm, to meet a delivery that otherwise it couldn't make. By the time the bank has to sell the securities back to the other party, it will hope to have obtained a further supply of them from somewhere else. This seething activity is invisible to the outsider below the other seething activity of trading and selling. The element of secrecy pertains to the technicalities of contracts and, presumably, the identity of lenders, though in general this can't be much of a mystery. The system provides a means of soaking up some of the surplus money found in every financial centre.

The scale is enormous. Around a hundred billion dollars' worth of repos and reverse-repos may be in existence at any one time. Because each type of agreement meets a need that is the reverse of the other, it is possible to use them for their own sake, to 'arbitrage' a difference in interest rates. This earns hundreds of millions of dollars in a good year for Wall Street. 'Interest' of one sort or another can be a large item in an investment bank's revenue, and the repo/reverse-repo element contributes handsomely. The fact that Wall Street firms can make such a profit in short-term borrowing from sophisticated lenders may be another reason for coyness; the lenders might squeeze them harder if they saw how well the banks were doing.

The risk involved in running the inventories which the repos are designed to finance remains in the banker's mind. It is adrenalin; it is also a small black cloud far away. It is the reason that the traditional trading houses like Salomon have moved wherever possible into the fee-earning business, such as M&A – 'Not to have always to turn on the lights every morning,' as a Salomon officer put it, 'and wait for the next opportunity to commit capital, and see when you roll the dice if you win or lose – even if you're good at rolling the dice and winning more than you lose, which is certainly the case at our ship.' A firm's capital is a tiny percentage of the money at risk. Just as the amount of interest to be paid on such borrowings is crucial, so is any movement in the value of the inventory. If some barely imaginable series of events wiped twelve per cent off the value of Salomon's average holding, it would find itself a billion dollars the poorer, and holed below the waterline. Perhaps disaster as a theoretical possibility is part of the reason for the adrenalin.

Traders themselves have a showy reputation. A man at Merrill Lynch phoned a colleague in a trading room to arrange a visit for me. 'He'd like to see what a live zoo looks like,' he said. In the event it was quite orderly, but traders like to regard themselves as the inhabitants of organised chaos. 'It's very quiet today,' my host said apologetically. In the usual caricature, traders drink too much and have problems with women. 'The trading floor is where the animals are,' an old-fashioned investment banker said at his Wall Street club. 'It's the dirty jokes and the four divorces.' His firm is small and doesn't trade much, and he might have been more than half serious. Scandalous stories about cocaine abuse by Wall Street traders surface from time to time. But one suspects that the industry is already too bureaucratised for the oddities to be much more than that.

The larger the amounts that a firm has at risk, the more consumed it is with the need to manage and control them. All trading departments operate within limits, arranged by category. Senior arbiters are never far from the action, with managing directors strategically placed. At Salomon, John Gutfreund has a desk on the Government-bond trading floor. The difficulty of supervising traders is that in the nature of the business they need to follow opportunity; too much supervision cramps their style. Exactly what happens at Salomon is not clear to those outside the firm, no doubt deliberately so. The annual report for 1971 said that 'traders have great flexibility in position taking, with authority going as high as $100 million in short-dated securities.' Gutfreund says that 'we leave them a lot of autonomy', but 'if someone is used to running a position of fifty or a hundred million dollars, long or short, and all of a sudden there is an opportunity to do four or five hundred million, they would discuss it with management.' A Salomon managing director, anonymous, said flatly that 'We have no limits. No trader has a limit. That is probably unusual in this industry. Hopefully they have something up here [he tapped his head] that tells them when they should be talking to somebody, but there's no formal limit to what he can do. We've had 'em abuse their freedom, but they don't last long.'

104

Salomon was a pushy firm of bond traders that in the last twenty years has successfully pushed its way into the full range of investment banking. In 1983 it displaced Morgan Stanley as the biggest capital-raising firm in the world, acting as lead manager to 176 issues that raised nearly $16 billion (three-quarters of it for bonds; Morgan Stanley still led in raising equity capital). Founded by three brothers in 1910, its present offices, which occupy nine floors of a tower at One New York Plaza, on the tip of the financial peninsula, are roomy and well decorated, but are not lined with the historical prints and portraits found at some firms. The contents of a bookcase in the waiting area on the forty-second floor include the works of Thackeray, a *History of Harlem* and some bound volumes of the *National Geographic* magazine, beginning with 1909. When I asked someone if the books had been chosen for their public-relations value, he said, 'What books?'

Salomon was soon dealing in US Government paper, making a reputation for handling large blocks of securities. It managed new issues, but was never in the first league of underwriters, a distant memory that some of its rivals still try to keep alive. When Judge Medina investigated the industry after World War 2, he had no interest in Salomon. However important they were as bond dealers, they were not members of the Club of Seventeen. During the 1960s the firm began to see the wisdom of diversifying, just as a firm like Morgan Stanley saw the same wisdom from the other end of things, where underwriting and relations with industrial companies were second nature, and it was trading that had to be learned. In persuading issuers to let it manage their underwritings, Salomon seems to have used two convincing arguments. One was that thanks to its long history of large-scale bond trading and selling, it could offer institutional customers the magic ingredient of 'distribution power'. The other was that in order to get new-issue business, it was willing to take a chance, 'commit capital', and buy an issue outright, without waiting to form a syndicate. This was to set the pace for everyone else. Before the 1980s, Salomon was in the Bulge.

It has only two overseas branches, in Tokyo and London (where, alone outside New York Plaza, the firm has a modest risk-taking operation). But it is stronger than this suggests in selling to institutions outside the US. Salomon is well regarded for its continuous research into the technical labyrinth of the bond market, and its analyses of particular items. Dr Henry Kaufman, the firm's chief economist, has been the most quoted man in Wall Street; a Kaufman hint about a change in interest rates can be an event in itself. Through the 1970s, borrowing via the bond market flourished as never before; as the succinct Dick Curvin at First Boston put it, 'Bonds is the business in an inflationary decade. You were a fool if you didn't issue bonds and pay them back over a period of years in shitty dollars.'

No one borrows like governments, and US Government securities remain the backbone of Salomon's business, perhaps half its trading turnover. The upper of the two big trading-rooms deals with them. Men in their shirt sleeves and a sprinkling of women wearing bright dresses sit surrounded by screens, dealing panels, telephones, notepads and electric fans, talking their lives away. Few are aged more than forty; many are under thirty. The securities world is inventive and frenzied. Bonds come dressed up with special features. Important markets have arisen from nowhere. Financial futures, quicker to catch on in the United States than in Britain, are widely used. A 'future' is a contract, legally binding, to buy or sell a commodity, in this case financial, at a fixed price on a specified day in the future. One use among many could be to hedge risks in the bond market, by a contract to deliver so many thousand bonds at a particular price some days hence. The 'future', once created, becomes a negotiable instrument in its own right, which trades in a specialised market where speculators abound. Another comparatively new market, peculiar to the United States, is in 'mortgage securities'. Pools of mortgage debt are aggregated into certificates and sold to pension funds and the like. The securities, once created, can then be traded. Salomon handles more than $100 billion worth in a year.

Strangers anxious to see 'pure' trading in action are advised to try the municipal desk. John Gutfreund, the chairman, came up through the firm in this specialty. Municipal securities are issued by states, cities or other local entities. They might be raising money to finance an airport or a hospital or a dam. They are exempt from federal taxes, and usually from local taxes in the place of issue. The market in them is large, but can't compare with the market in Government securities, where the supply is almost limitless, and traders can 'short' the bonds – selling what they don't possess – in the confident hope of being able to find them for delivery. Lewis Glucksman says that 'with municipals, you can go crazy trying to find bonds'. Traders have to work harder to match both sides of a deal.

The day I was on the section of floor at Salomon that handles them, a new issue of bonds for the Intermountain Power Agency was in the pipeline. So was an issue for the state of Florida. Nothing defined the syndicate area. The built-up desks and narrow alleyways continued in all directions. Forty people arranged over three rows seemed to constitute the group handling the issues. 'We do more here with less people than any other firm on Wall Street,' someone said. No conversation lasted more than a minute before whoever I was talking to broke off to talk to someone else. I lost track of them and failed later to identify voices from the tape. The only one I could be sure of was the chairman of the board of Intermountain, Reece D. Nielsen, a Mormon from Utah, who wandered on to the floor to get the feel of things. He said they had spent the previous week visiting major institutions across the country, with a team from Salomon, preparing the way for the issue. They hoped it would raise $900 million (it did) to build coal-burning power stations; they had a lot of coal in Utah. Their pre-selling tour began in New York on Monday and ended in Los Angeles on Friday afternoon, meeting people (he said) who represented 'ninety per cent of the investment dollars in the United States'. For the issue itself, the Intermountain team had flown up from Utah on Monday – it was Tuesday now – and they hoped to be away by Wednesday morning with the money in the bag. I said it seemed an expeditious dispatch of business. 'The American financial system has a lot of money out there,' he said happily, and told me about his son, a Mormon missionary who had knocked on many doors in Britain. Around us the voices squawked and whispered, 'What do you want to pay for a million?', 'Who's it for?', 'I'll make him two and three-quarters, three and an eighth', 'He needs to talk to you', 'Let's get the deal rolling', 'I'm doing some business here', 'Stan's got an order for ninety-nine', 'a million ninety-twos', 'ninety-eight to two thousand'. The bonds had different maturities. 'Ninety-eight' meant 1998, 'two thousand' was the year 2000, when the world would be different, but money wouldn't. The longest bonds, almost two-thirds of the total, would not be paid off till 1 July 2023. These were the most popular with investors; the syndicate status report that someone pulled off a desk-top printer for me showed that most of them had gone already. On 1 July 2023, I would be ninety-four, if anything. The sales staff would have moved on to something quieter.

John H. Gutfreund would be ninety-four, too. In middle age he is quiet, gruff, well manicured and rich. He joined Salomon in 1953, became a partner ten years later, and rose to the head of the firm in 1978 as managing partner. There were sixty or seventy general partners, their private capital locked up in the firm; altogether they owned but had little access to a fortune of between three and four hundred million dollars. In 1981 talks began with a possible purchaser who would buy them out and enable them to realise their wealth. This was not the only reason for the dialogue. The firm interested in Salomon Brothers was the large and secretive Philbro Corporation, a commodity trader and dealer in many countries, with annual sales of twenty or thirty billion dollars. Philbro and Salomon had done business for years, and there were logical reasons for combining the two. Philbro's staples included ores, metals, grains and the commodity that (with one exception) trades in the greatest volume, petroleum. The exception was money and securities. Salomon Brothers knew all about financial trading. The talks prospered and the deal was done by the autumn of 1981. Salomon Brothers Inc. kept its autonomy under a holding company that was itself called Philbro–Salomon. There were those who said that despite the size of Philbro, the bank might be the tail that wagged the dog. As for the former partners who changed overnight into managing directors, dazzling sums of money fell into their laps. Every partner seems to have become a dollar millionaire if he was not one already: not that a plain millionaire in the United States nowadays excites much interest. The money came from two directions. Philbro Corp. paid the partners $250 million in Philbro securities for the firm. Some got more than others. Securities and Exchange Commission figures showed that Henry Kaufman received just over $10 million worth. Gutfreund's share was worth more than $13 million. Their value fluctuated, on the whole upwards. The other source was the broken-up partnership capital. This must have been worth well over $10 million apiece to some of the senior Salomon people. John Gutfreund's total prize from both sources was widely estimated, a couple of years after the Philbro deal, to be worth more than $40 million.

He has a somewhat world-weary look. His grey hair is thinning. His heavy face and the almost sullen set of his sensuous mouth don't change much as he speaks. The hand looks too small for the cigar. Measured and lucid, he sounds the epitome of the Wall Street professional. If there is a trace of some different person, it is only a trace. Everybody knows who Gutfreund is. He has never worked anywhere else. I met him twice. The first time, he said, 'One of the problems for me in a proprietary business is that I'm really not very interested in removing the mystique. It doesn't serve our purpose to lay ourselves bare. A nice press is leaving us alone.' After that he was more helpful than his remarks suggested. He talked, when asked, about his progress through the firm. 'I graduated from college in 1951,' he said, 'was drafted into the army, went to Korea. When I returned I wasn't poor but I wasn't terribly affluent. I was thinking of going to graduate school, of teaching, of the arts. But I felt – I don't know, I thought maybe I wouldn't be the greatest, and I always had an affection for wanting to be the best in some way. In the arts it seemed to me that you really were starved emotionally and financially if you were less than the best. I met a friend who asked me down for lunch, and they said, "Would you like to try this, John?" I took the job, which was supposedly training. The training was watching other people working. Then when somebody died or got fired or they were expanding the department, they'd transfer you to that slot. And I got placed in the municipal department. At that time you had to understand simple numbers, have a good memory so you didn't make the same mistakes over and over again, and have the ability to respond to the broadest set of stimuli, which is what a good market person always has to have. I proved to have a pretty good memory and a simple knowledge of numbers, and I did it well for some years. As a result I was put in charge of sales and syndicate. I used to be very good at the syndicate business. It was a great deal of fun. It was a game I understood. In our firm at that point in history it was very important. My success was related to that, and to the fact that I had a great information base. If one is successful it is only because one knows more facts, not because one is smarter. I had a better feel, because of our trading activities, because of our sales force, of what might happen. And I guess I was fairly aggressive in my time – that is, trying to get the best terms. We didn't have much inherited underwriting business, so most of it was through competitive bidding.... I just used the resources at hand.' I asked how long it had taken before he felt committed to the firm. 'You get involved in working here,' he said. 'The world narrows, your horizons narrow. You drift – if you're like I am – you drift into something, then excuse it by saying, "Anything else I do now, I'm too old, I'm twenty-seven, I'm thirty-three, I'm thirty-six. I'm too old to try for something new."'

A ship's hooter was groaning in the bay. He said, 'I'm not one of the great adventurers of the world. I think I've become more so as I've got older. Probably because I *am* older. Also probably because I'm richer.' He said that one of the things he liked about the securities business was the certainty: 'There is no room for half-truths. It's not a grey world. There are no white lies. Either you made the bid or you didn't. Either you sold the bonds or you didn't. You lose money sometimes, you make money sometimes. It's a fairly simple-minded game. There is an absolute truth, which is rare in the human condition, that's quite satisfying for small people. Also, I would guess that I knew the people with whom I worked, better most of the time than I knew wife and family. The necessity for an absolute, unequivocal answer – I pay, I buy, I sell. It used to be *we* bought, *we* sold, but you get more egotistical as you get older. Which is an error, because it's not my money.' He smiled as he said it: the only time. He said that nowadays they hired people who were better versed in 'elementary business technique' than he had been, thirty years earlier. 'I was an arts major,' he said. 'I knew nothing about the business.' Such a person would not be hired by Salomon today, he said. He illustrated his argument by talking about the difficulties that 'natural' salespersons met, now that the firm made more technical demands on them. He had never been in that category himself. But in the past, gifted salesmen who were not necessarily very clever or creative at anything else had ready entry into the business. They were 'down here for one reason, to make money, and this is a business that throws up more money than selling shoes'. That had been sufficient. Now they were not always tolerated. 'The technicians of our trade,' he said, 'have become ever more powerful.'

I wasn't sure if Gutfreund was stating a fact or evoking a nostalgia for simpler times. He said human relationships continued to have a place in the business. 'The element of human judgement and human relations still is very important,' he said, and added after a pause, 'I think. It has to be for me because it's a great part of my skill,' and again he modified it, 'if I have any.'

As I was leaving I paused by a fine brass telescope that stood in the window. The eyepiece was muzzled. I asked what it was aimed at – it seemed to be a jetty on Governors Island. He didn't answer; perhaps didn't hear. He ushered me out to the humming spaces of the trading floor, and went back to sit at his desk.

*   *   *

After Salomon Brothers became a corporation, Goldman Sachs was left as the only major Wall Street partnership in the strict sense. Marcus Goldman was a Bavarian immigrant who set up as a banker in New York in the 1860s, lending merchants money against 'commercial paper', in effect promises to repay at some date in the future. He carried the day's securities inside his top hat. A hundred and twenty years later, Goldman Sachs was still the leading commercial-paper firm. The original

Goldman went into partnership with the original Sachs, who married a Goldman daughter in the 1880s; there used to be a comma between the names.

Goldman Sachs, with partners' capital of $500 million, safely locked up and out of reach, is thought to be among the most profitable investment banks. Its earnings in 1983, not revealed but intelligently guessed-at by competitors, were put at an enormous $400 million. Partners are millionaires many times over, but the bulk of their fortune constitutes Goldman Sachs' capital, and can't be extracted till they retire, and then not all at once. They receive interest on the capital, which keeps the wolf from the door, and there is income from other sources. But partners are not encouraged to flaunt their wealth. The firm drives ahead, a dedicated machine that appeals to other dedicated machines. Certainly its peers regard it highly; they see it as a predator. 'It's the Goldman Sachs Syndrome,' said a rival banker: 'what's mine is mine and what's yours is half mine.' In London, David Scholey of Warburg, itself a model for merchant banks, said the two Wall Street firms that appealed to them most as exemplars were Salomon and Goldman, for the way they had emerged in recent times. It may not be a coincidence that I found Warburg, Salomon and Goldman among the firms least anxious to have an observer in their midst; low profiles agree with them.

At Goldman Sachs they are aware of being regarded as a faceless machine, anonymous and efficient. Roy C. Smith is the partner who runs Goldman Sachs International in London, the firm's biggest office outside the United States; he is its managing director. The building it shares with another American bank is near the western edge of the City, at Blackfriars. It used to house two newspapers, *The Times* and the *Observer*. I had not been inside it since those days. The carpets had got thicker. Roy Smith was the only partner (of more than seventy in the whole firm) I was able to interview. He said their style underscored their reputation for being somewhat machine-like, 'feared but not loved. I'm not saying that should be our image. But I suspect there are parts of the United States that would think of us that way.' Personalities were not cultivated, he said, names were not well known outside. That wasn't necessarily so elsewhere. How many times did one hear about Henry Kaufman or John Gutfreund or Ira Harris? I said that as it happened, I had just been reading a long article about Goldman's John Whitehead and John Weinberg. 'Ah,' he said, 'John Whitehead is the head of the firm. And John Weinberg is the *co*-head. People get that mixed up. If we can't even get the co-heads straight, there is something lacking in the public-relations-projection part. Which is kind of our style. We are sort of shabby and low-key, low visibility in terms of personal heroes. We tend to resent heroes if any was to emerge. Because we all know that it is the team approach, the phalanx, that makes the difference . . . not letting our egos get out of line. I think frankly, that is a characteristic that does not dominate within Wall Street. As a result, by encouraging the heads-down, linked-arms approach, we produce a somewhat hard-to-classify sense of efficiency without too much identity. That sometimes frustrates us when we feel we have a lesser public image than some of us from time to time, in whatever moments of stress we're in, think we would rather see.'

Hoping this was a chink in Smith's armour, I tried to get him to say more about egos, but he wasn't having any. He waved aside matters of image as irrelevant. 'I tell you what,' he said. 'We have the largest number of corporate clients in investment banking. We are by far the most important distributor of equity securities to the institutions. We are by far the largest commercial-paper dealer. The way this machine is moving, we are probably in the top two or three houses in everything else we do. In good years we make a lot of money. In poor years we still make good money. If we're not in the top two or three, what are we doing wrong?' It was a sinful event, said Smith, not to be at the top; he was being ironical, but not as purely ironical as British merchant bankers within a quarter of a mile of his office would be, if they made such a remark. 'We will move people,' he said, 'or whip them to death or whatever if we're not up there. The competitive instinct says we have to earn it. We expect nothing less.'

No wonder banks have better offices than newspapers. I left hearing the ghosts of old reporters, grumbling on the stairs.

*   *   *

If the most visible characteristic of firms like Salomon and Goldman Sachs is that they are striving for more and more success, Morgan Stanley till recently proceeded on the opposite assumption, that blessings would continue to shower on it. This is mainly a question of style; Morgan is as hard-jawed as the rest when it comes to executing business. But it still enjoys its aristocratic overtones. And they still impress people, even in these cut-throat days. Take the BASF story.

Towards the end of January 1983 the Deutsche Bank, the leading all-purpose bank in the Federal Republic of Germany, set out to raise

$150 million for BASF, the West German chemicals group, by issuing bonds in the Euromarket. A small group of co-managers was invited to support the Deutsche Bank at the head of the syndicate. It happened to be a bad moment for Eurobonds, the result of a good moment earlier in the month, when so many companies decided that now was a good moment to borrow, that the market became choked with unsold securities. More than $6 billion had been raised since the start of the year. Borrowers included Texaco; Coca Cola; the Government of Sweden; Sears, Roebuck; Volvo; the British food-and-brewery group Allied Lyons, and Nippon Telegraph and Telephone. Investment banks, mainly the dominant American and Japanese firms with branches in London, strove to win mandates for these issues, before the stream of bonds began to overwhelm the market. Credit Suisse First Boston fought off competition for the Swedish Government issue, which was to raise a billion dollars. A dozen firms were telephoning and telexing Stockholm as soon as the issue was announced, begging to be allowed to do it more cheaply than CSFB. Goldman Sachs and Daiwa Securities won the mandate to raise Coca Cola's $100 million by undercutting Morgan Stanley. CSFB won another prize with Texaco, in the Eurobond market to borrow $150 million. Firms that failed to get mandates wrung their hands and cursed the supposed insanity of those who won business by offering to issue bonds with the interest rate shaved below a realistic figure. Wisdom laced with sour grapes spoiled the losers' lunches. Texaco, shaved down to $9\frac{3}{4}$ per cent, came at the end of a week that saw $3 billion worth of bonds issued. Banks that did badly spoke of bitter days, of their hope that interest rates would move upwards (instead of downwards, as the winning managers hoped), thus making the low-interest bonds even less attractive, and with any luck leaving the managers stuck with them. Texaco's $9\frac{3}{4}$, said one investment banker (it was not at Morgan Stanley), was 'what I call the irrational competitive urge of the Street. Somebody said, "Fuck it, let's get Texaco on the books as well." There's a lot of prestige that attaches to running these tombstones. Whoever leads Texaco is going to be identified with Texaco.' He writhed at the thought of this and other issues his firm had lost; it was the Monday after the Friday. 'The fact that issues are under water and people may lose money is a whole other story. There's always been in this market a crazy relationship between prestige and profit, the two Ps. At times the demand for visibility and market share runs ahead of a concern over profitability. The cycle goes its merry way until the red ink builds up and management says, "Wait, this is ridiculous." If I felt in a sadistic mood I'd wish the market would go against them. . . .'

His hopes were realised almost at once. Short-term interest rates in New York didn't fall as expected; with the market already glutted, two or three billion dollars' worth of bonds were rumoured to have been left with the syndicates. Eventually they would be sold. But 'eventually' is a long time in moving markets, with the prospect of underwriters having bonds on their books for days or weeks, and eventually having to sell them below the price they paid. It was just at the point when gloom was spreading and confidence had begun to ebb that the Deutsche Bank decided to press on with its BASF issue of six-year bonds at $9\frac{7}{8}$ per cent. A company ranked as high as BASF would expect to be supported by a group of leading banks, come rain or shine, and the expectation would usually be realised. Deutsche Bank made the phone calls and sent the telexes inviting seven or eight leading firms to join the management group. All said Yes except Morgan Stanley. Its reason was not (as it still would have been in New York at the time) that it didn't have first place in the syndicate; in Europe, Morgan Stanley International was willing to take a subordinate position, as long as it was not too subordinate. It declined to join in because it thought the deal was wrongly priced. According to a manager who did accept, this so upset BASF that it tried to find who had been present at whatever meetings inside Morgan Stanley had made the decision. Morgan had an existing relationship with BASF; it had done M&A work for the company. The price of being left with bonds it didn't want and couldn't sell might be half or even three-quarters of a million dollars. But given the mutual interests of high finance, that was all part of the game. The others grinned and bore it.

A couple of months later, a banker I asked about the BASF issue in January pointed stonily to a board that listed unsold securities. The firm still had \$11,620,000 of the BASF $9\frac{7}{8}$, of the \$15 million it was allocated. 'That was a stinker of a deal,' said the banker. Among the co-managers, Manufacturers Hanover Ltd, that bank's London subsidiary, said it knew it would lose money but thought the relationship of overriding importance. A Morgan Guaranty banker said tersely that 'we went in rather than taint our reputation in Germany'. Salomon Brothers, in the person of Thomas Strauss of the executive committee in New York, didn't recall the particular issue, but said that, in general, there were allegiances and relationships to be cultivated; firms did foolish things for strange reasons, 'and I'm sure we've been guilty of it more than once ourselves. That's the environment we're in.' It is not quite the environment Morgan Stanley is in. It feels strong enough to say No. But that too may be changing.

Presumably the firm's confidence has its roots in the history of J. P. Morgan's bank, from which it grew. Pierpont Morgan, probably the subject of more biographies than any other banker, was money incarnate. But he had moral authority too. In 1912, the year before he died, he testified to a Government committee in Washington that was trying in vain to find evidence of a 'money trust' through which he and others were supposed to dominate American industry. He used the occasion to make ringing statements about the moral content of business.

'Is not commercial credit based primarily upon money or property?' he was asked.

'No sir,' said the canny old banker, 'the first thing is character.'

'Before money or property?'

'Before money or anything else. Money cannot buy it. . . . Because a man I do not trust could not get money from me on all the bonds in Christendom.'

Twenty years later, his son, the younger Pierpont Morgan, spoke on similar lines before another committee, at hearings that paved the way for the Glass-Steagall Banking Act. 'The private banker is a member of a profession which has been practised since the Middle Ages,' he declared, and went on to talk about the code of ethics on which the banker's reputation rested. Another twenty years on, when the authorities were once more trying and failing to pin down those clever chaps in Wall Street, Judge Medina quoted with approval the younger Morgan on ethics. Morgan Stanley has a sense of its past. Tradition and anecdotes are handed down. From early times, everyone who went to a partners' meeting was paid fifty dollars, a considerable sum then, to encourage attendance. The money for those who didn't attend was divided among those who did. Only once was there a full house. That was in a blizzard. Each assumed he would be the only one there and could pocket the lot. As late as the early 1970s, when the firm was on the brink of the changes that were needed to preserve it, the custom was still in force. The reward had shrunk to twenty dollars, but a member of staff would stand at the door, handing every partner the money in cash as he went in to the meeting. Even the typographical style of tombstone advertisements derives from J. P. Morgan's insistence that the bank use a typeface called Ronaldson Slope. It is not unknown for a Morgan Stanley banker, travelling to arrange a deal in an American city where the local printers don't stock numerical fractions in Ronaldson, to take the pieces of type with him. The text of prospectuses always appears in royal blue, another cross for the printers to bear. Office wags say it is the first thing trainees in the corporate finance department learn.

In the early 1960s Morgan Stanley employed about a hundred and twenty people. Ten years later the staff had doubled, but it was still a small firm, with a capital of seven or eight million dollars. By the 1980s the staff was approaching three thousand and the firm's capital was above two hundred and fifty million dollars. Trading and distributing securities had become a central activity. The philosophy of the trader had to be absorbed into the nucleus of the firm. A banker setting up small numbers of big deals needs to be right most of the time. A trader lives with the errors he made yesterday, which are inherent in the business. All he must be is marginally more right than wrong. A trader who gets his position in Government securities right 55 per cent of the time can make a lot of money. This was not the way they made lots of money at Morgan Stanley in the past. You hear people say that J. P. Morgan must be turning in his grave, but by and large they sound amused at the thought, not worried.

An old story about Morgan Stanley, that any applicant for a job there needed brains, money and the right blood, was widely believed at one time, and was probably true. One of the present members was told it in a kindly way twenty-odd years ago by the director of placement at his university, who added, 'and at most, you've only got one of them'. Brains must have sufficed. The firm has no option but to be a meritocracy now. It might have been instructive to have sat in on meetings of the partner-style directors when they were electing a chief officer in 1983, a task they performed twice within twelve months. Robert Baldwin stepped down from the key post of president at the end of 1982, at the age of sixty-two. He became chairman, also a key post, though vacant for several years. In his place the firm chose S. Parker Gilbert, aged forty-nine, a member of the executive committee. Gilbert had tradition as well as merit on his side. His father, another S. Parker Gilbert, was a lawyer and US Treasury official turned banker, who joined J. P. Morgan in 1931. Gilbert senior died in 1938; his widow later married Harold Stanley, whose name had been incorporated into the breakaway firm when he helped to found it. Less than a year after the succession appeared to have been decided, Baldwin resigned the chairmanship to head a high-flown 'advisory committee' of big names. Gilbert took his place. Richard Fisher, the executive committee member in charge of trading operations, became president. Lewis Glucksman, the trader who ran Lehman Brothers until it was sold, was quoted as saying that Fisher's appointment was 'a very good move for Morgan', adding, 'unfortunately'.

One can only speculate what happened. But at the start of 1984, when Wall Street's analysts had spent Christmas with their computers, Salomon, the trader par excellence, was seen to have overtaken Morgan Stanley as underwriter in the new style. The firm found itself bottom of the Bulge. Morgan argued, with some justification, that its figure for total underwritings suffered because in capital-raising it concentrates on equity issues (like Telephone), where the profit margin is usually higher than in some of the high-volume business that its competitors specialise in. In 1983 Morgan was still the leader in straightforward equity financing. Nevertheless the league table hurt. A month earlier Morgan may have known already. The argument, long accepted, that it had to concentrate on trading and distribution, may have been enhanced by the gloomy news. Fisher, though very much a Morgan man in style and personality, helped convert Morgan Stanley to trading, and had climbed the firm on that ladder. Having been tipped before 1983 as the new president, he seemed to have been passed over, only to be chosen the second time round. It was Fisher, incidentally, who had been advised by his director of placement not to bother with Morgan Stanley.

*   *   *

Powerful as they are in Wall Street terms, neither Goldman, Morgan, Salomon, First Boston nor Lehman can match Merrill Lynch in size and variety. They would say in chorus that Merrill lacks their panache or glitter or historical experience when it comes to the 'investment banking' side of the business – that Merrill's size reflects its retail brokerage and other financial services for individuals. Sure enough, the figures show Merrill Lynch receiving much smaller percentages of its gross income from 'investment banking' (underwriting and advisory work) and from 'principal trading' than from brokerage commissions. At First Boston it's the other way round. But Merrill Lynch is so large that its modest percentage of investment-banking income is worth $746 million (1983) and First Boston's substantial percentage is worth only $198 million (1983). Similarly, trading as a principal, almost a sideline in the overall scene at Merrill Lynch, is worth $675 million; at First Boston, where it is a leading item, it produced $176 million. Merrill's figures hit you in the eye – gross revenue $5.6 billion, earnings $230 million, capital $1.9 billion.

Unexpectedly, Merrill Lynch feels less monolithic than the other Bulge firms. It sprawls; it looks untidy, in a friendly sort of way. A sales manager, who had to leave me in the office while he talked to a client, plugged a video cassette in a machine to keep me occupied. The film was about Merrill Lynch International, one of many companies within the family that owes its origins to Charles E. Merrill and Edmund C. Lynch. Men in dark suits and white shirts moved confidently about the world. The Tokyo bullet train rushed past, ships lay at anchor under the Hong Kong skyscrapers, a London bus stopped outside the Bank of England. Positive language came with the pictures, 'space-age communications', 'state-of-the-art technology', 'investors' paradise', 'poised to take advantage of'. This international presence is one side of the firm, represented by nearly fifty offices in more than thirty countries. Under the umbrella of Merrill Lynch International Inc. come trading, sales and capital-raising outside the United States. The film didn't say so, but in London there is a Merrill Lynch International Bank Ltd, whose parent company is Merrill Lynch International Bank Inc. of Panama. The man who tried to explain the structure to me later said it was a bit complicated, wasn't it? He said Merrill Lynch International & Co. of Curacao was used to book most of the investment-banking fees. These were all legal entities. Then there was an International Banking Group in London. This was not a legal entity but a management structure. It didn't seem worth pursuing. The construction of financial institutions tends to be puzzling, for tax and other reasons. With Merrill Lynch it often seems to be a product of size as well. Its employees understand the feeling. Changes are always occurring, as in a region of seismic activity. Bulges and squiggles appear on people's organisation charts. New bits are pencilled in. 'It changes all the damn time,' said a vice-president. 'I used to say that as a criticism. In fact it's an aspect of a firm that's changing, in an industry that's changing.'

A Wall Street firm with two or three thousand employees is considered large. Through its subsidiaries, the holding company, Merrill Lynch & Co. Inc., employs forty-five thousand, most of them in the United States. The retail brokerage side is what distinguishes it from the other Bulge firms, and will distinguish the new Shearson/Lehman conglomerate as it joins the leaders. The others' securities business is only with financial institutions. Merrill's, conducted largely but not solely through Merrill Lynch, Pierce, Fenner & Smith (the biggest securities firm in the world, if not always the most profitable), is with institutions as well, because it has driven itself in that direction. But its power base is made up of the four and a half million customers it claims to serve through 9,000 or so salespeople, or 'account executives' in the preferred language, operating from 430 offices in forty-nine states; the figures are sure to be out of date. The upper strata of this organisation are housed at One Liberty Plaza, a tower facing a draughty square near the foot of Broadway. The first time I went there, an advertisement in the long windows echoed public-service announcements that could be seen on television in the late evening, when an actor or well-known figure looked at you and said, 'It's 10 pm. Do you know where your child is?' The ad said, 'It's 2 pm. Do you know where your money is?' The ground floor is always thronged with people, but especially at the peak hours of morning, noon and early evening. The lifts, arranged in banks to serve discrete blocks of floors, soar away but crawl back as if gravity had turned against them. Once I went to the floor I had been told to visit, was redirected down one, then up two, and found myself in a limbo of stone corridors stacked with cardboard boxes. They seemed to have old trading tickets in them. No one I met knew where the department I wanted could be found. I had to descend to Information and start again.

Not surprisingly, rival firms make jokes about Merrill Lynch managers who have never met. A managing director at Morgan Stanley said it was not a joke: he personally had introduced two of them to one another. They both worked at One Liberty Plaza, but on different floors. I told this to William Clark Jr, Merrill's corporate relations manager, expecting him to say he had heard that story before. Instead he said, 'I would have to agree with him.' As Merrill Lynch grew, he said, it had to be decentralised; that had weaknesses as well as strengths. Clark's relaxed approach is a clue to the firm. Whether because of its origins as a broker to the people, or conscious efforts to avoid airs and graces, it has an agreeable character, forthright and bracing. Among the material handed out by Clark's department was an offprint of a magazine article, ranking Wall Street houses in institutional esteem. Merrill came top (Goldman was runner-up). One survey doesn't make a summer, but corporate relations keeps a good stock of offprints.

On the purely investment-banking side, Merrill did as the other ambitious broking houses in recent years, pushing its way into the business. Merrill had started his firm in 1914. He added Lynch almost at once, sold the retail side to Pierce in 1930, got it back again in 1940, and absorbed Fenner a year later; Smith, an early partner who ran the firm after Merrill's death, was tacked on in 1958. The firm was the king of the 'wire houses', so called because of their dependence on telephone and teleprinter lines. It used its retail base as the battering ram to become a major managing underwriter of issues. The retail network lacked the prestige of big institutional accounts, but what it lacked in quality of distribution it made up in quantity. Jerome P. Kenney, senior vice-president in charge of investment banking and research services, says they had to be accepted first as co-managers. 'We'd go to companies and say, "Your lead banker has something to offer, but we have something else to offer: the largest distribution of dollar-denominated securities in the world. It doesn't cost you anything to have us. The underwriters are going to split the spread at the same cost to you, and you get the additional benefit of all our muscle."' This logical argument appealed to many companies, though not to the existing lead bankers. 'They screamed and yelled,' says Kenney. 'But it worked, particularly in industries with hundreds of companies, where we could use our regional distribution.' When state utilities and banks and natural-gas companies were raising money, Merrill was able to use its branch network to sell the securities to local investors with a sentimental regard for local undertakings. The firm grew to be a leading underwriter, polished up its institutional connections and joined the elect.

But its special strength as a retailer drove it to expand in that direction as well. From about 1970 it began to dawn on banks and brokers that enormous profits were going to be made from offering the American public diverse services on the supermarket principle of everything under one roof. The resulting 'financial services revolution' is only now gathering speed. Merrill Lynch was an early convert to the cause, under the flamboyant Donald T. Reagan (no relation of the President), who later moved on to Washington as Secretary of the Treasury. It began to sell life insurance through one subsidiary and act as an estate agent through another; it now handles more house sales and purchases than anyone else in the United States. Another subsidiary, Merrill Lynch Relocation Management, arranges to sell and rent houses for business executives as their employers move them around the country. It works for large corporations on a contract basis. Some of the services offered sound bizarre to foreign ears. The uprooted can have 'area orientation' and 'relocation counselling'. But it is a serious business. At the last count the company owned property worth seven or eight hundred million dollars. 'We do fifty per cent of the transfers of IBM executives,' says William Clark. 'We'll buy your house, transfer you lock, stock and barrel to Dallas, Texas, or wherever, and buy you a house. All you do is hand over your old key and get the new one in Dallas. It's all set up. Some writer accused us of trying to capture the entire world from birth to grave,' and he paused again, as though this time he really did intend to refute these witticisms. But he only said, 'I guess that's what we are trying to do.'

Merrill Lynch has been grimly inventive. In 1977 it unveiled a brokerage service called the Cash Management Account, whose essence is that it reinvests any money accruing from investments, and enables the investor to borrow against his securities. This sort of thing excites more people in America than in Britain, where few invest directly in the stock market. The novelty of the CMA lay in the package, not the contents. Instead of having to persuade a broker to keep reinvesting surplus money, the account was swept daily as a matter of course, and any surplus put into a money-market fund. Borrowing to the agreed limit was automatic, using a special cheque book and debit card. There were other refinements, like a monthly statement. The packaged brokerage account was novel in the way that the packaged holiday was novel when first seen. Merrill Lynch didn't introduce it lightly. The concept was originally one of several suggested by the Stanford Research Institute, when the firm commissioned an elaborate study of investors' needs. Inside Merrill there was much opposition to the new product – 'negative reaction,' says William Clark, 'people protecting their turf. Don Reagan said, "Dammit, we're going to do it," and he was right. But he was wrong in thinking we might get a hundred thousand accounts out of it. So far we've got nearly a million.' The minimum an investor needs in cash and securities to open a CMA account is $20,000. The average account is three or four times as large. Merrill Lynch earns fees and commissions on $75 billion of investments owned by that million customers. To the broker, a disadvantage of such an account (other firms have introduced their own variants) is that customers' money is no longer left lying around for the firm to invest on its own behalf. Other people's idle money still makes a handsome contribution to brokers' income, but less handsome than in the past.

For my last visit to a Wall Street trading floor, I tried one of Merrill Lynch's. I arranged to visit the room where they handle equities – the basic investor's basic security. Merrill and equities go together like

Salomon and Government bonds. The previous day I had been to the New York Stock Exchange, just off Wall Street itself, where more equities are traded daily down on the ugly floor than anywhere else in the world. It is still the focal point of the system. If Merrill sells some IBM stock for a pension fund, or if First Boston buys them for its own account from Morgan Stanley, the deal goes via this or a regional exchange. 'Specialists' stand at positions under banks of hanging television sets, making markets in whatever stocks are their line. Bonds are traded elsewhere, out of sight on a lower floor, in as much as they are traded in the building at all. Essentially the bond market is electronic and has no centre; it exists only in the telephone and computer networks linking buyers and sellers. The same thing is happening with equities, many of which are now traded in an over-the-counter market called NASDAQ – the National Association of Securities Dealers Automated Quotations system. NASDAQ is a computerised network that has had a phenomenal growth, handling shares of many of the new technology companies. But for the present, it must co-exist with the old system of trading floor and personal contact. With certain exceptions, dealings in the stocks listed on the New York Exchange, among them most of the famous blue-chip names, have to take place on the open floor; Rule 390 says so. Around the specialists the floor brokers circle, bringing their buy or sell orders; some are employed by investment banks and brokerage houses, some are freelance, 'two-dollar' brokers. As in all stock exchanges, the figures you see slantingly through glass from the visitors' gallery belong to an exclusive set who have paid heavily for the right of admission. Over the next decade the electronic whirlwind may sweep them all away. Already the place has a whiff of anachronism. The block-trading of securities that has become a commonplace swamps the old mechanism of floor brokers and specialists through which everything is supposed to be channelled.

The spirit of Rule 390 if not the letter is breached all the time. Institutions have acquired a taste for dealing in quantities rarely seen a few years ago. A 'block' is anything above 10,000 shares. Samuel E. Hunter, senior vice-president in charge of securities trading at Merrill Lynch, says that 'five or six years ago, if we did a block of a hundred thousand, everybody in the room would turn round and wait to see it go up on the tape. Last year we did something like eight blocks a day over a hundred thousand. Institutions want instant liquidity on ten and twenty million dollar blocks. A lot of the trading has switched upstairs because the specialist system is not capable of accommodating it.'

'Upstairs' means the trading-rooms of investment banks. In effect the deal is done on the telephone and endorsed on the floor of the exchange. Other firms will tell you how they avoid the New York Exchange altogether for some deals, ratifying them through Pacific coast or Midwest exchanges so as to lessen the risk of the New York specialists interfering with a piece of business that buyer and seller merely want rubber-stamped. It is part of the traders' skill to know how to use regional exchanges without breaking the rules.

In the long room with a low ceiling at Liberty Plaza where Merrill Lynch trades equities, the future is arriving in sections. Screens produce complex information instantly, but the tickets to record transactions are still written out by hand. That explained the cardboard boxes in the corridors. Eventually they hope to write direct on screens with cursors. At present an endless conveyor-belt for tickets moves past the positions. More cardboard boxes stood against the plain yellow walls, alongside metal lockers. The place was utilitarian; the floor had fitted squares of durable carpet. My guide was to be the vice-president in charge of the room, Terry J. Arnold. He rushed up, said 'Gimme a second', and rushed away again. A trader said something and grinned. I grinned back. He said, 'You didn't hear what I said. I said, "I'd like to give you life."' He winked to make sure I didn't think he meant it. As far as I could tell there were about a hundred people in the room, men and women. A voice shouted, 'Twenty-seven cents! Get it!' but generally things seemed quiet. When Arnold came back he said he was sorry they weren't busier. You could see he felt he had let the side down. It was going to be a seventy-million-shares day, not a hundred-million day, as they had been used to recently. He meant the total traded by everyone, not just Merrill Lynch.

'Well,' he said, 'here we buy and sell stock for institutions, corporations and individuals. Block trading is the glamour spot, the bragging part. I also service and take care of all the retail, but only orders above two thousand shares.' Taking an average value of thirty dollars a share, it meant that only substantial retail orders came his way. 'And the reason I do that,' he said, 'is that with nine thousand retail salesmen in our system, if they're all out buying IBM at one time, they can get in my hair.' The thousands of small orders are not allowed to impede the work of attending to the above-two-thousand brigade. Someone else at the firm had spoken of 'a more automated, less personal system' of executing orders for small customers. Was this it? If two customers called at the Merrill Lynch booth in the concourse at Grand Central Station, one to buy 1,900 shares and the other 2,100, what would be the difference?

'Right,' said Arnold. 'The 2,100 would come to this desk and be professionally handled by traders. They are on the pulse all day long. The other one goes down through the machines to the floor [of the Stock Exchange]. It's just a fill-'em-and-bill-'em, that's the term we use. All they do is take the order off the machine, present it to the specialist, he writes down a price on it, and it comes back. It's automatic – whether it's up two points or down two points. Above two thousand shares we would bid for it a little bit. There's a lot of advantages you don't get when it goes through the machine.' So here, as in everything else, the large customer did better than the small one? 'Correct,' said Arnold. 'It is a function of necessity.' This is not the best possible news for the little old lady with a small order from Sun City. No doubt Merrill Lynch would point out that she has the benefit of the salesman's advice, backed up by the firm's research, before she decides what to do in the first place.

Arnold said that ten of his staff in the room were the 'position traders', who committed the firm's capital. Every morning he met them to discuss the day's strategy. The best safeguard was that they all had their own views of the market. 'I don't try to make 'em think my way,' said Arnold, 'because if I do and I'm wrong, we lose a lot. They all think differently – the hi-tech trader, the chemicals trader, the utilities, the oil. Though as manager of the group I may say, "I don't like this position, buy 'em back." That's my prerogative. We may change the strategy two or three times a day as news comes out. We have a research man who sits on the desk and all he does is read the news. We have wires to Washington and the West Coast so I can punch in directly and see what's going on.' The majority of his staff, the ones who are not committers of capital, spend their time looking for buyers and sellers. An inquiry for a block of shares needed to fill an order goes to seven or eight hundred institutions in the United States in no time. There are seven regional offices with trading desks. 'In each one of these,' said Arnold, 'I have at least five traders making calls at once. I've got sixty-some right here – all calling institutions. What this does is to create a monstrous network of telephone calls. We've canvassed the United States.' Some people in the room make three or four hundred thousand dollars a year (some don't). Arnold indicated a trader who specialised in Bank X, a commercial bank with limitless stock-exchange business to transact that paid a fortune in commissions to those lucky enough to

124

handle it. Merrill Lynch hired him from a rival firm because he knew so much about Bank X. 'He's a very good trader,' said Arnold, 'but you've got to remember, it's a public-relations business as well. You wine 'em and dine 'em, you go out and have nice times. I don't mean you *buy* business – you can't buy business – but it's much easier dealing with a friend than a guy you don't know. There is expertise and there is trust.'

Arnold distinguished between the money that a securities firm earned by trading with its own resources, the risk-taking, and the money it earned in commissions as a buyer and seller on behalf of others. The former was 'real' dollars, the latter 'soft' dollars. At the retail end of the business there are a lot of soft dollars to be earned. They are soft because they melt away in overheads, leaving the firm with barely a third of the original amount. Arnold said that every dollar earned in commission business took about twenty cents in adminis-trative costs, five cents in special bonus payments inside the depart-ment, and, the biggest slice of all, about forty cents to the retail salesman. This is how the nine thousand salespersons or 'account executives' make their living, all over America. They don't have to deal exclusively with Merrill Lynch; they have a franchise of the firm's products, but may need to be persuaded by a better-than-usual percent-age to sell a particular share to their customers. 'We force him to come to us when we want him to,' said Arnold. 'Again, that's soft dollars. So really, you're not giving anything away. The firm still makes a tremen-dous amount of money.'

The nine thousand or so retail salesmen give Merrill Lynch an extra layer of capacity. Individually they are of no consequence compared to the big investment institutions. Mobilised by the glint of money, they amount to a vast institution of their own. Arnold conjured up a new display on the screen where he had been showing me how he could monitor the firm's position in every security. Now he drew on its memory to show me how he had used the retail network a few weeks earlier. The security was US Gypsum, highly rated but not very active. An institution wanted to sell 600,000 shares. 'This stock does not trade in monstrous lines,' said Arnold. 'It's usually a very light trader. So to move six hundred thousand shares is virtually impossible in this market-place. But I can internalise it, take it in-house to Merrill Lynch, and sell it out in my internal system here, overnight. I entice the salesman by giving him a big buck. US Gypsum happens to be a highly recommended stock in our research department, OK? Without having that good research opinion, retail individuals would not touch it. But the salesman says, if Merrill Lynch likes the company, I'll take a shot on it. So he gets his grandmother or his aunt or his uncle or whatever to buy it.' All over America that day in February 1983, people were buying US Gypsum without quite knowing why. Figures came up on the screen. 'See, we bought six hundred and thirty thousand, two hundred shares at forty-five and an eighth,' said Arnold. That cost the firm something over twenty-eight million dollars. 'And here's where we sold it the next day,' he said, 'at forty-six and seven-eighths. The profit being a million dollars.' On each of the 630,000 shares, Merrill Lynch made one and three-quarter dollars. These weren't all hard dollars. To put the nine thousand in the right mood to find instant purchasers among the uncles and grandmothers probably cost sixty cents a share. A salesman who sold a hundred shares, price a shade under $4,700, would have made just sixty dollars. The trading profit left to Merrill Lynch after the salesmen's cut and other overheads would be well short of a million. I didn't think to ask for the exact figure until long after, and by that time the information had been wiped from the disk. Someone said that at most it would have been half a million dollars. Even so.

5
WALL STREET: ALL CHANGE

Mayday and after—Gunning for Glass-Steagall—
Grey pinstripes at Prudential-Bache—American Express and the real world—
Tom Saunders III and Rule 415—The three Lazards—
Felix Rohatyn meets all crises—Private lives at Brown Brothers Harriman—
Good works at James D. Wolfensohn—Scarecrows and castles—
An opportunist banker

Defining Wall Street is harder than it was. The place has a touch of frenzy. Old hands say there was always drama and restlessness, as in any market-place, but that this is different. Explanations are readily available. On 1 May 1975, the Securities and Exchange Commission finally had its way with the stock market and abolished brokers' fixed commissions. This is remembered as 'Mayday', a sort of holocaust; the consumers had broken through. As strong firms competed with weak to negotiate commissions, a long age of easy profits came to an end. 'Back in 75, when we had full commissions, an IBM trade would pay us sixty-five dollars a hundred shares,' says Terry Arnold at Merrill Lynch. 'Today on a block trade it may pay us ten cents a hundred. Scary, isn't it?' The strong survived, the weak merged or went out of business.

But Mayday was only part of a wider process. A comparable change on the capital-raising side of the business was the SEC's Rule 415. All financial institutions were changing. Business was more combative; Wall Street's clients, tormented by years of inflation, were beginning to wake up and expect their investments to be more efficient. Rock-bottom commission rates when dealing with institutions, Terry Arnold's scary ten cents a hundred shares, were one response. Another, for Wall Street houses that did retail business (the majority, outside the Bulge firms), was to solicit business from old-fashioned private investors. These were not as clever as the institutions, and went on paying bigger commissions. Unfortunately private investors had been dropping out of the market for years. Merrill Lynch found a way of tempting them back by inventing the Cash Management Account, with its surplus cash going into money-market funds. These funds, whether or not associated with investment accounts, became a sub-industry in themselves. Their interest rates were much better than commercial banks were allowed by law to offer. By the end of 1982, when the law has changed after frantic lobbying by the commercial banks, more than two hundred billion dollars had shifted over from them to money-market accounts of one sort or another. Merrill Lynch had $47 billion of it, nearly half in CMA accounts. Glass-Steagall laid down that investment banks couldn't be commercial banks, but the line was getting blurred.

Tension had existed between the two kinds of bank (and banker) since the 1930s, when the law created the distinction. The idea that banks had to be kept in separate compartments has been deeply ingrained in American thinking. The 1920s were a time of financial opportunism. The Crash and its aftermath confirmed suspicions of wicked goings-on. After 1934 the United States banking system was among the most regulated in the world. The legislation was never seriously challenged. When Martin Mayer wrote his impeccable book about Wall Street (1955) he misspelt the name of the Act, calling it 'Glass-Steagle'; it seemed ancient history then. Now 'Glass-Steagall' appears casually in financial headlines, shorthand for a moribund system. The commercial banks, arguing through a powerful political lobby, want to end the Act's restrictive practices. When investment banks invaded their territory with money-market accounts, they retaliated by offering 'discount brokerage' services. Discount brokers, now a healthy sub-industry causing anxiety to investment banks, appeared after 1975's Mayday, offering customers basic buy-and-sell facilities with no trimmings, such as investment advice. They are rarely Stock Exchange members, so they make bulk-purchase deals with brokers who are. The customer can pay as little as a quarter of the full brokerage commission that someone grander would charge. After a while it occurred to commercial banks that the existing law might allow them to offer this cut-price service, acting merely as a channel for customers' orders. Glass-Steagall implied that it could be done, probably with the intention of helping the investor in a remote community with only a local bank and no access to a broker. Hundreds of banks, among them the biggest in the country, Bank of America and Citicorp, assumed the Act meant them, and offered to do their customers' share transactions. The Securities Industry Association, which takes commercial banks to court when it thinks it can curb their excesses, has been unable to stop the tide. Another bit of Glass-Steagall crumbled. Soon commercial banks were toying with insurance and estate-agency services, lured, like Wall Street, into dreaming of a future as financial supermarkets. That was bad enough for those interested in the retail end of the business. But Wall Street's ultimate fear was that Glass-Steagall would be swept away, and the big banks would, in the twinkling of an eye, become full-scale brokers, traders and underwriters, competing with the Salomons and Goldmans. Then Wall Street might be gobbled up.

Barbed advertising began to appear from both sides. The broker was presented as lazy, the commercial banker clumsy in matters of personal finance. A New York commercial banker, No. 3 in the hierarchy at his glassy palace, made no bones about wanting to 'turn the situation around, so we can get at the Merrill Lynches'. He said Senators Glass and Steagall based their infamous Act on the British banking system, which they misunderstood, since Britain makes no legal distinction between banks that handle securities and banks that don't. In saying that, he misunderstood the City's merchant banks, which historically couldn't be members of the Stock Exchange, thus creating a British variant of America's split between 'banking' and 'broking'. But he was talking politics, not technicalities. He was just back from the American Bankers' Association meeting in Washington: four hundred extroverts, he said, and not one shrinking violet among them. 'We're not *entirely* bad guys,' he said, 'but if we start getting strapped because other guys get into the business, we've got to fight.' He made it sound as if commercial banking was the cottage industry, not Wall Street.

So Wall Street has two grounds for anxiety. Commercial banks threaten it from without. Its own difficulties of change and adaptation threaten it from within. Perhaps its past has caught up with it. Judge Medina spent seven years trying to see if there was any truth in the smear that investment bankers feathered their nest at the expense of America. He concluded there was not. But there were always aspects of Wall Street that angered those on the outside. The fixed commission was one of them; it seemed eternal, until the SEC decided it was against the public interest. Today the public interest is a noisier beast, and Wall Street has to offer a better service than in the past. It is more competitive. Issuing shares has become cheaper for companies and less profitable for investment banks. Under these conditions, the creatures of Wall Street must be that much more predatory. No doubt new kinds of banking lie ahead. ('When Glass-Steagall goes,' I heard a commercial banker say with a purr, 'it will go like the windscreen of a car.') Wall Street's rearguard hints at another dark age, like the unregulated 1920s, if that happens and universal banking returns; as though to concede that at the root of its trade lies something wicked, only waiting for deregulation to let mischief commence. But prophecy is futile. Better to catch glimpses of Mammon's people as they are, under pressure, before in their present form they become history, like the fixed commissions.

*   *   *

George L. Ball, a slightly built man with pale hair, in his middle forties, became president and chief executive of Prudential-Bache Securities in 1982. 'Bache' was a familiar Wall Street name, but in its new form the firm had been in existence for only a year. Articles in financial magazines wondered whether he and it were a contribution to the shape of things to come. Nobody knew. Nobody knows yet. Bache, founded 1879, was an old-line brokerage house, once among the leaders. In 1933, during the Depression, when America feared for its financial system, the firm felt itself important enough to publish reassuring advertisements headed 'The Worst Is Known'. It developed as a mainly retail firm, with many branches and far-flung salesmen, like a smaller Merrill Lynch. In recent times energy and earnings flagged, and in its weakened state it was threatened by an unfriendly takeover from Canada in 1981. Bache's investment-bank adviser was First Boston. The mergers-and-acquisitions group there found a saviour in Prudential Insurance. Bache fell into its arms and became a subsidiary. In this way, more or less by accident, the first of the new financial-service groups, mooted in Wall Street ever since Merrill Lynch showed the way, was created. Bache with its network of three or four thousand securities salesmen, Prudential with more than twenty thousand insurance agents, could offer services that complemented one another, or so it was said. Prudential, the nation's largest life insurer, with more private money to invest than any other institution in America, had all the capital that any investment bank could need. PruCapital, also headed by Ball, was put alongside Prudential-Bache, to provide money for industrial clients in the shape of loans and investments. Glowing castles in the air were painted. People spoke of 'synergy', the in-word of the time for combined effort. Ball had been hired from the prosperous firm of E. F. Hutton, another investment bank with most of its clout at the retail broking end, where he had risen through the ranks of salesmen to be president, the second-in-command. By 1983 the brokerage end of the business was spending a fortune on advertising, and angelic voices could be heard in Prudential-Bache TV commercials, singing 'America, bring us your future'.

The Prudential-Bache offices looked a long way from such lyrics. They were then in a glum building at 100 Gold Street, where Bache moved in 1971, almost in the shadow of Brooklyn Bridge, half a mile distant from the Stock Exchange, a long way in financial districts. Ball is reported to have stalked into the building the day he took over and said the lobby was a pigsty. It was clean but barren the morning I arrived for a 9 am appointment. I was directed to the 'executive offices' on the fifth floor. While I waited upstairs on a sofa, the hall man answered every telephone caller with a lofty 'Executive offices!' It was a longish wait. Ball apologised for the delay, explaining that his breakfast visitors had been delayed coming in from Philadelphia by a rail strike. He had to keep one of us waiting, them or me. They were in town to discuss a $350 million deal. 'So it was you,' he said. He had a graceful directness. 'What can I obfuscate for you?' he said presently. He talked about the importance, to an investment bank, of managing issues, because they guaranteed a supply of cheaply-priced new securities for the firm's sales staff to distribute. 'The brokerage arm,' he said, 'is like a nest of little birds, waiting for the mother bird to put worms in their beaks. The highest nutrient-value worm is a co-managed underwriting. So broking and investment banking are not separate.' He conceded that Bache was 'behind the pack' as a managing underwriter; but exciting prospects lay ahead for a company with Prudential-Bache's backing, to be unlike 'all the other thirteen grey pinstripes and white shirts'. It so happened he was wearing a grey pinstripe suit and a white shirt. He may have intended the joke. Ball said what a 'marvellous luxury' it was to be part of a group where the parent company's resources were so great that money was always at hand for days or hours to finance trading or underwriting positions. 'Somebody asked me the other day how much capital Prudential-Bache has,' he said, 'and I said I don't know. If your father is very very rich, you never really ask about money. The constraint is good business sense, not the amount of capital available. I think we have four hundred and fifty or five hundred million or six hundred million, I honestly am not sure. Actually we can run our business with substantially less capital. I'm always trying to send the money back to Prudential, to let them use it for something else. If we need three hundred million dollars for an underwriting commitment, I can always pick up the phone.'

What he envisaged was combined effort of one sort or another; he

131

didn't say 'synergy' once. Security analysts who knew individual companies well, because they had studied them intensively, could work more closely with the corporate finance teams at Prudential-Bache, opening up new business prospects at the companies. The bankers at PruCapital and at Prudential-Bache could work alongside one another, lending companies cash or raising capital for them as part of a grand strategy. The brokers at Bache might have the contacts with companies that PruCapital needed. The parent, Prudential, was going to buy a commercial bank (it soon did, and turned it into Prudential Bank & Trust Co.), which would offer finance to insurance and brokerage clients. Eventually his brokers and Prudential's insurance agents would co-operate to offer financial services. As for the brokers of the future, he saw them as counsellors, not just salesmen. The previous year, contributing to a magazine* his view of the financial world in the year 2000, Ball wrote ironically that a 'breathtaking' development was on the way, called 'personal counselling'. Ideas would be exchanged by 'something called conversation rather than data input'. This note of detached, rather flat optimism is the one he struck in conversation, as though he recognised, and wanted others to know that he recognised, that behind all the talk about change, the same old realities were at work. At one point he paused to investigate a small dead worm that he spotted on his desk, remarking that it was a strange thing to find in a Manhattan office. It was a strange thing to comment on, too. If our conversation was inconclusive, that may have been because it was a time of ifs and buts for a firm like his. (A year later, Prudential-Bache said its 'synergy' was working.) As he was showing me out, I asked why a gleaming sword and scabbard hung on the wall. We paused, he blinked. Bells were ringing; secretaries bore down on him with messages and the next visitor. He said the sword was presented to him at a function that a regional manager helped to organise. 'Unfortunately,' he said, and pointed me towards the lifts, 'I had to fire the poor guy about three months ago.'

I said that seemed appropriate, its being a sword.

'That's right,' he said. 'Yes.'

Bache's defensive sale of itself to an insurance company acted as a catalyst in Wall Street. Investment banks needed larger amounts of capital to back up gargantuan deals. Mergers might be the inevitable answer. No doubt firms concluded also that it was better to be swallowed by, say, an insurance company, which would leave its Wall Street

---

* *Institutional Investor*, December 1982.

arm to get on with trading and underwriting, than to wait too long, wake up one day to find that Glass-Steagall had shattered like a windscreen, and be gathered in by a commercial bank which would be far less likely to run it at arm's length. It was widely assumed that one of the reasons the likes of Citicorp and Morgan Guaranty had their Eurobond subsidiaries in London was to help them get their hand in at investment banking, ready for the day when it was legal in New York.

Within a few months of the Bache-Prudential deal, three more leading firms had been merged. Salomon Brothers became part of Philbro, the trading conglomerate. Dean Witter Reynolds was bought (for $800 million) by the Sears, Roebuck group of stores, which acquired a property group at the same time, a deal that made the 'financial supermarket' idea an almost literal possibility. Soon Sears, Roebuck was opening branches in its shops (it has more than eight hundred), to the sound of wisecracks about 'socks and stocks' and 'Half a pound of home loans, please.'

In a further variant on the 'supermarket' idea, American Express bought (for $930 million) the powerful Wall Street house of Shearson Loeb Rhoades, itself the product of a merger two years earlier, to produce another creature of a kind unknown to man or banker until now. Apart from its core business of credit cards and travellers' cheques (which has many competitors), American Express was involved in insurance, property and travel. Now it added underwriting, stockbroking and other financial services. Thus the holders of the seventeen million American Express cards around the world, many of them wealthy and none of them poor, their names and financial data already inside the firm's computers, were available as potential customers for the same firm's salesmen. Those earning more than $50,000 a year were the best prospects; those earning less than $35,000 were not significant, since when Wall Street talks of financial supermarkets, it really means something more superior, financial department stores. As a Merrill Lynch manager put it, when explaining to me the electronic services that the firm hoped to introduce into customers' homes, 'I'm talking about the guy with a hundred thousand dollars or whatever the breakpoint is going to be. The guy with the six-pack [pack of six beers, i.e. young or poor] doesn't have enough money to worry about investments, avoiding taxes, buying that many things. That's not the real world.'

American Express made further incursions into this real world in 1983 by merging its International Banking Corporation, until then not a star performer, with the empire of a secretive banker from the Lebanon, based in Switzerland, controlled through a company in Luxembourg, with branches throughout Europe and the Americas; the deal was agreed in Montreal. The shy partner was Edmond Safra, whose family for generations back were Middle Eastern bankers and gold traders. His full face, touched with a smile, appeared briefly in photographs, usually the same one, and disappeared again behind the colourless title of his organisation, the Trade Development Bank. This also controls a size-able commercial bank in New York, Republic National, while the same family runs the Banco Safra in Brazil. What American Express agreed to pay more than $500 million for were the non-US operations of the Trade Development Bank. As far as one could tell, Safra was not an investment banker. He took deposits from international customers, especially in the Middle East, traded in gold and foreign exchange, and was engaged in moving banknotes, the physical cash, around the world. But financial liaisons now have few rules to follow. In different places, wearing various hats, American Express was credit-card merchant, travel agent, stockbroker, insurer and gold trader, to name a few. With capital of more than a billion dollars, it was in the Merrill Lynch league. By the spring of 1984, with its opportunistic purchase of the ailing Lehman Brothers, the group had bought its way into the charmed circle of old-style investment bankers as well. Not surprisingly, one of the first reported acts of Shearson/Express, the entity that made the purchase, was to earmark thirty or forty million dollars in bonuses and pay for senior Lehman officers, whose goodwill was necessary if it was to be a fruitful acquisition.

American Express's high visibility to all, whether friend or foe, accounts for the extra layer of security that the visitor meets on his way to the office of James D. Robinson III, chairman and chief executive officer. American Express Plaza is on the shore, at the bottom of the financial district. The executive waiting-area, spacious and expensively decorated, is isolated from the offices themselves; the attendant must use a magnetic card to admit the visitor. Robinson is a trim dark-haired man in his late forties with a serious manner, educated at Harvard, whose father ran an investment bank in Atlanta. His office was palatial. He ran briskly through the strategy of acquisition. American Express had reasoned as follows. It possessed two leading products in terms of payment systems, the card and the travellers' cheque. It was involved with people who had money to spend. So when the firm sensed a coming shift back to saving and investing, it wanted to be involved. That was the reason for merging with Shearson. To offer a variety of products and services was to provide a hedge against any one of them losing favour. The deal with Safra would work in various ways. Overnight it meant that American Express International Banking Corp. achieved what had been a five-year target. 'Edmond,' he said, 'has been a highly selective banker, very conservative, a man who turns his assets over as frequently as possible. He will be able to develop an Asian business more actively. We have a presence there, our name is well known. As a participant in world trade, he's an active player, as are we. He is active in gold trading, with Shearson we are active in the commodity markets and in gold. Safra is a lead factor in the banknote business, shipping currencies to central banks – if the Bank of France wants US dollar bills, if the Philippines want Deutschmarks – and think of all the paper that we send around the world in the form of travellers' cheques.' Implicit in all Robinson said was the motto of the industry, that one thing leads to another. Get to know a central bank through handling its gold or banknotes, and it might be a customer for US Treasury bonds. Obtain access to those Safra depositors, and tap sources of personal discretionary income beyond the dreams of avarice. Or as Robinson put it, 'Overnight the Trade Development Bank acquisition brings us a major position in private banking around the world, doing business with wealthy clients.' Even Safra's inscrutability could be useful, the other side of the coin to the high profile of American Express. But with Shearson, Safra and Lehman all together under one roof, instant 'synergy' seemed unlikely. As at Prudential-Bache, it was early days yet.

It was always important for banks to live on their wits. Today old firms make new alignments to attack markets and continents; technology oils the wheels; 'loyalty' is a negotiable concept. In all this there may be, in addition, the unconscious response of an industry that must roll on defiantly, and to hell with the world outside financial centres, with its latent hostility to such rich men's games. But in the daily round of Wall Street it merely feels like tactical survival. The change in attitude that Rule 415* encouraged was towards the 'transactional', a phrase much heard in Wall Street. Relationships between investment bank and client shifted away from the stable towards the promiscuous. Large corporate clients would no longer go almost cap-in-hand to Wall Street and ask the financial magicians to raise money by special processes that only they could understand. The client knew how it was done. He might invite competing offers before deciding which bank to use.

* See p. 83.

His relative strength, and the bankers' relative weakness, narrowed the 'spread', the amount it cost him in fees and selling concessions. There was nothing in Rule 415 that told companies they had suddenly to activate an issue that was waiting on the shelf, and let banks bid for it; the issue could be negotiated with an investment bank in the old way. But it invited a more competitive approach. Many bankers felt that the SEC regarded Wall Street's syndicate system as a price-fixing mechanism. It had broken one of those already, the New York Stock Exchange commission structure. Now it would do another good deed and liberate the capital markets.

At first, when Rule 415 was mooted, no one took much notice. Tom Saunders of Morgan Stanley claims he was one of the first to see its implications, while jogging before breakfast – 'I do a lot of crazy running and stuff, and if you're out in the park, into your fifth mile, things sort of wander through your mind, and you say, "My God, is that what this is all about?" I came to the office and said, "Hold it, fellers, this thing is *unbelievable*. How will the capital markets respond to billions and billions of dollars piled up on the shelf that could just *come*?" We got in touch with the other firms and they all said, "Holy God, this is insane."' When these anxieties were aired, Wall Street firms were accused of being self-interested. Morgan Stanley took the precaution of explaining to the SEC that it believed the powerful firms (like itself) would benefit from 415 because they had both the capital to take risks, and the distribution network to find bulk buyers at the institutions; smaller firms would be the sufferers. This tale of woe was not believed at the time. Saunders shakes his head at such a low view of human nature. 'We got tainted,' he said. 'What came out of it was, "You guys are just worried about your own hides," and down that trail they went. Well, we were dead right. There was a loss of liquidity. Business was concentrated in a few firms. Guess who they were? Morgan Stanley, Goldman, Salomon, First Boston.' Nevertheless, viewed broadly, 415 was another nail in the coffin of Wall Street's privilege. Saunders talks with feeling about 'the spectre of innovation'. He thinks the capital markets are going through the most significant changes in their history – 'all excited,' he says, 'scrambling to be innovative, to be competitive, to be leaders. Issuers are fostering competition that may be detrimental to them in the long run. But corporate treasurers are the same as you and me. They want to be innovative, they want to tell the board, "Look what I did! I created this competitive situation, I got these five banks beating a path to our door, and wasn't it wonderful? I've taken the shackles off. The issuer is now in control of the world, and here I come." On the other hand, those of us on the investment-banking side don't want to be perceived as not being risk-takers, not willing to step up and do something for an issuer.'

It is no longer the cosy scene that Judge Medina investigated.

* * *

Deceptively cosy scenes can still be found. The partnership of Lazard Frères catches the outsider's eye with its name, its history, its air of comfortable living and its apparent indifference to the rat-race of Johnny-come-latelies. I collected more than one scathing reference to Lazard, as though people felt that its thirty partners had no right to be prospering without trying to be like everybody else. 'It is run,' said a trader at one of the Bulge firms, 'like a Jewish partnership was run a hundred years ago.' This sounded more insulting to him than it did to Lazard Frères which, in any case, sees its style, whatever it may be, as a wise choice, not historical accident.

There are three banks in the world called Lazard. In London, Lazard Brothers is a limited company, in other hands since World War I. The Bank of England wanted to see foreign-owned City banks anglicised, in case their assets came under German control. France might have been defeated; Lazard was a leading dealer in gold bullion. So the Pearson industrial group was brought in, and owned Lazard Brothers outright until 1984. In Paris and New York the firms continued as partnerships, closely linked. London, the largest, was the odd man out among the three. Lazard Frères in Paris owned some of London's stock, and London owned some of New York's partnership capital. But Lazard Brothers, a rather haughty bank, remained very English and quite separate, although in later years there was a degree of co-operation with the other two. Paris and New York had the same senior partner, a French multi-millionaire, Michel David-Weill, who, since he took control in 1980, made it his business to bring Lazard Brothers back into the fold: a logical step in the age of alliances. In 1984 the three firms were formally linked in an international partnership based in the US, Lazard Partners, owned half by Pearson, half by a combination of David-Weill's own interests and Lazard Frères New York. David-Weill himself was the leading figure. His New York firm, some of its financial details now disclosed for the first time, turned out to be almost embarrassingly profitable beside Lazard Brothers. Lazard Frères had made a pre-tax profit the previous year of $80 million. Lazard Brothers, employing far more capital (as well as more people), disclosed less than $20 million before tax.

David-Weill's family is descended from a cousin of the original Lazard brothers, three emigrant Frenchmen who began as shopkeepers in New Orleans in the mid-nineteenth century. They had no male descendants; it was the Weills, later known as David-Weills, who kept up the original name. Before Michel David-Weill took over, the New York Lazard Frères was run by André Meyer, perhaps Wall Street's best-known investment banker in recent decades. He died in 1979; he didn't think much of the British, and it was only after his death that Lazard Brothers and Lazard Frères began to drift together. Meyer had been hired by the David-Weills in Paris in 1927. He escaped to the United States when the Germans invaded in 1940, and ran the American partnership for more than thirty years, making it, and himself, rich and influential. An autocrat with a sharp tongue, he was primarily a deal-maker and strategist, advising companies, fighting and fixing. Illness had sapped his authority before he died. Michel David-Weill, who already headed the French bank, took over in New York as well, reorganised the firm and restored morale. Peace reigns now in the utilitarian offices in Rockefeller Plaza. ('Is it true that Lazard is proud of being a bit parsimonious with its furnishings?' I asked a partner, Frank Zarb. '*Cheap*,' he said gleefully. 'It's true!') Michel David-Weill, even when speaking English with an accent as soft as a Camembert, sounds precise and very sure of himself. He goes to and fro between Europe and New York by Concorde, a few weeks here, a few weeks there. He wants to be like the rest of Wall Street about as much as he wants to be poor.

Major risk-taking does not appeal to Lazard Frères in the ordinary course of business. David-Weill says he is open to any idea as long as it doesn't tie up capital or more than a few people. This means he is not open to half the bright ideas that appeal to investment bankers. He offers 'a pretty impressive list of the things we do not do. We are not in arbitrage. We are not in block trading. We don't lend money to our customers, including margin loans. We don't take huge positions in the bond market – or the futures market, or the equity market. The fact that the firm is not engaged in its own trading doesn't prevent us, and may make it easier, for us to be an adviser to corporations when they have mergers, acquisitions, reorganisations. Relative to our size, there are more people available for clients.'

Given the firm's modest size, few leading Wall Street houses are as profitable. Lazard doesn't thirst after publicity; it gets on with the business of making money. The trader who, in talking to me, sneered at it as a 'Jewish partnership', worked for First Boston. In 1983, First Boston's before-tax earnings were $108 million, barely a third more than the $80 million of Lazard Frères. For all its activity, and the slightly theatrical air of excitement in which it operates, First Boston's enormous revenues of half a billion dollars are offset by similarly enormous expenses. Frugal Lazard Frères plods along in comparative obscurity, money sticking to its boots. Corporate finance, the 'advisory' role, produces about half its earnings in New York. In a 1981 interview,* David-Weill said that 'a few' of his partners would earn half a million dollars 'in a very good year'. He was probably being conservative, even then. Managing investments for clients is important business. The firm also does some capital-raising. David-Weill says that by acting only for selected issuers, Lazard is seen to be discriminating; institutions will share its enthusiasm and buy the securities. However that may be, Lazard hasn't tried to beef itself up with traders and salesmen, any more than it goes in for reception areas like cocktail bars (in New York a male attendant sits at a small wooden desk; wind moans between the glass doors. In Paris, where Lazard has an important commercial-banking business, the offices are larger, with a touch of marble and chandeliers). But Lazard is regularly invited to underwrite, and given a prominent position on tombstones, because it has strong relationships with so many important companies. 'They have a lot of business that we want to be in,' said a banker at a Bulge firm, explaining why his firm gave underwriting to Lazard.

For all the talk about 'transactional' deals, the old connections are not dead yet. An investment banker at Manufacturers Hanover Ltd, the London arm of the parent in New York, has a story of the 1970s engraved on his heart. 'For some time,' he said, 'we had been toying with a company where we had a prime commercial-banking relationship. Eventually they said they were happy for us, here in London, to go ahead and do a Eurobond issue, I think it was for fifty million dollars. One of my colleagues was literally on his way to the airport to see the client when he was told to hang on a second – the client's finance man had gone to see his chairman, and the chairman said they'd better check with Mr X, partner of a long-established Wall Street house, who had a seat on the client's board. Mr X said, "Sure, Manny Hanny is a good

* 'The making of Lazard's', *Euromoney*, March 1981.

commercial bank, but *investment* bank? They don't know what they're talking about." To cut a long story short, after a week of immense emotion, and our banging the table and saying it was our deal, that we'd worked on it for two years, we got screwed. We had our deal taken away. The only change they made in our arrangements was to change it from English law to American. Instead of having all the cake, we got twenty-five per cent of it. It was their deal. That wouldn't happen today.'

Perhaps not. I asked David-Weill if Lazard ever did that kind of thing, but he shrugged his shoulders: there were many deals over the years. He seemed contented. 'The Lazard universe,' he said, 'has become a little unique. It is a minor miracle that these three firms have managed to remain themselves, not to be transformed.' He didn't hold with working for glory. 'Glory is size,' he said. 'If you look at the magazines, all the time banks speak of size. But we are in this business to make money, not to be the greatest in the world, not to see our name in the newspaper all the time, not to be the first in Eurodollar lending.' People thought their letter-heads had to say New York, Tokyo, Hong Kong, Singapore. There was an obsession with glory. 'Most people who have a big office in Tokyo have not made a penny out of it,' he said. 'Why do they do it?'

One of Lazard Frères partners is Ian MacGregor, loaned to Britain in recent years, to run state firms, latterly the National Coal Board. His confrontations with the miners' union no doubt owe something to the miners' (not surprising) perception of him as a dour, ruthless figure from a world of high finance, come to ram the language of capitalism down their unwilling throats. But Lazard's best-known partner in New York is Felix G. Rohatyn, born in Vienna in 1928, who reached the United States via France, Portugal and Brazil during World War 2, and later joined Lazard Frères as a trainee; his stepfather was a friend of André Meyer. Rohatyn, Meyer's pupil, and his heir had he chosen to be, was at one time Wall Street's king of mergers and acquisitions. Now he represents an earlier, soberer generation of M&A men, who dislike confrontation between companies if it can be avoided. 'The macho dynamic,' he murmurs. 'Who's-got-the-balls-to-do-this?' The vast takeover fees paid to bankers for advice that leads to 'victory' pain him. 'I don't think any responsible investment banker will knowingly skew his advice because of the compensation. On the other hand, you're asking people, many of whom are young, to achieve a level of dis-interestedness in their own finances. If you don't make a deal, your firm gets five hundred thousand dollars. If you do, it gets five million. That's a difficult thing to ask for – a level of asceticism. You know, we don't expect people in our business to be canonised.' At Lazard, he says, 'we have advised our clients to walk away from a great number of deals'. Rohatyn takes a puritanical view of the way securities markets have expanded recently, using such devices as options, commodity futures and venture-capital funds. 'Every kind of financial instrument is being created to lure individuals into believing they are investing when they are really speculating,' he said in a speech in 1984.

Rohatyn, like his bank, avoids the mainstream. The reason his name is known outside financial circles is that in 1975 he drifted into the role of 'the man who saved New York'. The city was well on the way to bankruptcy. There were even respectable arguments at the time for letting it happen; many Americans have always regarded the city with hostility, a profligate place. Rohatyn first heard of the problems privately and by chance. He let himself be drawn in after meeting Hugh Carey, the Governor of New York State. At first he was purely a backroom expert, sitting on Carey's advisory committee and helping to set up a rescue agency called the Municipal Assistance Corporation to sell bonds. A statuette of what looks like a rampant bronze bulldog stands (with other medals and awards) on a table in an ante-room to his office. Its collar is labelled 'MAC', and the initials are further rammed home by the inscription underneath, which reads: 'Meeting All Crises. Hugh L. Carey, March 1976.' As time went on, Rohatyn became more deeply involved in reforming the city's budget. 'I moved into another world, of labour leaders and newspaper people and politicians, which is kind of heady stuff.' I said he had been quoted as saying that he 'felt like the wandering Jew come home'. He said, 'I do love New York City, and I am a refugee. It is not something you ever stop being. The city was very good to me. So the whole exercise became both a professional challenge and an emotional experience, paying back a debt.' New York survived, at the price of dilapidation. The seedy subways are a monument to careful housekeeping. When I mentioned that side of it, Rohatyn said sharply, 'You can't judge what we did by some mythical perfection that is unachievable.'

I asked him about getting rich on Wall Street. He said that accumulating piles of money had no great charm for him. 'In terms of everyday standards I am clearly very well off,' he said. 'In terms of the world in which I live, I'm not. I need a certain amount of capital so that I can provide for my family. But I have no great desire to build up a huge financial empire in order to leave a great deal of money to my children. I think it's probably bad for them. And I don't have enough faith in the way the world is going to have any real notion what money is going to be worth in ten or twenty years' time.'

A chilly note to end on.

At the cosy firm of Brown Brothers Harriman, which describes itself as a private bank, the country's largest and oldest, there is still a partners' room with roll-top desks. Their owners pull down the lids and lock them at the end of the day; 'a blessing for dealing with clutter,' says one of them. There are thirty partners, exactly the same number as at Lazard; but no one bothered to be rude to me about Brown Brothers Harriman. The bank, in Wall Street itself, with branches in ten cities in the United States and Europe, is a financial anomaly, a partnership that is also a commercial bank that is also (because it is a partnership) allowed to have a seat on the New York Stock Exchange, so that it can handle its own brokerage. Founded in 1818 as Brown Brothers, it looks after US banking business for many foreign banks, manages investments for clients, at home and abroad, deals in securities and advises many companies. One of its specialist services, small but doubtless lucrative, consists of paying the senior executives of firms direct, bypassing their own accounting procedures so that prying clerks don't know what the bosses earn. 'Well,' said Robert V. Roosa, a BBH partner, 'the idea occurred to me when I got here, that many firms like to have their executives' compensation handled separately and confidentially, and would keep a pool on deposit of three, four, five million dollars. We mail the cheques to their senior executives. We can do little things like that, tailor them to special needs with the emphasis on quality and personal attention. In amidst all these canyons of the great banks, we fill a niche.' A fee-earning service that also brings in millions of dollars of other people's money on deposit has a merchant-banking ring about it. Roosa himself is a man whom it would be hard to visualise on the trading floor at Salomon Brothers, but easy enough to see against mahogany and brass lamps in Lombard Street. Partners are not appointed much before they are forty, but, once there, remain till the age of seventy. 'A pleasant way to conduct business,' said Roosa.

He was a plump, stately, Chestertonian sort of man, jolly, with a twinkle in his eye, dressed in a comfortable suit with a waistcoat and bow tie. His occasional 'Shucks' and 'Oh my gosh' were in keeping. When John F. Kennedy was President, Roosa was an Under Secretary of the Treasury, and a figure in Washington. His signed commission from Kennedy was on the wall of his room at the bank. Among the photographs was one of Kennedy that was waiting to be autographed, as a gift for Roosa's parents, when the President was assassinated. The room had two doors, both of which stood open all the time I was there. One connected with a bigger room, where nine of the partners were said to work; I could see half a roll-top desk and a small American flag; voices murmured out of sight. The other was the way I had come in, from a banking hall via a carpeted reception area, where an attendant in dark clothes was on duty. That was pure City, too. Roosa talked about Japan, where the bank had connections in high places, and the Persian Gulf, where he was going soon for a couple of weeks. He said he couldn't talk much longer because he had to leave at 5.15 for a meeting of the bank's steering committee in mid-town at six. They met at a club, The Links, to get away from the office. For years someone from BBH had been either the president, or chairman of the membership committee, 'so in that way we keep up the relationship'. He said he belonged to two or three such clubs. He seemed to be talking of old families, old money, old Anglo-Saxons. 'A little bit of the old-boy net,' he said, 'but nothing like the UK.'

A young man appeared from the hall, a candidate for the job of assistant to Roosa. He had been seeing various people at the bank. If successful, he would work with Roosa for two years, then move on through the firm.

'Excuse me,' said the candidate. 'I'm sorry.'

The banker waved him in. They exchanged pleasantries. It was a benign scene.

'Well,' said Roosa. 'I hope they didn't swamp you out.'

'No, they might have chewed me up, but they didn't spit me out. It was a good day. Nice to have met you.'

'Well, it's fine,' said the banker. 'And I guess Bill indicated that we're going to do our best to finish all the interviewing and make decisions no later than the middle of March. I'll meditate in the Middle East.'

'Great,' said the candidate. 'Thanks so much.'

'Well. Grand to see you.'

And the dark-coated man like a butler let him out into Wall Street.

* * *

My first view of New York investment bankers, and almost my last, months later, was through the eyes of James D. Wolfensohn, who sits high up in a skyscraper on an expensive stretch of Park Avenue, advising companies and arranging deals. By accident or temperament

Wolfensohn has moved on from two careers in other people's money-machines, in the City and in Wall Street, to run a modest money-machine of his own. Born in Australia in 1933, he was an investment banker there before joining the London merchant bank of J. Henry Schroder Wagg. It sent him to New York, recalled him to be the firm's number two, and lost him in 1977 when he was not appointed number one. He was invited to join Salomon Brothers and returned to New York, ostensibly a 'banker' in a firm of 'traders'. His job was to develop Salomon's weakest department, corporate finance, where business with companies, in particular raising capital for them, was fostered. Five years later he decided he had had enough of the traditional Wall Street. People said you never knew what Jim Wolfensohn would be up to next. He has interests outside banking, among them music and the arts. He plays the cello, has musicians as friends, and is chairman of the board of Carnegie Hall; he says that running it has changed his life. The outside interests cost him money. There is the international federation of multiple sclerosis societies (he is president), the Rockefeller Foundation (chairman of the finance committee), the Institute of Advanced Studies at Princeton (president) and the Jerusalem Foundation. He is even a trustee of the Population Council, whose aim is more and better family planning in underdeveloped countries; early travels in Asia and Africa introduced him to poverty.

His suite of offices was conventionally smart, the outer doors labelled with his name in large metal letters; the peephole was in the first 'O' of 'Wolfensohn'. Paintings by the Australian artist Arthur Boyd decorated the waiting area. In the most striking, a man in a dark suit sat under a tree, absorbed in a book. Beyond him was desert. In the middle distance a figure bound to a stake was being flogged. On the left, a couple were copulating. Wolfensohn was a stocky man with grey-streaked hair, his accent more English than anything; there was a trace of Australian. He seemed a little tired, and said he was about to go to California to lose thirty pounds and have a winter holiday. He dwelt on change. At Salomon he had transferred people from corporate finance and put them on the trading desk, where the action was. Now everyone had caught on. Technology modified attitudes. Look how sophisticated companies were. 'When I started coming to the States for Schroder, I would get my morning telex from London and speak to the chaps there on the phone about the Euromarkets. There was a fair chance that when I went to Dearborn or Minneapolis, I could tell people what was going on in Europe. You'd say that Mobil had done an issue and it was going

144

terribly well, and they'd say, "That's very interesting." They'd be impressed. There is no *possibility* of doing that today. There are three people sitting there with screens who can tell you a bloody sight better than you can conceivably tell *them*, what's happened in the last five minutes. They have direct lines to banks who are flashing quotations on their screens. Buzzers go off if there's a news alert. Anyone who's interested can get a list of the last twenty Eurobond issues and what's happened to yields in the last three weeks, and how they compare with the yield on his own securities. He doesn't need it from a banker who comes to see him. He's buying it for five thousand dollars a year from Telefax.'

Wolfensohn thought investment banking was less fun; the scale had ceased to be human; it was the age of the specialist and the technocrat. 'Maybe it's because we're all getting to the age of fifty,' he said, 'so we just *feel* there'll never be people like us again. Which is entirely possible. But it's a fact that the environment has changed.' It was a few weeks later that I met John Gutfreund at Salomon Brothers and heard him think aloud on the same theme, the technocrat and the new age of Wall Street.

Wolfensohn has seven or eight people working for him. His first deal as an independent to be publicised was itself a part of the new scene. Aetna Life & Casualty, one of the largest US insurance companies, with assets of $40 billion, wanted to expand into financial services around the world. Consultants in California and London were instructed to look into the future and see what it held for capital – who was going to need it, who was going to have it. Trade, politics and military thinking were included. The wise men concluded that Aetna's best bet was a merchant bank. Aetna was using another consultant, James Wolfensohn. It was he who proposed to the company that it look at Samuel Montagu, the City merchant bank that had been bought a few years earlier by a commercial bank, the Midland. I asked Wolfensohn how it came about. 'As these things often do,' he said. 'I was talking to senior executives of Aetna in London and put the idea forward. Then I picked up the phone, talked to the Midland Bank, walked around the corner thirty minutes later and saw Geoffrey Taylor, the chief executive elect. I said, "Geoffrey, I think I've got a decent idea here." We had a thirty-minute conversation in which we agreed on the back of an envelope, literally, that it was worth doing.' This sounds like a caricature of the way in which the City of London is supposed to do business. But Wolfensohn, who sees his firm in a merchant-bank tradition, offering a personal endorsement of whatever it does, says that it happened exactly like that, Aetna bought forty per cent of Samuel Montagu; both firms had been founded in the same year, 1850. Eventually newspaper advertisements appeared in both countries to record the deal, using the investment-banker's deadpan formula to conceal a shout of 'Yippee!' – 'We initiated this transaction and acted as financial adviser to Aetna Life and Casualty Company during the negotiations leading to its completion. James D. Wolfensohn Incorporated.' The price paid was $115 million. Wolfensohn received a large fee and was retained by Aetna to advise on international affairs.

When I visited him the second time, it was still winter, but Wolfensohn had a tan; he had lost weight, as intended. The erotic painting had gone from the waiting area. 'I thought I'd better move it,' he said, 'in case it alarmed visitors. Especially the English.' I asked him to elaborate on the story of how he came to leave Schroder in London. City merchant banks in general had failed so far to match the Americans on the world stage. The passing over of Wolfensohn might be taken as symptomatic of that failure. He was not keen to discuss the Schroder affair. The story, he said, was 'broadly true. If I'd got the chairmanship, I'm sure I would still have been there. And Schroder would be a very different place, because I had a lot of my heretical thoughts eight years ago about what should be done at merchant banks. In fact it turned out to be the greatest good fortune for me. Who knows, maybe the best good fortune for Schroder as well. This is not defensive, but I was not required to leave the firm. I was chief executive, but they didn't want to give me plenipotentiary powers, because they were scared that if I was chairman *and* chief executive, I would do these terrible things, like getting them into distribution. I've never talked about this. But I had a different perception. I knew the merchant banks were vulnerable....'

I asked about Salomon Brothers. He said that when he went there, 'I told John Gutfreund that I had this latent desire to own my own candy store, and that I had a lot of outside interests.' As James D. Wolfensohn Inc, he has absorbed the interests into the firm. He is a serious benefactor, that most difficult of men to write about; how does one fit him into Wall Street, with his chairmanships and his cello? When he left Salomon, and apart from anything else, his cashed-in partnership capital must have made him a millionaire several times over. Wolfensohn diverts a quarter of his firm's resources and a quarter of its profits into 'non-business activities', that is, charities and good works of one sort and another. These, he said, are reported on at the daily manage-

146

ment meeting 'in an unselfconscious way, alongside the mergers and acquisitions'. He doesn't pretend that the good works have no practical value to the benefactor. The boards of charitable institutions are convenient meeting places for people whose paths may cross again next week or next year. The one purpose is wrapped within the other.

*   *   *

A stranger sees Wall Street through images of power and activity. They are what he expects to find, and he is not disappointed. But contrary images persist. A mobile food van stands outside One New York Plaza labelled 'The only fresh frozen custard on wheels'. A dog barks in a cobbled street, almost alongside the twin skyscrapers of the World Trade Center. The cobbles seem time-warped from another age, as anomalous as anything in London's City; above an old-fashioned four-storey building is a sign that reads 'Masters, Mates and Pilots Local No. 88'.

At the water's edge, near the south-east end of Wall Street itself, workmen lounge by a bit of wall in the winter sunlight, watching empty Budweiser cans lurch with the tide. Brooklyn across the water is a haze of buildings and a cargo ship with yellow masts. The only sound is traffic overhead, drumming invisibly along an elevated road. This is the route that taxis and chauffeur-driven cars take, coming down to Wall Street from the rich men's apartments along the East Side of Manhattan. The waterfront is half abandoned. Cars use the piers for parking. A scarecrow figure rummages in a pile of sodden cartons and comes up smoking a splinter of cigarette. He wears a black lace-up shoe on his left foot, a white gym shoe on his right. A hundred yards inland the cliffs of glass begin. Yet the river, merging into sea, retains the power, in some lights and some moods, to make the skyscrapers look ghostly and episodic, deserted castles by the shore.

It is not like that from the inside, looking out. I was in a room with broad windows and wide black ledges, high above the street. Snow was falling, whipping over the ledges and into space. It was late on a Friday afternoon. I had come to ask a banker about mergers and acquisitions. I had been in New York only a few days. He said that where we sat was the heart of a secure area, with locked doors and locked file cabinets, electronically swept to detect alien devices. 'You got in easier than usual,' he said, not pleased that no one had stopped me. He blamed the snowstorm. Everyone was going home early.

The banker talked about companies that were busy merging and de-merging, often not sure what they really wanted. 'Like, you know,' he said, '*the best lack all conviction, while the worst are full of passionate intensity.*'

The phone rang. He listened and said, 'Something weird's going on here.' From a man thinking of going home he turned into a man playing a game with telephones and people. He didn't want me to identify the conversations. His interest turned on an industrial corporation. A colleague had alerted him to the fact that its stock was up a few dollars on the day, on trading of fifty thousand shares. It suggested someone knew, or thought he knew, that Industrial Corporation was going to be the subject of a takeover bid. I asked if the firm was a client. 'Not really,' he said. 'I've been trying to warm them a little bit.' The chief officer was on his way to the Caribbean for a weekend's sailing. Two or three phone calls found the hotel where aides had already arrived. 'Do you have a Mr Grandiloquent?' said the banker. 'No, *Grandiloquent*, G as in God.' Contact made, the banker told them what was happening, reading details of share movements off his screen. Perhaps they knew already. 'Anyway,' he said, 'I'm at home this weekend. You're lucky to be out of town.'

Then he rang someone he knew at a company he didn't identify, that he thought might itself be interested in Industrial Corporation if things were happening. 'Yeah,' he said, 'they're sailing this weekend. I decided to ruin their vacation by telling them. Up ten per cent on the day is pretty damn strong. You might want to dust off the file.' The company sounded far away. 'The market's closed here,' he said. 'New York is pretty well closed. There's the worst goddam snowstorm I've seen in a long time.'

Between calls he grinned at me and said, 'I'm trying to stir up some trouble. See how bad I am?' Did he mean trouble for the sake of trouble? 'Well, no,' he said. 'I don't know anything yet. But if I can get myself into a position where I'm helpful to one or other of the companies, that's good for this firm. Assuming that Industrial Corporation doesn't need our help, which I think will be the case, and assuming that something *is* going on, the chances are better, from what I've been doing, that we can represent the potential white knight, the company that comes to the rescue. That's why I suggested he dust off the file and stay on the qui vive. It's all in the long-shot category. Anyway, it's sort of fun.'

The rest of the department was deserted, as far as I could see. In the distance a telephone rang, unanswered. There was only this banker, his lighted windows streaming out into the dark, operating in a cloud of snow. We seemed to be there for the night. He liked to talk about the business; who was I to object? From time to time he made or received a phone call to keep the pot boiling. He brought coffee from a machine and talked about the nature of clients. They were opportunists, he said, so a banker could afford to be no less. Gazing into the screen for some last flicker of information, he was as rapt as a clairvoyant with a crystal.

6
EAST WIND

Tokyo's investment bankers are used to being caricatured in the West as an army of salesmen with smiles. Their range is broadening now, but the four firms that lead the industry, Nomura, Nikko, Daiwa and Yamaichi, remain hard-selling stockbrokers at heart. They are still powered by straight commissions earned from customers in Japan, as buying and selling roars through the hall of the Tokyo Stock Exchange, the second busiest in the world; it is like the concourse of a great railway station.

Nomura Securities Co. is the biggest of the four. Earnings of nearly $300 million make it the most profitable financial firm in the country, including the commercial banks. Its headquarters is a cluster of newish buildings in the Nihonbashi district, near the Exchange. The men, most of whom are at their desks by 8 am, wear the bankers' universal dark suits with white or pale blue shirts. The women wear the Nomura uniform, blue tunic with striped shirt and orange cravat tied in a floppy bow. Women are employed as clerks, secretaries and assistants to salesmen. 'There are no, so to speak, professionals among the female staff,' says a company spokesman. 'It is company policy.' Nomura is no different to anyone else. If anything, its pretty secretaries seem less inclined to bow deeply after bringing green tea, or to go down on one knee beside a manager's chair to deliver a message, than at other firms. But selling securities is – almost – a male preserve.

'The salesforce drives the company and makes the profits,' says Mitsuo Goto, a general manager in market planning. He is middle-aged, with a thin face; a bright pink plastic pen rises from his breast pocket. 'To give an example,' he says, 'one basic difference between

Nomura and Morgan Stanley is that most of our general managers will
have worked in sales offices.' He makes the comparison in an offhand
way. Nomura, after all, is a lot bigger than Morgan Stanley. The current
president, the chief executive officer, came up through the firm as a
salesman, and so did his three predecessors. Some of Goto's colleagues at
the meeting – every interview was a meeting, with tea and sometimes an
agenda – check the list of forty board members to see how many were
once salesmen. The answer is all but four or five. I remark that it will be a
long time before the partners of Morgan Stanley elect anyone but a pure
banker to be president. (This turned out to be wrong; six months later
they elected Richard Fisher.) Goto gives a long 'Ah-h-h!' Selling is the
game. Brokerage commissions bring Nomura $700 or $800 million in a
year, nearly half the firm's gross revenue. Much of this is retail business,
from people who don't spend their income to the hilt. Americans, one
hears it said, have forgotten thrift. They have four or five per cent of
income after tax. The prosperous Japanese salt away five times as much.
Nomura is an engine for sucking up surplus wealth.

In Hong Kong a week earlier I had been told about the thousands of
Nomura saleswomen who sell securities on the doorstep in Japanese
suburbs. My informant, a British stockbroker who thought it was
funny, said that Nomura handled it like a military operation. They were
an army, obeying orders to sell a particular item that the firm had in
stock, as it might be a grocery supplier with too much tinned salmon or
tea biscuits. According to Mr Goto, women were minions at Nomura.
So was this a fictive army, an uncomfortable Western joke? No, they
said, it was quite true, Nomura had a 'very unique group of ladies' who
visited selected clients to sell newly issued Government bonds and
other fixed-interest securities. But they were not on Nomura's full-time
payroll of eight or nine thousand that they had spoken of earlier. The
firm had 1,800 salesladies, working on two-year contracts: women
employed from 10 am to 4 pm to sell regularly to other women, house-
wives with savings from family income. They were based in Nomura's
hundred or so retail branches throughout Japan. The 'army of
thousands' was shrinking, but I clung to the stockbroker's vision of
ruthless matrons on the march, and a few days later it was agreed that I
could visit a branch and meet some of the ladies.

It had to be in the afternoon, when the day's doorstepping was over.
A company car with a driver in white gloves was summoned. Mr K, a
young securities analyst not long with Nomura, came along as trans-
lator. Nomura has battalions of analysts. On the journey – to the port of

Yokohama, part of the Tokyo conurbation – Mr K said work began officially at 8.30 am, but he arrived earlier, and ended officially at 5 pm, but he was often there till ten or even midnight. He lived in a company hostel an hour's rail journey from the office, paying £50 a month for rent and two meals a day. The journey to Yokohama took nearly an hour through heavy traffic; the motorway skirted Tokyo Bay, which now and then appeared like metal in gaps between buildings. The Nomura office block was on a town-centre corner. A window opposite said 'Coffee-ya Hamburger Hotdog', 'ya' meaning shop. Another had the laconic message, 'Sex Drugs'. Inside Nomura, minions in their seemly blue and orange were busy with customers at the front counter. It looked more like an airline selling holidays to the sun than a securities firm. Upstairs the manager, Mr Morishita, was waiting in an airy room decorated with purple flowers. White venetian blinds subdued the light. The chairs had lace arm-rests. We talked about the 'quotas' that are said to haunt sellers of securities in Japan, especially Nomura's. There is a laborious pun on the firm's name, that it is really *Norm*-ura Securities, after the Russian production norms. Someone at head office had already assured me that seven or eight years earlier, Nomura's sales were 'conducted in the way a machine works', but that nowadays each branch chose what securities to sell. Mr Morishita, looking hot in his suit, said through the interpreter that there were no quotas, only targets. But 'a rough plan' *was* made at head office. I asked about the saleswomen. Mr Morishita and his deputy shook with laughter. While they went to see what they could do, Mr K, the analyst, found literature that the women hawk on the doorsteps, and translated it for me. One document, a sheet of pink paper, featured a railway train with a puff of red statistics emerging from the stack, and showed what a small investor could do with 100,000 yen, about £300. Another spelt out the virtues of three-year Government bonds: they were safe, they were high-yielding, and investors could hold up to six million yen in Government securities, about £18,000, without paying tax on the interest. This resounding offer was on a scrap of yellow paper, duplicated from a handwritten original; two little humanised birds looked down from a branch by way of illustration. Presumably it was meant to be intimate, avoiding the impersonal gloss of investment-bank literature. If there is anything amateurish about the branch's twenty-three part-time saleswomen, it will be there by design, not accident. When a European banker makes an envious joke about the Japanese capacity to swallow securities, the sales force at Yokohama – bright, cheerful, demure, alien – is a thread in his uneasiness.

152

Five of them sat in a row and we talked as best we could through Mr K. Their ages seemed to be from late twenties to late forties. A woman in a salmon-red jersey and white trousers, with a pink stone on a gold chain around her neck, and gold-rimmed glasses, was spokesperson. Mr K said they each had 300 to 500 customers. Established customers did their buying on the doorstep, but with new prospects they liked to go inside and talk about Nomura. Before they spoke to anyone for the first time, they knew the age, occupation and income level of household members. Did they all set out together? No, they left one by one. The stockbroker's army had turned into twenty-three Hondas and Toyotas driving around suburban Yokohama. I asked if they had quotas to fulfil. 'Yes,' said Mr K, 'but it is very interesting.' In desperation I asked a shy woman in a blue skirt if she liked the work or did it only for the money. She smiled and rubbed her forehead with the back of her hand. 'She says she has to accumulate knowledge about her business,' said Mr K. That was as far as I got. But one way and another, Nomura underwrites and distributes seven or eight billion dollars of Government bonds in a year. The ladies do their bit.

In the firm's business generally, stocks are bought and sold more frequently than bonds, so this is where most of the brokerage commission is earned, in Nomura's case two-thirds of the total. The ranks of young men at the branches who spend their time encouraging customers to buy a little of this and sell a little of that contain the directors of thirty years hence. The headquarters office of Yusaku Kobayashi, the public-relations manager, was decorated with full-page advertisements published in newspapers to promote individual Nomura branches. This particular campaign was based on seminars run by Nomura in provincial centres for the benefit of local industrialists. 'We like to make friends with the companies,' said Kobayashi; 'making friends' is the Japanese solution. 'Then they become brokerage customers. It may be for the company's own account, or it may be that the owner is a wealthy man.' There is a national appetite for stocks. When Merrill Lynch's Milton Beard in Tokyo began attending classes in Japanese, his teacher soon learnt who he was and wanted any tips that were going.

Foreigners in Japan come up against numerous brick walls – of language, culture and general disposition – and the financial community, although friendly enough to strangers, has an indefinable air of screens and labyrinths. Nomura Securities is widely believed, among western investment bankers in Tokyo, to enjoy a special relationship with the Ministry of Finance. The words 'special relationship' and 'preferential treatment' are spoken with emphasis, a suggestion of sinister collusion that works to the stranger's disadvantage. A British banker thought it was 'not the MoF advising Nomura, it's Nomura advising the MoF'. Given the absolute authority of the Ministry, this was meant as a complaint, not a compliment. But it looks different to the Japanese, who seem to enjoy dissecting their quirks as much as foreigners do. I asked a Japanese manager at the Lehman Brothers International office in Tokyo. He said it was nonsense to suggest that Nomura received favours. Of course, he added, if one of the smaller security houses went to the MoF with some market innovation, it would not get a hearing. If Nomura did the same, it would be listened to with great attention. I said, 'But that's preferential treatment.' He said, 'No, it's only natural.' Nomura is the senior firm and so it commands automatic respect. A Nomura manager, one of the few I managed to talk to informally, away from the rooms full of men and green tea, said that when new officials were appointed to the securities division at the Ministry, they called in Nomura people who could brief them on the industry. This was more or less what the British banker had told me. But my friend the manager saw nothing special about such a relationship. It was the obvious course to follow.

Daiwa Securities wasn't such hard going as Nomura. This may have been chance, or perhaps reflects an informality more likely to be found at the second investment bank in the pecking order than at the first. Daiwa's revenue (1983) is rather more than half Nomura's, its earnings just over a third. But those earnings, $105 million, are three times that of large London merchant banks. It has ninety-three branches in Japan. The head office is north of Tokyo railway station, not far from Nomura's. Guests are received in a handsome fifth-floor room decorated with paintings and vases. A low table has soft chairs placed either side. It is necessary for a Japanese guest to be seated at the farthest point from the door. This involves a moment of farce when it is discovered that the guest is wrongly positioned, just as the chairman arrives, and he has to be propelled into the place of honour. The chairman, Yositoki Chino, was a lean, friendly man with a striped tie and a gold pen. Twenty-five years ago he translated Martin Mayer's book about Wall Street into Japanese. Chino said that Tokyo was becoming a world market-place, and the securities firms were already internationalised on a scale that no one dreamt of when he joined Daiwa after the war. Sitting next to him was Yasuyoshi Fujisaki, a senior managing director. Fujisaki said the reason that some of the Japanese investment banks were regarded in the

West as aggressive was that they had exported traits developed in Japan as they fought to increase their market share. 'We in Daiwa,' he added, 'never undertake aggressive sales activities.' A short debate ensued between him and the chairman. It might be that an investment bank should not entirely avoid aggressiveness. They reached consensus on the ideal. '*Reasonably* aggressive,' beamed the chairman.

Also at the meeting was the general manager of Daiwa's international finance department, Masanobu Nakamura, stocky, sardonic and westernised, who talked to me at intervals throughout the day. His contribution to better understanding by foreigners included a list of twenty questions about business life in Japan that arose over lunch at an embassy, followed by his answers, some with tongue in cheek. Question, 'Why do people sitting in the train sleep?' Answer, 'Even people standing sleep, but it is more difficult to do so.' Question, 'Why are the Japanese authorities so domestic [i.e. parochial]?' Answer, 'It is more profitable to remain domestic than be international. Simply that. It is very dangerous indeed for a government official to be internationalised.' It is a serious answer. Investment banks, like all financial institutions everywhere, are prime targets for regulation by national authorities. In Japan they suffer more than usual. This is why it pays to be on good terms with the Ministry of Finance. Nakamura, in common with every manager on the international side, is a product of the last decade or two. Daiwa operates in Asia, Europe and the Americas, and earns perhaps a fifth of its profits outside Japan, chiefly from selling Japanese securities, and doing business in the Eurobond market.

Another piece of literature that Nakamura hands to visitors is a chart produced in his department showing 'Image Profiles of Capital Markets'. This is based on the answers to a questionnaire at a Daiwa seminar in Tokyo that was attended by Japanese industrialists, bankers and government officials. Stock exchanges are characterised by the gut reactions they aroused. Thus London's line on the graph shifts towards warm and rosy, easy, flexible, quick, normal and strong. New York's inclines to cold and grey, slow, difficult, normal and even stronger. What this proves isn't clear, but Nakamura is a tireless expositor of the need to think internationally. When a client company of Daiwa is raising money in the Eurobond market, the bank sees it as an opportunity for senior company officials to travel to the signing ceremony – for their own benefit and for Daiwa's. 'Japanese people are very curious as to what others say of them,' said Nakamura. 'The chance to find out is one

155

of the secret and never-mentioned reasons for going abroad. For the securities house that is managing the issue, it is a chance to make a strong contact with the senior management. In his office in Japan the president says what he is supposed to say. In his hotel in Europe he is more open.' Nakamura tries to persuade the client company's top man to take his wife with him, unbusinesslike as this seems to a Japanese. If it is a leading firm, Daiwa will send a couple of senior men to accompany the borrower's party. Sometimes a Daiwa representative boards the plane in advance to make sure everything is in order in the first-class section for a demanding client. (Colleagues in the room laughed when Nakamura said this. He waved his hand and said, 'It is no joke. It happens.') The hotel suite and the view are checked by local staff. A client firm pays its own travelling expenses, but the securities house tries to provide the extras – hired Daimlers, theatre tickets, night clubs. Rival Japanese firms, co-managers to the deal, will be imploring the client to patronise their Daimlers and night clubs instead. Bankers' time, not money, is the real investment. Daiwa says it's worth every penny.

It is in this outside world that the securities firms spread their wings and become more like the multi-purpose Wall Street banks that they admire. They make no secret of their admiration. 'It has long been a dream of ours to become a big investment banker such as Morgan Stanley or Goldman Sachs,' says Nomura's Zurich manager, quoted in the firm's house magazine. 'The time is getting closer for us to catch up with them.'

The time should be getting closer, too, for Tokyo itself to operate as a world financial centre on the scale that Japan's commercial prosperity merits. If Tokyo allowed foreigners to deal freely in its financial markets, using yen, dollars or whatever currency suited them, it would assume its obvious place alongside London and New York as the Asian leg of a global system. As it is, outsiders wanting to arrange finance through Tokyo have some freedom to use the local currency, yen, but none to use the international currency, dollars. To be a successful 'offshore' centre, the Japanese authorities would have to let interest earned on dollar deposits and bonds be paid free of a withholding tax in Tokyo. This, and in general the 'flexible' outlook that international bankers rate so highly, has been too much for the Japanese temperament so far. Investment bankers in Tokyo who have lived abroad, and realise the opportunities their firms are missing at home, have to stay within the confines of the system. Even in their own firms they work alongside colleagues who are often as conservative as officials at the Ministry of Finance. Question, 'Are the controls imposed by the authorities really necessary?' Answer, 'No, the controls are a hindrance rather than an aid. . . . The ministries are perfectionist. All information is gathered (this burden is on the private sector, really a useless loss of time and energy), and all "negative" points should be resolved before the green light will be given. All procedures are carefully designed to avoid mistakes so no blame can be placed on the authorities.' The outward-looking bankers, who would like to see Tokyo take its rightful place, lobby and manoeuvre, and make excursions abroad to examine other offshore centres.

Hong Kong, where controls are few and dollars pour in and out with little hindrance, offers an Asian model. A delegation contacted the Banking Commissioner, Colin Martin, and asked if they could visit him. He says there were thirty-seven of them, but he couldn't face more than three. They wrote down everything he said. When they asked what he saw as the chief obstacle to Tokyo's becoming an offshore centre, he replied, 'The language'. The delegation nodded agreement. They knew the language was a disadvantage, but no one had said so until Martin did. Their painstaking seriousness may be itself a part of the problem. At one securities house in Tokyo, an English-language copy of a Japanese report on 'World Financial Centres' – perhaps produced by the same delegation – had been left in a waiting-room. It was open at a page devoted to the Isle of Man, 'located between England and Ireland in the Irish Sea'. A tax haven of limited appeal, the little island emerged here as 'internationally known . . . an offshore banking centre'. There was even a potted history: 'At one time when the island was inhabited by Celts, Manx was the language of the island, but it is no longer in general use. . . .'

Meanwhile, the domestic market keeps them all busy. The investment houses appear in orderly syndicates to raise capital for Japanese firms, a comparatively new way of doing things. After World War 2, and during the years of the US occupation, the financial system, formerly dominated by the *zaibatsu*, the industrial holding companies, and their attendant banks, was reformed along American lines. But underwriting new issues lacks the drama of capital-raising on Wall Street; it is not where reputations are made. There is little jostling among syndicate members. Fees for domestic underwriting may account for as little as ten or twelve per cent of Nomura's earnings, hardly enough to get excited about. The figure may not be much lower than at some Wall Street banks. But on Wall Street the managing underwriter still has traces of glory, walking his (sometimes illusory) razor's edge between risks to achieve the goal. In Tokyo, raising capital has no legendary past, no gallery of Pierpont Morgans. It is a humdrum activity, with firms taking their pre-arranged place in the pecking order. 'They are clerks,' someone said at Nomura, when I asked about the syndication department. The idea of 'risk', as in shuffling around blocks of bonds and shares, doesn't carry the same mark of virility. Nor is trading securities (as opposed to selling them) perceived as especially big business, as it is in New York.

It is 'selling' that matters, and where all the best stories are. Some of them are slanderous and hard for strangers to verify. In a word, the well-regulated Japanese are said to manipulate the stock market. A lot of them are supposed to do it or acquiesce in it, members of a vast conspiracy, pushing shares as it suits their book, sometimes inciting turnover purely for the sake of turnover (and the commissions thereon), making the market at times more like a lottery than a sober stock exchange. 'Ramping' a stock, artificially producing a rise in the price, with the speculator selling out just before it crashes, is a common practice – or so the story goes. The well-regarded *Far Eastern Economic Review* in the course of a damning article* suggested that 'the ramping of stocks in Japan is not something which is done now and again by a few fringe members of the financial establishment. It is an everyday occurrence perpetrated by many groups . . . securities houses . . . professional fund managers . . . leading figures in the corporate sector, and . . . some speculator groups formed especially for the purpose.'

The mildest allegation is the one mentioned earlier (Chapter 3), that Japanese investment banks, bulging as they are with security analysts and analysis, will never look a customer in the eye and recommend him to sell a stock. Western banks and stockbrokers put it about that this shows how unreliable they are. The Japanese say that, on the contrary, it merely proves them pragmatic. A manager at Yamaichi Securities (bank number four in the pecking order) pointed out that if Yamaichi raised capital for a company, this meant 'a close relationship that must be maintained at all times'. In such circumstances it was tactless for Yamaichi's salesmen to say things that might lower the price of the company's stock. 'But overseas investors know what's happening,' he added. A British manager at a Japanese investment bank in London said

---

* 'Tokyo's Managed Market', 19 March 1982.

158

that western brokers soon got used to interpreting shades of meaning. If the question, *How is X doing*? produces the answer, *Oh, good. But Y is doing very good*, it means: Sell X. 'I thought at first they were sharks,' he said. 'But it's not dishonesty. They do sort of tell you, but you have to pick it up.'

'Ramping' stocks and 'churning' them – inducing clients to buy or sell when it may not be in their interest to do so – are sterner subjects. Mr Q, a former broker with a western firm in Tokyo, said it was a sorry scene. He would talk about it if neither he nor his firm was identified. He said there were seven foreign brokerage firms licensed as dealers in Tokyo, five American and two British. They sell western securities to the Japanese, and Japanese securities to the West. He would not find it helpful if the Japanese knew who he was. 'Q' isn't his initial. He said, 'There is no question about ramping stocks. It is absolutely lethal. It was amazing to me how long one could keep a veil over such goings-on. You must understand, they have hordes of investors who are quite unsophisticated. What the market wants is volatility. It's no good trying to persuade people to buy stocks that don't move. So how do they do it? By concentrating on a stock that seems to suit the mood, quietly accumulating a position. People begin to notice that a stock is being pushed. But whoever is doing it can only go so far. If it's a securities firm, it has to make the stock sufficiently interesting to topple another securities firm into following it. Then it can get its own clients out.

'The manipulation isn't for the benefit of individuals at the firms. I think politicians get a better-than-average slice of the cake. So do managers of finance departments at certain industrial corporations. But really, the manipulation is to increase people's interest, to bring in as many small speculators as possible. The object is to work up excitement. There are comparatively few outlets for investible money in Japan. You can't invest in land. There's no market in antiques. Even horse-racing is regarded as a low-class activity. But until recent times stock-exchange profits carried no capital gains tax, and it's still very low. A great deal of the money invested is grey money, undeclared to the tax authorities. That's a whole subject in itself. Everyone is allowed one account at the Postal Savings Bank, which is quite vast, twenty thousand offices or something, I don't know how many hundred billion dollars invested. There's no tax payable on interest on the first three million yen in your account, say twelve or thirteen thousand dollars. So there are two or three times as many accounts as there are Japanese citizens – dummy accounts to get the tax break.'

Mr Q returned to manipulation. He became understanding. He shrugged his shoulders. 'Once you get the hang of it,' he said, 'it's a perfectly predictable aspect of the market. The foreign broker can take advantage of it or not. I have sympathy with the Japanese authorities. How do you draw the line between a free market, which is what the United States told them they ought to have, and what I've described? What have I described? Only an unreasonable, by some standards, abuse of power. . . .'

The formal response of a senior manager at a securities house, who would certainly know if these things were true, was to say that they are not. Either they never happened, or they happened years ago. I tried a less senior manager and talked to him at a safe distance from the office. He said more or less what Q said. His word for it was 'running up'. Stocks were regularly 'run up'. He didn't like the word 'manipulation'. The object of running them up was (a) to make a capital profit for the firm, and (b) to stimulate investment. It seemed obvious to him. All salesmen had targets they must reach, whether or not the market was performing well. There were popular financial newspapers, the *jiba shimbun*, not entirely free from influence. 'They don't always tell the truth,' he said. He added, 'But people know what's going on.' Articles in these newspapers helped to stir up interest. 'As you know,' he said, 'to raise its revenue, a securities firm must have a certain number of transactions every day.' I was watching a uniformed road sweeper outside the café, which had chairs and tables on the pavement, facing the gardens of the Imperial Palace. He was brushing tiny scraps of twig from a spotless gutter. It was the way they did things. 'In any case,' said the junior manager, 'we cannot force investors to buy stock. We can only recommend. It is up to the investors, simply speaking.'

He spoke without guile. Japanese investment banking is quite straightforward, once you get the hang of it.

*   *   *

In Hong Kong, a time-expired remnant of the British Empire, now resigned to its reabsorption by China when the lease runs out in 1997, everything is different. They are all there, bankers and brokers of every kind and colour, making or losing money, few holds barred, a zoo of financial services. Manufacture and trade generate flows of cash within the colony that are out of all proportion to such a winkle of a place, an island off the China coast, at the mouth of the Pearl River, together with a sliver of mainland. Before political uncertainty diminished the flow, other funds poured in from a dozen countries in South-east Asia, as entrepreneurs channelled profits into a safer place, usually breaking the law at the far end because of exchange controls, but doing nothing wrong at the receiving end. For a long time Hong Kong has been the money-centre for overseas Chinese in South-east Asia, no questions asked; there are twenty or thirty million of them, an expatriate community with a core of manufacturers, traders and fixers, the Phoenicians of the Far East. The history of Hong Kong makes it a convenient valve for the British as well, letting them condone and profit from ways of doing business that they might frown on, or feel they ought to frown on, in Europe. Thirty years ago when Britain was racked with 'sterling crises', and rigid exchange controls were employed to protect the currency, Hong Kong was one of the centres where those who knew how could sell their pounds for dollars with impunity. British banks used a 'comprador', a kind of Chinese supervisor who was part of the firm yet separate from it, to do the business in an office around the corner. The right hand was not supposed to know what the left hand was doing. In the 1950s newspapers in Britain often referred to the 'Kuwait Gap' and the 'Hong Kong Gap', through which sterling leaked away. In 1983 I heard a Hong Kong Government official say it was 'exchange control from the world of Lewis Carroll', rather nostalgically, I thought.

The Hong Kong Gap (and the need for it) has long since gone, but the spirit lives on. Company law in the colony is out of date. 'Insider trading' flourishes on the stock exchanges. Ownership of companies need not be disclosed; as the deputy commissioner for securities and commodities trading, another Government official, put it in a speech, 'Even the company itself may not know who its real owners are!' Financially Hong Kong is a dangerous place for the weak or inept. But its singular freedom from cant makes it oddly attractive, after the pious professions of virtue that are obligatory in most financial centres, where standards may be higher, but not always *that* much higher. Hong Kong is as things were when the world was young, unreformed and more honest about its dishonesty. Even its public-service posters are unequivocal. There is one of a flower with the words, 'Keep Hong Kong beautiful. Report corruption.' The parallel worlds of pretence and reality seem closer. As Europe was once, South-east Asia is now. Western bankers on three-year contracts like it there: if their system flourishes even when confined by officialdom, how much better when officialdom is lax? Conrad, the right author for the place, noted 'the strong life of white men, which rolls on irresistible and hard on the edge of outer darkness.'

Commercial banks from Europe, the United States and Japan, as well as local banks both Chinese and post-imperial British, compete to handle the billions of dollars that still pass around and through the place. There are too many of them for their own good, but twenty years of up-and-down prosperity, with more ups than downs, have drawn them in. There is no such thing as exchange control. Interest on deposits of foreign currency at licensed banks is paid tax-free. It would be surprising had merchant banks on the City pattern not developed there. The busiest are indigenous, although British, not Chinese; others are the local branches of London houses. Young bankers speaking in City accents but wearing lighter suits earn £50,000 or £60,000 a year, worth twice as much as in London because tax is so low; the highest rate for individuals is 15 per cent (it is only 16½ per cent for companies). Fifteen per cent is still too much for local tastes. 'I used to live in Spain,' said a European banker. 'I thought the Spanish were the champion tax evaders, until I met the Chinese.'

Surrounding the foreigners, the hundred and fifty thousand *gweilos* – a Chinese word that is usually said to mean 'foreign devils', but according to some old hands means more like 'foreign bastards' – is a population of more than five million Chinese. These provide an active workforce, like something from a Victorian dream of diligence, that pumps out goods as directed – clothes, transistors, toys, jewellery, watches, plastic flowers, rubber spiders. The harbour with its creeks and bays unfolding from Hong Kong itself into the South China Sea is alive with ships, a setpiece of restless water. The Chinese entrepreneurs who direct the manufacture, and who usually turn out to have been dock workers or printed-circuit solderers before they crossed the shaky bridge to affluence, run companies with good-luck names that sound funny, but are not meant to be. Wonderful Manufacturing Co., Super Intellectual Computer Co., Glorious Concrete Ltd, Very Good Electrical Co., Ever Rising Trading Corp., Glorious Watch Co., Happy Plastic, Up & Higher Ltd, Super Glory Co. and the Marvellous Investment Co. are all in Hong Kong Telephone's business directory; it has three and a half columns of names that begin with Lucky.

Bankers are not immune to the spirit of the place. Wardley, the biggest merchant bank, has a propitious telephone number. In Cantonese, the dialect spoken in the adjacent part of China, where most of the inhabitants come from, the numeral '8' can sound like a bleat, *Ba-a-a,* and be mistaken for a word that means 'booming', *Fa-a-a*. This makes it lucky. The Wardley telephone number is 841–8888. Its chief rival is Jardine Fleming, on a different exchange; the number to ring there is 843–8888. (Hong Kong's third merchant bank in order of importance is Schroder & Chartered, set up in 1971 by Schroder in London, the Chartered Bank and the powerful Kadoorie family. It doesn't go in for lucky numbers.) Hong Kong's Chinese are not only diligent but optimistic, always on the look-out for short cuts to wealth. Gambling is a major industry. The Royal Hong Kong Jockey Club, which controls both horse-racing and betting, has a betting turnover of about £1 billion a year. It is said that police patrols are doubled in the tunnels under the harbour on race nights to make sure traffic gets to the Sha Tin course on time, not in the interests of punters so much as the economy. As a result the Jockey Club is an investing institution in its own right, much solicited by brokers who want its money.

Hong Kong offers unreformed capitalism. Property has made more fortunes than anything else, but the stock exchanges attract local Chinese speculators, great and small. Mr Chau Kar Pak is manager of the Far East Exchange, the largest of four. As he tells his visitor from Britain with many smiles, 'In your country the people are being taken care of from the time they are born. Here the Government will not subsidise the lazy-bones.' He shakes his head; his English is excellent, but Britain is a long way off, probably all lazy-bones and cricket. 'In your country a person will leave behind his money with the institutions who have the expertise. In Hong Kong they like to have the tangible touch of their transactions. They like to keep the shares in the drawers at home. Every night after dinner they pick them up. "Ah-h-h! This is my investment!" They have the touch of it.'

Sun Hung Kai (SHK) is a large banking and broking group, founded by a refugee from mainland China, Fung King Hey, and still staffed mainly by Chinese. In good times (1983 on the whole was bad times) investors have to be issued with admission cards for the customers' room at head office, where they sit shoulder to shoulder on rows of hard seats to watch stock prices on six TV screens. The corridor outside is windowed off and full of people with opera glasses, studying the prices. Merrill Lynch, long established in Hong Kong to sell US shares to Asians, owned a quarter of SHK by 1984, giving it a foot in a different door. (The French investment bank, Paribas, owned a similar share, and they controlled the group jointly.) Somewhere near the edge of Merrill Lynch's nervous system, a filament runs out to SHK's little branches, where customers stand outside in shabby pants and tunics, even in a bad year, waiting for the doors to open.

Outside the Yuen Long branch at nine o'clock in the morning, they looked like young unemployed, waiting for the clerks to arrive and start paying out social benefits. But they would wait a long time in Hong Kong. They were early speculators, reading the papers and looking forward to the daily gamble. Yuen Long is in the New Territories, the piece of mainland which lies between the central sprawl of Hong Kong island and the border with China. Ten minutes' driving, and you would be in sight of the wire fences and the rice fields going on for ever. Unlike central Hong Kong, where the street signs are bilingual, Yuen Long doesn't have much Anglo-Saxon on show. It is a jumble of crowded streets and concrete buildings, set in a landscape of building sites, factories, offices, apartment blocks, power lines and cranes. A western face is still uncommon enough for two small boys on their way to school to pause and shout, 'How do you do? I am very well thank you,' hysterical with laughter.

Inside the Sun Hung Kai branch, business is soon under way on an upper floor. A dozen men sit on shabby, doctor's-waiting-room chairs, facing a board chalked with stock prices and a TV screen showing Chinese characters. They give their orders to salesmen behind desks and telephones at one end of the room. If the excitement dries their mouths, a water dispenser with paper cups is to hand. The board lists about eighty local securities, more than enough to cover the active stocks.

If all Hong Kong's stocks were shown, there would still be only two or three hundred of them. This handful of securities, dominated by property shares, is enough to make Hong Kong one of the world's busier exchanges at boom times. New York's is the busiest, with Tokyo a poor second, and London an even poorer third. On a good day in Hong Kong, when the colony is vibrating with inside information, the turnover is supposed to be more than London's. Someone in the Banking Commissioner's department told me that during the boom of the early 1970s, civil servants had to be forbidden to use official telephones to talk to their brokers because no one was able to get through to Government offices. He said that one day the main stock exchange was so crowded that the police were worried about public safety. A government clerk was told to make an anonymous phone call to say the building was on fire. The brigade turned up and the stock exchange was evacuated. 'No water was actually squirted,' the official said reassuringly. A dozen years after that, China was making it implacably clear that it intended to reassume a kind of benevolent control of its lost island when the British lease on it ran out, Hong Kong had the jitters, the property-based Carrian group had crashed spectacularly, and the stock exchange, at least for the moment, had gone limp.

The Yuen Long branch, however, was still doing well enough to justify a staff of seven. Most of the day's customers were windfall men who had recently come into money. The Government had taken their land around Yuen Long, where they would otherwise have spent their lives scratching a living, and compensated them with Hong Kong dollars. This is why they sat absorbed in front of the blackboard, grains on the capitalist shore, watching the prices move. The manager pretended to be ashamed of having these emancipated farmers sitting there all day, bringing their tea and rice with them, plonking down thousands of dollars at a time on rumours. 'Theoretically,' he said, 'we hate that person. He is not a proper investor. It is a scandal.' He looked disgusted. Perhaps he had been told this was the thing to tell visitors. An official at SHK's head office had been suspicious when I asked to visit a small branch, 'in case you make it sound like a Mickey Mouse operation'. The manager added that he scolded his customers and told them they ought to take a long-term view of the market. But he knew that without them there would be no need for the cosy, stuffy little office with its clerks at the back and its cash-in-hand trading.

Gold offered a diversion. Would we like to see some? No problem. Hong Kong is a world centre for gold trading. Where physical money has to be smuggled, gold is still the most convenient way. But most of the trading is respectable. It is simply that gold is reality, part of Asia's way of thinking. The manager said that his customers speculated in gold as well as in shares, using the busy Gold and Silver Exchange, and sometimes took delivery of the stuff. It was in his safe; he would go and fetch a piece or two. He disappeared behind a closed door, and discreet clicking noises were heard above a partition. When he returned he was carrying a five-tael bar, six ounces, say $19,000 Hong Kong dollars, or US $2,500. It sat comfortably in the palm, stamped with a lion's head. He also brought a one-tael piece, like a fat yellow peppermint with a hole in the middle, a mere US $500 worth, and a Krugerrand, something over US $400. All were needed for the shelves of a well-stocked broker in this dusty township.

The clients politely ignored the gold. 'In practice,' said the manager, 'without this kind of person, the branch cannot survive. It is kind of ridiculous. We scold them. But,' and he smiled at his paradox, 'we are afraid that they go away.'

In the long run, SHK may be important to Merrill Lynch and Paribas as a means of helping them come to grips with new aspects of South-east Asia. In the short run it hasn't been a happy investment, at least for Merrill. The Americans' original deal was done in 1982 (Paribas had taken a stake in 1978). Merrill paid SHK with a four per cent share of itself that soon increased in value. At the same time, its own investment in SHK was depreciating, as the Chinese firm, along with others in the colony, ran into difficulties over property and a general loss of confidence. Fung King Hey, the founder, remains the nearest thing to a Chinese investment banker. No doubt Merrill Lynch saw him as a financier who could go where Americans feared to tread in Asia. Like many of China's expatriate capitalists, he keeps faith with the homeland – what option has he got? – and tells visiting journalists what Hong Kong has known all along in its heart, that the colony belongs to China. He revisits China bearing friendship and gifts, and is thought to have enviable commercial connections there. Fung made SHK into the biggest brokerage house in Hong Kong, and built up a large commercial bank as well. Before the French and American connection, Sun Hung Kai International was set up to venture into investment banking. This seemed logical enough. But a successful Chinese-run investment bank on western lines has yet to emerge. Capital-raising in Hong Kong offers limited scope. The British trading and property firms, imperial left-overs, use the British or British-linked merchant banks. Hong Kong had no national debt until recently, so the Government had no need to raise money through the bond market, which didn't exist. As for Hong Kong's Chinese industrialists, they depend on their lightly taxed cash flow and on bank loans, or even on loans from family and acquaintances. Financial affairs are private. The idea of selling off pieces of one's company to investors, in public, is not attractive.

SHK International looked elsewhere and tried to enter the Eurobond market. Fung and the marketing men travelled in Europe and the US, and the firm's name began to appear on tombstones in the late 1970s. 'It was good in terms of publicity,' says Raymond Lee, an executive director, 'but a disaster in terms of profit. Our Chinese clients were not interested in Triple A bonds, especially when prices rose. In the bond market at that time, we in Asia were novices, wanting to play a grown-up game. We didn't realise the amount of money and commitment that was needed. In Hong Kong, and to a lesser extent in Singapore, there is an aversion to a "steady income" from fixed-interest securities.' Later SHK had more success doing corporate-finance work for Chinese companies in the colony. All along, the firm has been handling export finance for the Peking Government, many of whose cargoes are trans-shipped through Hong Kong, and arranging finance for projects on the mainland. Whichever way the western banker turns in Hong Kong, he is always facing China.

As straightforward brokers for US securities, Merrill and other firms do good business. There is intense competition, both for local money and for funds smuggled in from Taiwan, Malaysia, the Philippines and elsewhere. The Japanese are after it; so are the Australians. Not much goes to London. Hong Kong brokers learn to give customers advice when it's asked for and keep quiet when it isn't. The investors who put their money in New York or Tokyo are more substantial than the typical small investor in the Hong Kong market. But they still want to make their own investment decisions. Stanley Wu, the Merrill Lynch man-ager, tells a story of his previous branch, in Singapore. He was trying to persuade an Asian manufacturing company to hedge its risks in pur-chasing raw materials by speculating in commodity futures. He and his colleagues made a two-hour presentation to the directors, who were so pleased at the end that they applauded. Two days later Wu was called back – as he thought, to be told the firm was going to adopt the Merrill Lynch strategy. A director greeted him with effusive politeness. Wu said, 'When do you want to start?' The director said, 'We don't. The chairman has said No.' Wu asked why. It was simple, said the director. The chairman had built up the company by his personal skill in buying raw materials at the right time. If that were taken away, what was there left for him to do?

Another US broker said, 'The so-called managed fund can never take off. We have filthy rich clients with ten million Hong Kong dollars to invest, but they won't leave it with us. It's not that they don't trust us, but win or lose, they want to make their own decisions.' John Wei at Bache is Chinese, like all but two of the twenty brokers on his staff. He said goodbye to Shanghai, eight hundred miles away, when the Com-munists took over, and has not been home since. But he is proud of China's march to power, as are many who ran away from the system; it is an odd paradox. 'I can tell you a joke,' says Wei. Not long after Bache started operating in Hong Kong, in 1960, Wei opened five accounts in one week. 'I was the eager beaver,' he says. Suddenly, within days, all five closed their accounts. Wei made anguished phone calls. He found that Bache in New York had followed standard practice and referred the names to an agency for a credit check. The agency contacted bankers in Hong Kong, who, it being that sort of a place, rang up the investors who were under scrutiny, Chinese to Chinese, and said, 'What do you want us to say about you?' Bache's procedure offended the investors. The idea of being spied upon was abhorrent, a loss of face. If they weren't trusted, why did Bache want to do business with them in the first place?

The British find themselves in the oddest situation of all the foreign devils. They have been in from the start, when Hong Kong was not much more than rocks, rain and fishing boats. They came to regard themselves as original inhabitants: it is their architecture, their trams, their language. Central Hong Kong presents no problems to English-speaking visitors, who find the placenames clearly marked: Queen's Road, Queen Victoria Street, Ice House Street, Connaught Road, Aberdeen Street, Pottinger Street. The Mandarin Hotel is alive with western accents, and western comforts for their owners. The White Ensign flies from the naval base down the road. But all this is becoming an illusion. The British-run trading houses, of which Jardine, Matheson is the most famous, developed as part of a colonial system that has become an embarrassment; few in Hong Kong use the word 'colony' today except in inverted commas. Jardines, now an international conglomerate, is still large and flourishing, but not in the old way. Its headquarters but not its legal residence are in the Connaught Tower, a dominant new structure low in gracefulness but high in prestige, that stares across the harbour with rounded windows like eyes or holes; the Chinese have an obscene epithet for it. The Jardine, Matheson offices retain a spacious air. The Chinese attendant hovering near the lifts on the forty-eighth floor wears a dazzling white uniform and cap, like the chief engineer of a pleasure boat that never puts to sea. A long wall has sepia photographs of former directors. Old prints displayed in the reception area include 'View of a Burying Place', and, even more discouragingly, 'The Punishment of the Bastinado'. Jardine, Matheson owns fifty per cent of the second largest merchant bank in Hong Kong, Jardine Fleming, whose offices are two floors down; these are slightly less spacious, with a motif of crumpled yellow structures on the wall of Reception, like damaged gold bars. Jardine Fleming began in 1970 as a modest investment venture with Robert Fleming, a London merchant bank; the Jardine and Fleming families had connections in Scotland and went shooting together. The idea was to manage British investments on Far East stock exchanges. Out of this grew a merchant bank that has raised capital for local clients, and operates as the largest broker on the Hong Kong stock exchanges, channelling British and other investment into the colony. Jardine Fleming operates independently of its proprietors, which is important for the Jardine half of the ownership, because Jardine, Matheson is so deeply a part of Hong Kong's colonial past.

The Jardine, Matheson director with special responsibility for Jardine Fleming is P. L. Macdougall, formerly of Rothschild and American Express. He said the problem for a Chinese businessman who is thinking of using a British merchant bank is that 'as he perceives it, he has a horrible choice. Whichever he goes to, he is afraid that his affairs will be known. It isn't true, but it's how he perceives it. The Chinese have all got a strong secrecy wish. The businessman is afraid that if he comes to Jardine Fleming with a deal that involves a possible takeover, Jardine Fleming will do him down in some way. In other words, the merchant banks here tend not to be thought of as fully independent, although they are.' At that time (1983), Jardine Fleming Holdings had only one Chinese director. Macdougall said it was the best they could do. Promising young Chinese joined the firm, but after a few years, 'if they're really good they go out and set up a finance company. They see how much entrepreneurial money there is to be made, and they won't stay to work their way up.' Hong Kong-Chinese tycoons have begun to make their presence felt. Besides Fung King Hey, the banker, there is Li Ka-shing, whose empire rests on property, and Sir Y. K. Pao, probably the biggest shipowner in the world. All are interestingly rich.

The tension between the British, who made the place, and the Chinese, who are inheriting it, hovers beneath the surface. I asked Macdougall what I should look for in Hong Kong. He said, 'Chinese interests versus non-Chinese interests'. Later a Chinese banker, cosmopolitan but firmly based in Hong Kong, invited me to lunch to meet a variety of commercial bankers, both Chinese and British. At one point I asked what the word 'Hong' meant – the British trading houses were all known as 'hongs', Jardine, Matheson as 'the princely hong'. The banker said with a smile that it meant 'company': just that. I said I had always assumed it was something grander – 'the princely company' sounded rather flat. There were more smiles. 'Walk along the road to an industrial area,' someone said. 'You will see many hongs.' The host said there was another word that confused the stranger: that was 'taipan', the big boss of the hong. The British master was the 'taipan'. 'Well,' said the banker, 'it also means the minder at a girlie bar who looks after the topless waitresses.' They nearly died laughing.

Not long after that, the princely hong decided that Hong Kong was no longer safe. The Chinese were coming. Jardines, always ruthless and direct, decided to transfer its legal residence to Bermuda, an act of symbolic force for the local community. It was, said someone, as if the Queen had moved to Australia. The physical company and operations would remain. The spirit had flown.

The leading merchant bank is Wardley, a subsidiary of the Hongkong and Shanghai Banking Corporation. The Hongkong Bank is the colony's financial heavyweight, a part of the British establishment, though with a growing number of Chinese in senior positions. It ranks in the first twenty commercial banks of the world, with extensive interests in Europe, the Middle East and the United States. It is a 'bank of issue', and its red hundred-dollar banknotes are popular as currency because red is a lucky colour; they still circulate freely in the 'PRC', the People's Republic of China, and are hoarded there in socks and under mattresses. Wardley, like Jardine Fleming, began in the early 1970s, when Hong Kong was expanding its trade and finance. The troubles of a few years earlier were forgotten, or at least brushed out of sight. In 1967 Hong Kong had suffered serious anti-British riots. But Peking, which probably fomented them, drew back from direct confrontation. The colony – whose financial affairs were so shaky at one point that no physical cash was available for issue, and a chartered plane flew in British banknotes from London, ready for distribution under an emergency law that made them legal tender – found that the end hadn't come after all. Wardley was invented by the Hongkong Bank to handle capital-raising business that arose as the stock market boomed. The name, taken from a nearby street, was the one the bank kept for occasional use; the bank's No. 1 boat, to be seen at noon on a Saturday, along with all the other banks' boats, picking up guests from the Queens Pier to go picnicking off Lamma Island, is still the *Wardley*. The new subsidiary also lent money, for longer terms than the parent, which left it painfully involved, along with half the banks in Hong Kong, when the Carrian group collapsed in 1983. In size Wardley compares with a large merchant bank in London. One of its former officers, Michael Roberts, says that the fee-earning business in the 1970s, when companies were in the market for capital, brought Wardley 'incredible profits'. 'The department had a staff of seven or eight people,' he says, 'and in one year

I think we turned in ten million quid. They were halcyon days. We knew they were halcyon days.'

Roberts has since moved on to Samuel Montagu, which was upgrading its Hong Kong operations. They all seem to know one another, the Rothschild men, the Kleinwort Benson men, the Hambros men – dealing in specialised loans, foreign exchange, corporate finance if they can get it, bullion and anything else that comes their way. They are a bit marginal; as amusing as ever, poised to take advantage of whatever happens, but not the lifeblood of the place. 'The merchant banker here shouldn't be seen as any great figure,' says Roberts. 'The commercial banker is that. Our lot are very much mechanics. The deals are done late at night, in the bars, in the clubs, around the private dinner tables. It's often very simple – "I'll buy your building" – and the argument is about the price. Next morning I find I've bought something I can't afford, so I go and borrow the money. That's it.'

Whatever place western bankers have in Hong Kong, both before and after the Chinese assume sovereignty, the character of the place will come to reflect, more and more, its Asian surroundings. Michel Barrett was Paribas' executive vice-president in Hong Kong when I met him (later he became chief executive of the banking side at Sun Hung Kai as well). The Chinese temperament interested him. They were not emotional about loss. Even when swindled by someone, they accepted it as part of the game; cleverness was a virtue. They were pragmatists. In Hong Kong it was school children aged fourteen and fifteen who committed suicide because of the pressures to succeed. Businessmen who failed went on living. What could be more pragmatic than that? Europe, of course, they had discounted: 'to them it's a lazy place,' said Barrett, 'full of government controls. Boring.'

He said the Sun Hung Kai connection had already given Paribas access to many substantial Chinese investors in the region. He spoke wryly of the Hong Kong ethos. 'The middle-class Chinese here are very good at looking like the British,' he said. 'The striped shirts. The external discipline.' But whatever veneer they had acquired, at a time when it was politic to acquire one, they behaved like Chinese: more Latin than Anglo-Saxon. 'Don't be fooled,' said Barrett. 'Hong Kong is audited to Hong Kong standards.'

7

THE LONDON BANKER

A century of habit—Anglo-Saxon attitudes—
Chips Keswick airs a prejudice—Acceptable bills—Codes of behaviour—
Hidden reserves—Rewards and profits—The bankers' turn—
How not to get a bloody nose—Envying Wall Street—Raising capital—
Princes' favours—The plumbers move in—New generation—
Schroder alters course—Montagu wakes up—The hand of Siegmund Warburg—
A non-attributable pencil—The late Saemy Japhet—The great Woolworth sale—
Victor Blank perseveres—Champagne at Paternoster Row

The upheavals that are reshaping and americanizing the City have not
yet altered its persona, and perhaps will always leave something
untouched. It is too early, in 1984, to do more than see the outline of
things to come. But the merchant banks are clearly marked down for
change. They represent one of the oldest traditions in the City, excellence brushed with idiosyncrasy, growing out of a solid, comfortable
past. If there is such a person as a characteristic merchant banker today,
he is still a man from a southern county who was educated at a good
public school and displays a kind of friendly arrogance that assumes his
is the best possible way of doing things.

A few of the firms, like S. G. Warburg, while still staffed largely by
bankers answering to the same title of 'English gentlemen', began long
ago to rethink their role, as they realised how finance, like industry, was
becoming a game for international players. The Wall Street investment
banks had their revolution a decade earlier. They became multi-purpose brokers, issuing houses and securities-traders, operating around
the world. The Japanese are developing in the same way, with large investment houses whose capital strength is sufficient to let them bid for
deals worth hundreds of millions of dollars at a time. It is the same
principle of bigness, bringing 'economies of scale', that produces jugger-
naut lorries and 100,000-ton oil tankers. It is how the world has gone.

In the City, the securities business, the heart of investment banking,
has been traditionally split up. The merchant banks organise syndicates

and raise capital, but leave the distributing of shares to stockbrokers. The stockbrokers, in turn, don't 'make markets' in the securities, but deal through another specialist sub-breed, the stockjobbers; these are the wholesalers, the equivalent (though with far smaller resources) of the trading desks at First Boston and Salomon Brothers which run their aggressive 'positions', risking large losses to make large profits. The unified securities firm on the Wall Street pattern couldn't exist in London while brokers and jobbers enjoyed a monopoly of their functions. It is the breaking of that monopoly, begun in 1983 after years of dithering, that is expected to lead to 'all-purpose' firms, British versions of Wall Street originals.

In one important area, the international business of Eurobonds, change had already slipped into the City through the back door. Because Eurobonds are not 'local' securities, the London Stock Exchange had no powers of monopoly. A merchant bank could issue the bonds, trade in them and distribute them to buyers around the world. But the merchant banks missed the boat – whether because they were too conservative, or (as some observers believe) because they lacked the nagging greed of the true entrepreneur. In practice, only S. G. Warburg has emerged as a British-owned force in Eurobonds. The rest of the leaders, although they run their operations from London, are the offspring of parents in New York, Paris, Frankfurt and Tokyo. The merchant banks who have begun to buy stakes in brokers and jobbers, forming alliances in unCity-like ways, know that the end of the Stock Exchange's monopoly will admit the enemy as well. The size of leading investment banks in New York and Tokyo will take some matching. The 'boutique' argument has been heard in the City: that merchant banks can't all try to become like Salomon Brothers with any hope of success, so why not settle for a smaller excellence, a British niche of specialist advice and services? No doubt this is the route that some firms will take. But as a deliberate course for proud men to set, it has undertones of defeat that are themselves debilitating. Not surprisingly, merchant banks are taking time to make the psychological adjustment to the new order. A century of habit is not easily overthrown. Like the container lorries that sometimes get lost in the City, on their way to or from the docks, and find themselves nosing into alleys that were built for the horse and carriage, change has to inch its way along.

The 'typical' merchant banker may be decisively modified by the events of the next decade. For the moment he still regards himself as sensible and a little cynical; he and his forbears have seen it all before.

173

There is the matter of foreigners. Most merchant banks were founded by immigrant Europeans, and usually they have cultivated their overseas connections. In spite of this, or because of it, men with funny accents doing business in other currencies than sterling used to be regarded with suspicion in the banking parlour. All that has changed, of course. The world turns out to be full of men with funny accents doing business in dollars, yen and Deutschmarks. What hasn't changed is the merchant banker's long memory of something nasty that happened in Ruritania a lifetime ago. 'Watch out when making loans to princes,' said 'Mr Lombard', the chairman of a fine old merchant bank. 'They tend to renege when it suits them.'

The day I visited Mr Lombard, the papers were full of bankers bewailing the enormous loans they had made to countries that now seemed incapable of paying the interest, let alone thinking of repaying the principal. It was more of a crisis for United States commercial banks; most of the loans were theirs, and most of the defaulters were in South America. European banks were not unscathed. Mr Lombard's was, though, and so were most of the merchant banks. Their lending business is comparatively small, in any case. But it is important to them as bread-and-butter business. And because they are small they have to be careful.

Mr Lombard said it was fifty years, give or take, since the last wave of national defaults by banks: before his time, but he knew who did what. 'Who didn't default in Europe?' he said. 'The Scandinavians, by and large. Most of the continent of Europe defaulted. Certainly the Spaniards, the Portuguese, the Czechs and the Belgians. The Dutch didn't, but they didn't have any foreign loans. Australia and New Zealand didn't default. Canada didn't, except that I think Newfoundland did. French influence, question mark?' He smiled at his small anti-Gallic barb. 'Latin America defaulted, almost without exception. The Latin view of debt obligations is to say, "The silly mug, he lent me the money. Doubtless he's got rich on it. We shall default if it suits us." The Anglo-Saxon thinks a little bit further ahead and calculates he may need to borrow again one day. If he has defaulted, his terms will be worse.'

Mr Lombard slandered nations without losing his negligent air. They were not the sort of remarks I had been reading in the papers. 'I think bankers should have history lessons,' he said. As a young merchant banker in the 1950s, he was told how lucky he was, not to have lived through the traumatic thirties. International lending by banks had not resumed on any scale when he began his career. The world was still recovering from the war. Then surplus dollars laid the foundation of the Eurodollar market. 'Market lending' began again. 'And then,' he said, 'you had all these kids aged thirty-five dashing around the world with their buttoned-down shirts and their little briefcases, sticking loans on Zambia and Costa Rica and Bolivia. It's curious how the business of risk-assessment in domestic lending is passed on from generation to generation. We do learn a bit from the mistakes of predecessors. But not in international lending. It is absolutely mad.'

Mr Lombard had an authentic City voice. Chips Keswick at Hambros, where he is a deputy chairman, in charge of the banking department, has another. The Keswick family is well-known in the City. I was told that J. C. L. Keswick is called Chips because the 'C' is said to stand for 'Chippendale', and he was conceived in a Chippendale bed. This may or may not be true. Nicknames and leg-pulling are what you expect at those merchant banks where the need to be earnest and emulate Wall Street is not yet paramount. 'It's like the prefects' library at school,' said one of them, as he tried to sum up life at the top. Chips Keswick is more austere than his way of talking suggests. Hambros wouldn't want another Reksten affair, which was the result of decisions (not Keswick's) that were as unwise as anything the commercial bankers did in South America. 'Prejudices,' said Keswick, 'are one's greatest strength. There are lots of people I wouldn't trust with a bargepole and won't do business with. Whole nations of people. Never lose a prejudice. It saves you millions. There are certain gentlemen who don't pay you back. They've done it through history.' Hambros had about £700 million lent out, more than half of it in foreign currencies, but there were continents where they didn't have a penny, and never would have as far as he was concerned. 'I was lucky,' he said. 'I had a relative who was swindled in South American railways and lost some of my family's fortune. My wife had a relative who was locked up by the Persians, and that always struck me as a very poor place to do business in.' He rubbed his chin and said, 'Of course, you're only hearing the good side. Nobody gets it right all the time.'

Few commentators on the City fail to compare its central institutions to a series of clubs for Englishmen. London has no monopoly of privileged groups. But the City's have presented a close-knit appearance because of the narrow social background shared by so many of the inhabitants. The formal organisation for the inner core of merchant banks is the Accepting Houses Committee. Its members, fewer than twenty, are the 'accepting houses'. The phrase defines an historic activity. Their guarantee of a bill of exchange – a form of 'commercial paper' or I O U – by writing 'Accepted' across the face, made it as good as cash. It could be sold, for slightly less than its value at maturity (usually three months ahead), to a specialist bank in the money market, a 'discount house'. For a century the 'bill on London' was the City's way of providing short-term loans, as simple as it was profitable. The exporter got his money, less the discount, straight away; the importer had three months' breathing space before the bill matured and he had to pay whoever now owned it. This middleman's activity, routine with a trace of skill, sustained dynasties. Membership of the committee, which dates back to World War 1, came to mean that bills accepted by a member were safer (and thus cheaper) than anyone else's. If they found their way to the bank of last resort, the Bank of England, through the money market, the Bank would buy them at its 'finest rate'. An accepting house could earn a margin of $1\frac{1}{2}$ or 2 per cent on the value of each bill. The committee's close connections with the Bank of England, which is the City's club of clubs as well as its central bank, brought social as well as banking benefits.

Bills are still discounted, but the privileges of the accepting houses (which were shared by some commercial banks, all British or Commonwealth) were ended by the Bank of England in 1981. No longer did their endorsement confer a special status, making their bills alone 'eligible paper' that the Bank of England would buy. Soon more than a hundred banks, many of them American, were on the list. Competition between them reduced the profits. The accepting houses groaned and said goodbye to what had been, often enough, money for jam. 'We all lived like fat cats on it for donkey's years,' says Chips Keswick. 'It was one of those gloriously English institutions which grew from power and privilege. I'm all in favour of monopolies. It was amazing it lasted until 1981.'

The Accepting Houses Committee, however, is still there, jealous of its status. The members are not the banks themselves but the banks' representatives, one apiece, usually the chairman. No foreign bank is allowed to join. 'Mutual solidarity,' said one of its apologists, is the committee's real benefit. 'We are an elitist club, if you like.' The idea is that they would support any member bank that found itself in difficulties. But so would the Bank of England. The real point of the committee has dwindled to the ghostly standing that membership still confers. It is said that the Bank of England, if asked about the character of any committee member, will answer with the single word, 'Undoubted'.

Present members include all the front-line merchant banks like War-burg and Kleinwort and Schroder, but one or two of the names are very small fry. Never mind, they are all accepting houses. Not only are non-British banks excluded; if a member comes under overseas control, it is promptly asked to leave. This happened in 1980 when one of the City's oldest merchant banks, Antony Gibbs, founded 1808, was taken over by the Hongkong & Shanghai Bank.* Had the buyer been in London, the committee might have agreed. But the Hongkong Bank, although British in tone and history, is based in the colony. Its roots are far away. The fact that it is a commercial bank didn't help. The club looked down its nose. Even worse, Antony Gibbs refused to go quietly. Its chairman, Sir Philip de Zulueta, visited members and tried to persuade them to change their minds. Then he argued his case before the committee. A few members thought Antony Gibbs should stay, but the vote (of which no details are ever available) was for expulsion.

Another merchant bank, Samuel Montagu, had problems with the committee when the Midland Bank bought control of it in the 1970s. If a committee member needed substantial help, might the Midland fail to sympathise with the old-boy system, and persuade Montagu to take a harsh commercial view? Assurances were given and the committee let Montagu stay. In 1982 the committee shivered again when the Midland sold forty per cent of Montagu to the US insurance company Aetna. In the words of the same apologist for the committee, the system to be preserved is one of 'intimate relationships' among City people who are 'answerable for themselves'. Does this mean anything more than it would in Wall Street, where rival firms nevertheless have common interests? The City thinks it does. 'If a merchant bank becomes foreign-owned,' says the apologist, 'the other members will still know its management because they meet them around the City. They may have gone to the same school. But a management may not be running their own shop any longer. They may be taking orders from the United States or wherever. Now, they may *profess* that they would be honour-able. But they may be ordered by a court in New Jersey or somewhere to behave dishonourably. Stockholder suits against directors of banks are not unknown in the United States, to oppose bailing-out operations by subsidiaries. That is unthinkable in high banking practice,' and he thumped the polished table with his fist. 'If the thing carries your name, you bail it out or go under. Therefore foreign ownership is something

---

* In 1983 the Hongkong Bank relaunched Antony Gibbs as 'Wardley London', using the name of its merchant-banking subsidiary.

the committee is very sceptical about.' Aetna's large shareholding was a problem, until Samuel Montagu's autonomy was guaranteed in writing – in itself an unfamiliar way of doing things in London, the capital of winks and nods. A brief document was drawn up to guarantee an inner management structure inviolate to alien influence. Montagu stayed in the club.

The merchant-banking community is an odd mixture of informality contained within codes of behaviour. Its members, the older more than the younger, share a delicious sense of being set a little apart. Having developed in the nineteenth century as both 'merchants' and 'bankers', they let the first definition turn into an adjective to qualify the second. Technically meaningless, it serves its purpose, of describing specialist firms that evolved to serve the trading and capital-raising needs of clients. Such banks were once common in northern Europe. Few of them are left, and fewer have more than local significance. The once powerful 'private banks' of Germany are small in number and over-shadowed by the big 'universal' banks, which handle both commercial and securities business. I was urged to see the house of Merck, Finck & Co. in Munich, once regarded as the Rothschilds of South Germany, though when I approached it, the bank seemed less than keen. The fortunes of princes were said to have been its specialty; nowadays it is the fortunes of industrialists. Merck, Finck, though, like Sal. Oppenheim or Trinkhaus & Burkhardt (which is now owned by the Midland Bank), was in the wrong country to start with. Some of the famous names of merchant banking originated in German towns – Rothschild, Warburg, Schroder. But they had to go elsewhere to become internationally famous, and especially to the City, as it developed as a world centre. To have been in the right place at the right time accounts for much of the merchant banks' historic success. A curious lassitude on the part of the commercial banks helped. On the Continent the greater banks tended to swallow the lesser. The same could have happened in Britain, where no legal distinction exists between clearing banks like National Westminster or Midland, and merchant banks like S. G. Warburg or Hambros. The former chose to concentrate on retail business and become 'High Street banks', the latter went in for specialist finance and corporate clients.

This account of what happened, which is the one invariably given, doesn't explain why the clearing banks were so slow to combine the two kinds of business under one roof; it is only in recent years that a couple of the 'clearers' have set up their own merchant-bank subsidiaries, or, like the Midland, have bought their way into an existing firm. Perhaps the clearing-bank managements, drawn from modest social backgrounds, were secretly in awe of the upper-class City bankers; stranger things have happened. Merchant bankers had an unmistakable stamp. Win Bischoff, a director of J. Henry Schroder Wagg, told me that when he joined the bank some years before, sixteen out of twenty managing directors had been educated at Eton. Bischoff is of German extraction. Soon after I met him, he was made chief executive, over the heads of various Old Etonians. But at Schroder and most of the other merchant banks, the unmistakable stamp will be seen for a little while yet. Leisurely lunches with a couple of wines are regarded as a thing of the past, but I enjoyed one or two (though not at Schroder). There is still a virtue in not being seen to be too busy. 'The City is successful,' I heard one veteran say, 'because the English are so idle. They never do anything that's unnecessary.' He was bored with the place but devoted to it. 'If I visit a Swiss bank,' he said, by way of illustration, 'about fifteen days later I get a letter from the chief general manager, thanking me for my visit. In fact I've probably been to see an assistant general manager who's a pal of mine. But their system demands that a chief general manager has to sit around at night signing all those bloody letters.' The English live by knack; rules are for foreigners. He remembered how astonished a German had been to see bills of exchange casually handed over at a counter in return for an enormous cheque. 'The German said it wasn't how they did it in Hamburg. Well, I've been here many years, and I can't recall anything going seriously wrong in that department. A few bills got lost in the backs of drawers, that's all.'

The casual style is sometimes a pose, and in any case conceals a serious interest in making money. It is why merchant banks are there. I visited one the day after a few hundred anti-nuclear demonstrators had marched up and down the City, protesting at profits from the arms trade. Some American banks had security guards riding in the lifts, but nothing much happened. Next morning there were pamphlets trodden into the pavements. 'No Cruise' had been painted on a bank's wall in an alleyway, the 'S' made into a dollar sign. A manager and two workmen were discussing how best to remove it. I found the bank I was visiting. While I waited in the hall for my banker, I mentioned the demo to the attendant. 'Loonies,' he said. I didn't have much sympathy for them either, but you can see why radicals hate the bankers, inviolate in their parlours; I remember thinking the same when I first put my nose in the City, twenty years earlier. My banker emerged from a meeting – oiled

179

hair, pink cheeks – gave me a nod, said 'I must take a walk,' and seemed to go straight through the wall. The door in the panelling led to a lavatory; it was invisible except for a hinge when you knew where to look. When we finally arrived in his room, he said he didn't want to be quoted by name without his approval. There seemed no point in asking him to approve for publication his views on the subject we somehow came to, private finance for impoverished parts of Britain. Investment in Liverpool, troubled with high unemployment, had been suggested. He shook his head at such madness. 'Politicians hire buses and take businessmen around Merseyside,' he said. 'Well. Would you invest there? In a lot of bloody-minded Liverpudlians? People complain that the City doesn't invest in places like Liverpool. Why should it? It isn't efficient.'

An ingenious case can be made for saying that when it comes to making money, merchant bankers in general are more ethical, or at least more restrained, than their Wall Street counterparts. Merchant banks (virtually no others) are allowed to use a provision of the Companies Act that entitles them to transfer undisclosed sums from their profit-and-loss account to reserves, and to keep part of those reserves hidden. Thus both the earnings and the reserves are likely to be understated. In some cases the true figure, both of earnings and reserves, is probably half as much again as the one disclosed. (At least, that is the impression that merchant bankers give. Perhaps what they conceal is embarrassingly small. 'Hidden reserves' may have an element of bluff – City showmanship at work.) The theory is that by manipulating figures behind the scenes, a merchant bank can even out its performance between good and bad years.* This, runs the argument, makes for a less frenzied approach to profits. Instead of being goaded, like a Wall Street firm, by the need to maintain the price of the shares by showing improved earnings, the accepting house can manipulate its figures and relax. So it is nicer to do business with, less inclined to pull a fast one in the interests of success. But many New York investment banks are private companies whose profits are concealed, and they seem to behave no differently to the rest.

A simpler proposition, also heard, is that merchant bankers somehow inherit higher ethical standards. This is not Mr Lombard's argument of 'Anglo-Saxons versus Latins', because Wall Street runs on the same Anglo-Saxon lines as the City. Rather it rests on the self-indulgent

---

* It also helps when negotiating with staff. A manager at an accepting house said that staff might get unsettled if they knew the extent of the profits.

assumption that where Americans by nature are greedy and take the short view, Europeans are thoughtful and see themselves in the context of history. 'At the crunch point,' said another banker, 'you simply say to yourself, "One has been in business since eighteen hundred and something. There have been bad times and good times. If it means I must have leaner expectations, so be it."' This stoic is a senior manager at an accepting house. Given the undistinguished record of his bank in recent years, he has something to be stoical about. 'Wall Street has much greater orientation to personal gain,' he said. 'London wants to be successful, too, but the rewards are more in respect. They don't necessarily come through the wallet.'

One reason money may be less of a temptation in the City than in Wall Street is that there's less of it around. Jacob Rothschild, who likes to tease the City with statistics, says that his search of published figures in 1983 showed the highest-paid financial-services executive in Britain received £126,000 in a year, while the chairman of Merrill Lynch was paid $1,500,000. Comparisons can be multiplied. A senior director at a prosperous accepting house will hope to get within hailing distance of £100,000 a year. N. M. Rothschild paid seven directors between £85,000 and £100,000 in 1983; four received between £100,000 and £115,000. It sounds a lot in pounds; rather less in dollars. A comparable executive at Salomon Brothers or Morgan Stanley who wasn't earning five or ten times as much would feel underprivileged. Securities traders and salespersons on Wall Street can be paid hundreds of thousands of dollars. Since earnings in this area are more easily geared to performance, the coming boom in securities trading in the City will presumably have similar effects there. Accepting houses already reward their Eurobond dealers on an unBritish scale. At Samuel Montagu an experienced trader expects a salary of £30,000 or more, plus bonuses worth between a quarter and a half as much again. Fringe benefits like health insurance and a car are usually available. If the City follows Wall Street, fringe benefits will shrink and earnings will become more closely related to performance. A fully americanised City, in which the underperformer, no matter how senior, finds himself demoted or fired, is out of character, but no longer unthinkable.

As banks go, in the world league tables that bankers study so carefully, merchant banks are far below the giants, although a few of them have respectable positions. Using capital and reserves as the yardstick, Kleinwort Benson is the biggest – eighth in Britain, 233rd in the world (sandwiched between the National Bank of Dubai and the Hanil Bank in Seoul, Korea).* But this is a league of commercial banks, in which Kleinwort and four or five of its colleagues appear almost by accident, because they have a substantial lending function. Merchant banks are small, usually employing at most a thousand people (Kleinwort has eleven hundred), in some cases no more than a few hundred; there are no armies of clerks in many locations. Much of the revenue comes from fees, received for underwriting or advice of one sort or another; the cost to the bank is mainly the salaries of the comparative few who execute the business. Merchant banks can produce healthy profits. In 1984 Kleinwort Benson disclosed earnings of £21.6 million in the previous year, and capital and reserves of £215 million; so 'earnings' as a percentage of 'capital', one of the commonest measures of profitability, were a little over ten per cent. In Wall Street they wouldn't think much of 'ten per cent on capital'. But Kleinwort is regarded as a highly successful bank.

As for a breakdown of earnings into categories, as shown by some Wall Street firms (Merrill Lynch, First Boston), a merchant banker would as soon be seen in public without his trousers. The inquirer will be told that the banking side, which includes foreign-exchange dealing and the damaged trade in acceptances, is 'important'. Corporate-finance fees for arranging mergers and company reconstruction are 'sizeable'. Asset management is 'profitable'. Underwriting is 'useful'. The answers vary from place to place, but the fog is uniform. It is only fair to say that privately owned Wall Street firms (Goldman Sachs, Morgan Stanley) are no more anxious to publish details of earnings than are the merchant banks. But the Wall Street climate encourages leaks and informed guesses, and the general picture of how investment banks are making their money is much clearer.

Competition among banks has narrowed the 'bankers' turn', the margin between the rate he pays and the rate he receives for money. The Kleinwort Benson balance sheet shows the bank borrowing between three and four billion pounds. Some of the money represents 'natural' deposits by customers – a trading corporation, an oil trader – seeking a safe temporary home for funds. It is comparatively easy to lend such funds out again at a profitable rate, to finance a building or a cargo. Where the margins are narrowest is in 'wholesale' lending and borrowing. A banker creates the deposit by borrowing it more expensively in the interbank market, hoping to find someone who will pay him a

* Source: *Euromoney*, June 1984.

slightly higher rate. He is dealing in money, with a careful eye on interest rates and forecasts, 'lending long' (say, for six months) and 'borrowing short' (say, for a week), or vice versa, depending on one's estimate of how the rates are likely to move. 'You can make a lot of money,' said a Kleinwort director. 'But the margins are small. In the 1980s there will be much more emphasis on fee income.'

The smaller the margins, the larger the amounts must be if they are to generate worthwhile earnings. An executive in charge of these hour-by-hour operations in the money market is never unaware of the limits beyond which his dealers may not go. He is securing the deposit base of the bank, making sure there is money to lend out at wholesale rates, then watching in case it is lent imprudently. I spent an hour with Mr A, at the house of Z, hearing him say that danger might always be around the corner; that as markets had grown in size, so had the scope for disaster; that 'one is aware there may be an international catastrophe, but by definition it should not be able to bust Z's – it's not very big, is it?' He didn't sound as if it kept him awake at night. But they never lost sight of the limits. There would be a limit to Z's exposure in particular categories – say, to the Luxembourg subsidiaries of German banks. There would be limits for particular currencies and for individual banks, however large and reliable. He had a limit for banks all the way up to the likes of Chase Manhattan, whose capital runs into billions of dollars. The idea of Chase failing is either a joke or an international nightmare. The Chase limit with Z's in any one day is, or was then, $50 million. Z fiddled with buttons, and a screen displayed the Chase situation. The word 'Full' was flashing; Z's had $50 million lent to Chase. 'We must ensure that if some accident occurs,' said Mr A, 'it is not terminal to us. We could stand the loss of fifty million dollars. We couldn't stand two hundred.' The screen also showed that Chase had $23 million lent to Z's, but apparently that didn't count.

Computerised information has made it possible to prescribe, vary and adhere to exact limits. 'The dealer expects to get what he wants on his screen within three seconds,' said Mr A. 'Quite honestly, ten years ago he couldn't get it in three days.' Z's, like other accepting houses, was better regulated than in the old days. Foreign banks no one had heard of cropped up in the money market, which was dominated by the dollar and dealt in many currencies; only a quarter of Z's deposit base was in sterling. 'With a new name,' he said, 'a dealer is not allowed to do business with him until we get hold of a balance sheet. If he does, he's fired. We find it's a rule that's easily grasped.' In 1974 a small but apparently solid West German bank, I. D. Herstatt, collapsed because of fraud, for which senior executives were later convicted. Some unfortunate banks were left with substantial bad debts. Mr A said it would be a while yet before people forgot about Herstatt.

Chips Keswick at Hambros supplied the raciest overview of the lending business from the merchant banker's desk. I first saw him in action in the chair of the banking meeting, which takes place every morning at 10.30. It is here that Hambros' balance sheet is managed, day by day. A dozen people sat around a table in a room near the main staircase; it had a clock with a loud tick and a bookcase of fake books. I had no idea who any of the people were. Keswick consulted them in turn, asking what they had in the way of new business. A woman in a purple dress talked about extending an acceptance credit on which they were earning one per cent. A man in a grey suit said a borrower with a £200,000 overdraft wanted it increased by £50,000. The Deutsche Bank had offered a 900,000 Deutschmark slice of underwriting. Someone hurried in and said he was sorry, he'd gone to the wrong meeting. He was only just in time. There was a flurry of exchanges I couldn't follow. A man with a soft voice said the dollar rate against the pound was 1.594. 'We think the Bank's stop is four,' he said. While I worked out that this probably meant the Bank of England was prepared to let the pound, at that time under pressure, fall to 1.4 to the dollar, there was an elliptical reference to a loan, and the meeting ended.

When I said to Keswick later that it was all over quickly, he said Yes, but not so quickly that anything went unnoticed. 'There was a chap reporting on our sterling position,' he said, 'on our foreign-exchange position, and a whole raft of people putting up lending propositions. It's almost impossible to describe the way a bank runs because eighty per cent of it is instinct. It sounds a woolly answer. But say someone had wanted to put up fifty million dollars for financing a ship. I would instinctively ask, "When do we have to pay?" Or I would know already that we're not going to have to pay for three months. Then I relate that to what our cash position is. It's a juggling act. In order to lend you've got to borrow, and on top of that you must have a cushion of liquidity. The banking meeting is a long-stop. I'm sitting there in case I don't like the sound of something. It's normally the last point where you can blow the whistle. You *can* do it later, but that's your catchment area. No risk can be taken in the bank without it going through there.'

Hambros has about eight thousand banking customers. There is still a Hambros cheque book and a handful of retail customers. Ten years ago, when merchant bankers' margins were bigger and they did well out of commercial customers, individuals were not encouraged to go on holding accounts. As margins shrank, the wealthy customer who wants to be able to wave a Hambros cheque book was back in favour. Rather less than half the money on Hambros' books is in the form of 'natural' deposits – 'the sort we like best,' said Keswick. 'In other words, we've got a manufacturer of something who sells his product, doesn't have a requirement for his money immediately, and gives it to us.' 'Give' didn't seem quite the right word. But Keswick said they still had substantial customer deposits, even today, where no interest had to be paid. The total came to twenty-odd million pounds, he said. Was that the same twenty million all the time? No, said Keswick, it represented customers' funds that were on deposit overnight. It just happened to work out at an average of around twenty million at any one time. This is promptly lent out into the money market. With lending rates at ten per cent, that would generate a painless £2 million a year for Hambros. Humble customers of British deposit banks have grown used to being fleeced via current accounts that pay no interest. But even the sophisticated customer is unable to squeeze the last drop of interest from his cash-flow.

'Take a supermarket chain,' said Keswick. 'Money pours into the tills, and every day it pours out again because they have to pay their suppliers. There's always a balance in between which they can't refine down sufficiently. They may put it out overnight in the market, but there's always a little bit of a tail which isn't lent.' He embarked on an illustration about a shipowner leaving money with Hambros to pay for oil tankers, whose loading is delayed because of a dead whale in the harbour of Rio de Janeiro. His face shone with the story. The whale is enormous – shipping is delayed – hundreds of thousands of dollars linger in the Hambros computer. 'It's the flypaper of banking,' he concluded, as though to say, *and they all lived happily ever after*. 'Leave the door open and these little things come in. If you're efficient, you catch 'em.'

The remainder of Hambros deposits, rather more than half the total, is borrowed in the money market from other banks or from companies with cash to spare. There is no physical money market; it is just a phrase. All the banks are doing it, running 'ladders' of borrowings and lendings with multiple objectives: to service corporate customers immediately, to anticipate needs, to speculate among themselves by taking a view of interest rates next week or next month.

The money market happened to be hectic the day I was with

Keswick. The front-page story in early editions of the London evening paper was 'LOAN RATES: CITY IN TURMOIL'. 'Wholesale' rates for money were being pushed up, and one of the clearing banks, Barclays, had raised its base rate, on which interest charged to customers is calculated, from nine to ten per cent. London bankers had been taking the view that base rate, which had come down from sixteen per cent in just over a year, would continue to fall. They were heavily invested in short-term Government securities, bought on that assumption. Then the wholesale, interbank rate began to rise, because there were signs that base rate itself would have to go up to coax international money-men to put some of their currency into sterling, which was having one of its periodic bursts of unpopularity. Keswick said bankers had to look out for that sort of thing. When the market saw interest rates going up instead of down, alarm bells sounded. Everybody wanted cash; nobody wanted short-term securities.

'Then,' said Keswick, 'we had a curious situation this morning. Base rates were still at nine per cent, but the interbank rate was ten. There-fore a customer who had a base-rate-linked overdraft from me could draw on it at nine per cent, and lend it to some other bank at ten per cent, without any risk. It's called round-tripping. Now, what fright-ened the hell out of me was that if all these things happened at once – people over-invested, nobody buying the instruments, a kink in the rate structure making it attractive to people to borrow – there might be a classic shortage of money. Quite fun, quite interesting. But that's where you get caught.' I asked what he had done about it. Well, he said, he made the Hambros dealers push up the margins to anyone who wanted to borrow, which drove them away. 'In fact,' he said, 'I got it right last night. I borrowed twenty million.'

He added that he was often wrong, anxious in the English way not to sound boastful about having anticipated the day's mini-crisis. 'But yesterday I was right. So we had twenty million quid. I expect other banks were doing the same.' There was no fundamental threat to the bank; even if Keswick had got it wrong, it would have been only a temporary crisis, though an embarrassing one. I asked what was the worst that could have happened to Hambros, or to any bank of modest size, if it had found itself unable to obtain wholesale money to balance the day's borrowing and lending. 'If the worst comes to the worst,' he said, 'you'd have to go round cap in hand to the Bank of England, saying you need money to meet your commitments. I've never had to do it yet. I wouldn't want to. You'd get a bloody nose, be told you're a bloody

186

fool, got no business to be running a bank.' I said, so money was always available at a price. He said, 'Yes, but you've got to live with reality.'

Basic banking still pays the rent at most of the accepting houses. It is the least glamorous activity. The rest of the business is a mixed bag. A few firms make a specialty of packaging international credits, putting together loans from commercial banks that have the money but in theory lack the expertise to arrange the deal themselves. Most of the big syndicated loans, though, are arranged by commercial banks. But 'project finance', where a complicated package is assembled to build a dam in Africa or a power station in Asia, can still reward the merchant banker. The firm of Q has made many millions here and there with its elegant arrangements. Typically, the government of the 'exporting' country will guarantee most but not all the finance. In Britain, the banker who wants to arrange a £500 million package would hope to have £400 million of it covered by the Export Credits Guarantee Department. The man from Q's said it was basically an insurance concept – 'the person who benefits must also have part of the down-side. The ECGD has had to meet substantial claims – think what's happened with Poland and Iran. So the exporter has to take some of the risk, and he tries to pass this on to the banks. If he's exporting aero engines to Canada, that's a risk any bank will gladly take. If it's a project in Black Africa with payment over fifteen years. . . .' He made the kind of face that Black Africa prompts in bankers. Work began, he said, long before the contract was awarded. The merchant banker's client might be tendering for the contract against groups in two or three other countries. The financial groundwork had to be done early.

So what if the contract went elsewhere, and the work was in vain? The man from Q's said that in every race there were non-winners; by and large they would expect successes to pay for failures, unless it was obvious from the start that the client had only a slender chance, in which case Q's would ask to have its time and travel expenses guaranteed. He did a little sum on his fingers: if a team comprising a director, an assistant director and a junior spent one week per month over the negotiating period on the other side of the world, it would cost £100,000 a year. At least, he added. As for remuneration when a client won the contract, there would be a negotiating fee, plus commissions on the raising of finance, and an annual management fee for running the credit over whatever period of years it covered. I asked how much the bank might earn in a lump sum, excluding the management fee. 'It could be half a million pounds,' said the man from Q's. 'Or three-quarters. Say, up to a million and a quarter.'

Million-pound fees make outsiders lift their eyebrows. At last, the merchant banker is seen in his true colours, coolly pocketing a fortune without having any of his own bank's money at risk. This is not how it appears to the banks, who say that on the contrary, and considering their overheads, they are often grossly underpaid for their corporate-finance services. On an international scale of comparison, they are certainly better remunerated than Continental banks, which complain loudly about tight-fisted industrialists. It is when they compare themselves with American investment banks, as they do, that they feel deprived. Mergers-and-acquisitions work provokes the keenest envy. Fees of a couple of million dollars, rising to double figures, are common at the top end of the US mergers business. An M&A fee of £1 million in the City is almost unheard-of. The difference is partly explained by the size of some American takeovers; partly by the nature of the business, which in Wall Street frequently, and in London rarely, is initiated and elaborated by the bank itself, and is not seen merely as a passive 'service function'.

Nor can City bankers always be sure they will get all their money at the end of the affair, if they find themselves on the losing side. An episode at Schroder in 1979 is cited as a cautionary tale. The bank acted for Avery, a company that made weighing machines, when it tried to resist the advances of the British General Electric Co. GEC won, after paying more for Avery than it intended, and found itself expected to pay the Schroder fee for having acted on behalf of the victim. This didn't appeal to General Electric, which felt that Schroder had made it pay more than the company was worth, for the benefit of the Avery share-holders. In Schroder's experience, firms in that position grumbled but paid up. 'Perhaps we relied too much on the old-boy approach,' said a director. 'In New York, on the day a bank came in to defend on a thing like that, it would sign a written contract.' A compromise was agreed to, but the bank was not happy. 'We won't make that mistake again,' said a colleague.

The old-boy approach is no longer regarded as sufficient. J. A. Caldecott, then a vice-chairman of Kleinwort Benson, said that nowadays merchant banks were inclined to agree their takeover fees in advance, and 'not wait for the gentlemanly tendencies of the winner'. Kleinwort has a successful corporate-finance division. But according to Caldecott, 'if we handled a fifty-million-pound takeover, the fee would be something like a hundred thousand pounds.' This is a trifling 0.2 per cent of the value. The more aggressive firms, Kleinwort among them, are now breaking away from the orderly, low-key style that has characterised corporate finance.

Some accepting houses know that changes are coming but have done little to put their firms in order. 'I'm afraid', said one corporate-finance man, 'we find we can take longer negotiating the fee than doing the deal. We have companies who are good banking customers, who say they'd like us to help them acquire the perfect widget company. But when we try to talk about a fee, they say, "We don't expect to pay a *fee*". We say, "But don't you charge customers for your widgets?" and there's a stunned silence. It happened to me here, in this room, not long ago.' The room had a table, a creaking heater and a few old maps of Europe. 'We like to be seen as nice people,' he said wryly. 'To talk about something as dirty as money at one's first meeting with someone is regarded as bad form. We wish we could be more like the Americans, aggressive, or what they nicely call "assertive". On the other hand, you can easily get labelled as being too assertive or too aggressive, and we don't want to be. We are so, in quotes, steeped in history. When the Americans got going in London, we found they were going out and finding banking customers in the Midlands, while we were still sitting here, asking customers to look in when they came to London. Now they're starting to poach our corporate-finance clients as well.'

Raising new domestic capital earns useful sums in management fees. The issuing bank doesn't form a syndicate on the American pattern, with members anxious to be allocated as many shares or bonds as possible, so they can sell them at a profit. Because merchant banks have had no direct access to the London Stock Exchange, they leave the distributing to the stockbrokers. The British equivalent of the syndicate, the 'sub-underwriters', are paid a fee for agreeing to take securities if the stockbroker can't dispose of them. But the shares or bonds are not sought after as greedily as in New York. Sometimes the object of the exercise is not to take any securities at all.

Traditionally the merchant banker has been unable to see himself as either distributor or trader on a large scale. He has had to deal via a stockbroker and pay him a commission. A 'trading mentality' has not been encouraged. 'Certainly we all do a bit of trading of one sort or another,' said an accepting-house chairman, 'because we find ourselves at the centre of markets in every conceivable financial and material commodity. If as a result of our connections somebody feels that copper is strong and getting stronger, we might have a plunge and buy ourselves a few thousand tons, just to make a short profit. Or we might buy some gilt-edged [British Government securities] or some American Treasuries. But it's bad-quality business. It's not repetitive. It depends on a fluke of judgement and timing, and you get it wrong once in three times. If this bank got more than twenty per cent of its profits from dealing, I'd think it was too high.' Why was that? 'We ought to be getting our profits from our skills and client connections and creative work. They give rise to a more dependable stream of profits. Who was it said that a skilful dealer is a quick telephone and a rising market? Some wit. What I'm saying is that it's too dependent on the market.' This may be an outmoded view of trading, to put it mildly. It leans towards the merchant bank as specialist boutique, not investment-bank factory.

Among traditional sources of income still going strong is capital-raising by a 'rights' issue. This is an offer of new securities to a company's existing shareholders, a cheaper method than making a public issue. It usually pays a fee of one-half per cent of the amount raised, for a piece of routine work with no risk. It is an unexciting, painless way of making money – 'Immensely profitable,' says a Samuel Montagu banker, 'two hundred and fifty thousand pounds on a fifty-million issue.' It can be even more profitable than that. The biggest rights issue he knew of was for British Petroleum in 1981. This raised £600 million. The fee was 2 per cent, shared between merchant banks and brokers. Three merchant banks were paid a total of £4,500,000.

For a few years, some merchant banks will profit from a specialised kind of capital-raising, as the Conservative Government sells state-owned enterprises to private investors. Such issues are large and unconventional, and the merchant banks sometimes have to sweat for their fees. 'Privatisation' attracts publicity, and a badly priced offer (which has been made more than once, leaving millions of shares with the underwriters) takes place in a blaze of light. But the prices paid for undertakings like Britoil, British Aerospace, British Airways and Cable & Wireless mean that, whatever happens, the bankers' fees are based on capital values running into billions of pounds. Warburg, N. M. Rothschild, Kleinwort, Morgan Grenfell and Schroder are among the leading beneficiaries. The sum being guessed at as the eventual price for just over half British Telecom, the nation's phone and telex system, was £4 billion, unheard of for a single issue anywhere in the world, let alone the City. Two merchant banks were appointed as advisers, together with Morgan Stanley of New York, that expert on telephones, as if to

190

remind the City how times were changing. One of the London banks was the ubiquitous S. G. Warburg, the other Kleinwort Benson, which had set out a few years earlier to capture a slice of the privatisation business that it expected from a right-wing government, and succeeded to a degree that set its rivals' teeth on edge. Many a little banker yet unborn, his name not down for Eton, would come to benefit from the fractions shaved off the privatising billions.

There is always something new. The merchant banker's old boast of ingenuity, of living on his wits, of 'finding space between the wallpaper and the wall', does have some substance. Advising foreign governments and their agencies on how to manage their financial affairs emerged as a new specialty in the 1970s. Against a background of inflation, recession and the instability of world finance, a merchant banker who can present himself as a friend and counsellor, not as a rapacious creditor who wants his money back, can collect good fees for his solicitude. Prestige, too, comes from sitting in the company of kings, or at least heads of state and their ministers. Some of the clients are rich, and want help because wealth is still a novel experience. Here the work is simply a new version of an old game, advising a central bank or a finance minister far away instead of an industrial corporation or a wealthy investor at home. Thus N. M. Rothschild advises the investment arm of the Singapore Government, not actually managing the $15 billion or so that is said to be involved, but taking a 'strategic view'. Schroder advises a number of central banks, not all of them rich. Samuel Montagu admits to contracts with the central bank of the Dominican Republic, and with the governments of Jamaica, Zambia and Sierra Leone; there are others, but unless the government concerned talks about it, Montagu follows the banker's rule and says nothing. Baring Brothers has its advisers with the Saudi Arabian Monetary Agency; Merrill Lynch has a finger in the same pie.

Geoffrey Bell used to be a merchant banker at Schroder; earlier he was with the Treasury in London. He left the bank to handle the affairs of international clients from New York, and has a special interest in Venezuela. Bell is an archetype of the global banker, a lean man with a deep suntan and an easy mid-Atlantic accent, who seems to know everybody and travels relentlessly, as if his life depended on it, which no doubt it does. He encountered Venezuela when he was with Schroder, and the government wanted advice on handling its oil revenues. He says the bank went into the work not expecting to make a quick fortune, which was sensible, because it didn't. 'But we knew that if we could get into Venezuela, advising the government and the central bank, then we've got the Good Housekeeping seal of approval. *Then* what we could do was really something. Schroder made a great deal of money there. It led to new clients, to dealing with bond issues – the things you actually make money on.'

Banks that hang on princes' favours avoid publicity where they can. It is not a business they are willing to jeopardise by anything that might offend important, often self-important, clients. Their shyness is even more apparent when the client is a poor – or, in the tactful jargon, a 'less developed' – country, which wants advice about its debts. The issue of 'debt rescheduling' involves most of the world's major banks as creditors, and through them the financial systems of the countries to which they belong. Politically it is a minefield, and the merchant banks (together with some New York investment banks which have joined the sovereign advisers) keep the lowest possible profile. When a country in Africa or Latin America has debts of hundreds of millions of dollars, the creditor banks don't always take kindly to the team that slips in through the back door and tells the debtor how best to deal with them. The larger the debt, the more insignificant the advisory banker's little slice of a million dollars, or whatever it is, will appear to the debtor. But merchant bankers operating in faraway places insist on having their fees guaranteed from the start. The work is expensive in directors' time, with much travelling.

Much of what they do is unsensational. In its early stages it may be a matter of producing a financial profile of the country from muddled statistics. Apocryphal stories are told of closets jammed with documents that no one had bothered about for years, or old men peering into ancient ledgers. Geoffrey Bell says that in a small country whose finances are in a shambles, 'there may be one overworked governor in the central bank, and one permanent secretary in the treasury. Sometimes people don't know how much they owe. The merchant banker has an important role in pulling the numbers together. Then he can go to the commercial banks and say, "This is the problem. Now we can start negotiating."'

The best known of the advisers has been a group of three banks working together in an unusual alliance: Lehman Brothers in New York, Lazard Frères in New York and Paris, and Warburg in London. The three were in competition in Indonesia in 1975, when the state petroleum company, Pertamina, needed rescuing. They decided or were persuaded to co-operate, and developed a joint operation that

192

came to be called the 'Troika' or 'Triad'. About sixty people are employed full-time. Most of the work they do is not strictly debt-rescheduling (the vast debtors like Mexico and Brazil would be unlikely to employ them in any case), and the firms resent the idea that they are a burial party, come to dispose of the corpse. A managing director of one of the Troika banks said he saw them as plumbers, whizzing in to save countries from the consequences of being at risk in a complicated world, where borrowing from kind gentlemen had seemed an agreeable alter-native to reorganising the economy, until incompetence or corruption or acts of God overtook them. Clients include or have included Turkey, Panama, Gabon, Zaire and Sri Lanka.

'Just as commercial banks were keen to lend in the first place,' said Mr Troika, 'so they are keen to extort what they can when the country is on its beam ends. In Costa Rica [where the plumbers are said to have been paid at the rate of $200,000 a month], when the crisis breaks, the puny forces in the central bank aren't equipped to stand up to the chappies from New York. We are in the second row, whispering advice over the client's shoulder, making sure he isn't conned. It's an example of the classic merchant-banking function – finding a space between the wallpaper and the wall. . . .'

*   *   *

A new generation of younger men – not women, needless to say – has been taking over at merchant banks. Rupert Hambro was forty when he became chairman of the family bank in 1983. Christopher Castleman, thirty-nine when he was made chief executive of Hill Samuel (1981), was also an insider, although most of his career at the bank had been spent running subsidiaries in Australia and South Africa. Win Bischoff, in charge of Schroder at forty-two (1983), was brought back from Hong Kong, Schroder's principal base in the Far East, a year earlier. The fact that Bischoff is German-born is less significant than it would be at some merchant banks, since Schroder itself is of German origin, and the family is still the chief shareholder. Nevertheless, Bischoff brought a breath of change with him.

J. Henry Schroder Wagg – the bank itself, and the chief company in the group – was founded in London in 1804. It has a distinguished history and remains one of the inner circle of accepting houses, with a strong presence overseas. Its declared earnings in 1983 were £21 million, a very respectable figure. But in a way difficult to define, the bank had come to be thought of as worthy but unexciting. Bischoff himself, not long after he returned from Hong Kong, described it to me as 'professional and careful, with a good client-base, perhaps not getting into new areas quickly enough. We are unadventurous – doing the right thing by the client, but perhaps not seeing fast enough where the business ought to be going.' If he said that to me within ten minutes of meeting for the first time, he must have been saying rather more along the same lines to his colleagues on the board. In 1984 Bischoff was almost as explicit in public, telling a conference that the City had missed an opportunity to restructure its institutions, as the Americans had done, in the previous decade. That was the period when James Wolfensohn was denied the powers he sought at Schroder and resigned, an event that one of its younger executives still remembers as 'devastating'. Bischoff was at the bank then. In 1983, before he took over, I heard a Schroder traditionalist explain that the key to understanding the difference between the banker in London and in New York was that 'people are measured here by the quality of the man rather than the ability to make money. It is a fundamental point.'

Like all accepting houses, Schroder has been anxious to safeguard its name. At one time there was talk of using television to advertise the bank's unit-trust services to small investors. An advertising agency suggested filming several hundred one-pound notes on a table, with a thing like a vacuum cleaner fixed to the ceiling above the money. The idea was to suck the banknotes up into a pyramid; viewers would see the money grow. Nothing came of the vacuum cleaner. It is hard to think of any merchant bank, however profit-hungry, where it would. But Schroder's need for sobriety seemed to weigh on the mind of the person who told me. He brought up the matter of life-insurance business, backed so successfully by Hambros through Mark Weinberg's Hambro Life. He said Schroder had gone about it cautiously. 'So far,' he said, 'it hasn't been comparable to Hambro Life, which is a star performer in that respect. We have taken the slow road to developing the business. We were very careful not to change our style – even though we may not be earning in years three, four and five quite the profits we could have earned if we had taken the hard-sell route. We're very satisfied, provided we know it will be a quality product in year ten. Because we are totally committed to the long term.'

Such views seem to contain the essence of the London banker's tradition of honest conservatism, his strength but also his weakness. I asked him why he insisted that the Hambro Life type of operation would not have been possible there, even if another Weinberg had come on the scene. 'Because', he said, 'we would have had long debates about letting our name be used in a commercial sense, without a strong measure of control. We would have imposed constraints.' Oddities like the vacuum cleaner may have been part of some subterranean confusion as the bank's role was debated. Dignified banks and their associates have to be careful. At the time of the Queen's Jubilee celebrations in 1977, Schroder Life, which is based in Portsmouth, had agreed to underwrite the cost of a fireworks display on Southsea Common, alongside the Solent. As part of the Naval Review, the royal yacht *Britannia* would be at anchor. Among the guests on board would be the chairman of the Schroder holding company, the Earl of Airlie, and his wife Lady Airlie, who is a lady-in-waiting to the Queen. Shortly before the event, Schroder Life became aware of plans for an unusual finale. The Queen's crowned head would blaze out in fireworks. Loyal crowds would cheer. Underneath it would appear the firework message 'Schroder Life'. 'We all had absolute kittens,' said the director who told me. Schroder Life, which hadn't intended this juxtaposition, took hurried steps to have it changed.

Another new broom was at work at Samuel Montagu, in the shape of J. Staffan Gadd. Gadd, forty-six when he went there as chairman in 1980, was neither a merchant banker nor British. He was recruited, by an American consultant, from the Scandinavian Bank, a London-based consortium of which he was managing director. In City terms, this made him an outsider. A magazine article once described how he entertained Scandinavian Bank customers, inviting them to sporting occasions with a touch of class – racing at Ascot, tennis at Wimbledon, shooting birds in the country. I asked him if he meant to out-English the English. He said he was interested in tennis because of Bjorn Borg, had been to Ascot only once, and went shooting because he liked it. The flatly factual answer was itself somehow unEnglish. 'I remember when I came to the City,' he said, 'people used to say you shouldn't wear a topcoat. If you never wore a coat, even in winter, everyone would think you had a driver and a car. It was said in joking fashion.' His eyes looked sharp behind his glasses. 'But never brown shoes.' Brown shoes were serious. He was aware of the thin ice that a foreigner might still find himself walking on. 'I assume there are many people who say that a Swede running an accepting house is something outrageous. I'm sure that's said behind my back.' He thought the colour of his hair, which turned grey before he was thirty, had been a help; it made him look older.

The problem with Montagu, an old sleepy house, was that its absorption in the 1970s by a commercial-banking group seemed to substitute one dead hand for another. Merchant banking is not the commercial bankers' game, and success seems to depend on letting the subsidiary float away on a long umbilical. This is what has happened with County Bank, a healthy offspring of the National Westminster. In the case of Midland, there were difficulties at first in the way of allowing the subsidiary its freedom. But changes had already begun before Gadd took over; his appointment was part of the process. The management consultant who recruited him was Peter Giblin. Giblin says his brief from the Midland had been to find 'someone who was international, who could open up the bank. Many of the London banks have become too British or too insular.'

Having found Gadd, Giblin was in turn recruited to the bank, where as a managing director he began 'looking for individuals who are broad-minded and aggressive, who want to expand their role – somebody who's trying to figure out how he can use Swiss banking expertise in the UK, for instance, rather than waiting for the perpetual customer to call up and ask for assistance. Because the world's going the former way, not the latter.' The Midland Bank's deal with Aetna, which left the US insurance company owning forty per cent of Montagu, opened up new connections and, by dividing the ownership, helped Montagu feel more sure of its independence. The bank ceased to languish. It developed its presence in the United States and the Far East. The place began to fill up with clever young men like David Potter, recruited from Credit Suisse First Boston, and Mitchell Shivers, from Merrill Lynch; there was even a clever young woman, Barbara Thomas, until her recruitment a member of the US Securities and Exchange Commission – a creature from outer space for merchant bankers past and, in some cases, present. Much of the new talent was deployed in the Euromarkets, raising loans and capital, and building up securities trading. Montagu in the past had been seen as a 'trading' house. It was a leading dealer in gold and silver bullion, with a strong foreign-exchange department. From the early days of the Eurobond market it was more active than the majority in trading those securities. By accident, Montagu found itself with a tradition that was no longer a liability.

Many of the changes that are reshaping the City in general, and the merchant-banking community in particular, were foreshadowed by one man and his bank as early as the 1950s. The man, Sir Siegmund Warburg, is dead; his bank, S. G. Warburg & Co., is still among the two or three best names in the City. Sir Siegmund (1902–82), occasionally 'The Headmaster' to his staff, more often 'SGW' or 'Siegmund', was both the cultured Jew (leaving his native Germany as the horrors began) and the professional of iron in whose flashing enterprise a new version of the London Banker was born. He had none of the languid attributes traditional in the upper crust of City banking, and he was resented there before he was respected. For years he made little impact on the place. He came from a family of private bankers (though his father, like Samuel Montagu's Lord Swaythling, chose to be a farmer), and busied himself in London with a firm called the New Trading Co. After the war he put his name to the firm, and then, a crucial move, merged with a bank that was a member of the Accepting Houses Committee, Seligman Brothers. In that way he joined the inner circle, denying, to the end of his life, that it was the reason he acquired Seligman.

His place in City legend is long since established as the man who broke in. Staffan Gadd said with feeling that 'I can imagine what problems Siegmund Warburg had when he came here. He wasn't only a German, he was a Jew. But he had superior intelligence and built a superior fighting machine, and in the end he got established. Whether he was accepted by the *real* establishment or not, I don't know.' When I raised the point with a Warburg director, he looked dubious and said the last thing Siegmund would have wanted to hear was that the establishment ever accepted him. On the contrary, perhaps, Warburg saw himself as a patrician figure whose family bank, founded in Hamburg in 1798, entitled him to as much respect as any Hambro or Kleinwort; this would explain his reluctance to come to terms with the Seligman episode. Towards the end of his life he spoke of how the City had regarded him as 'a damn foreigner, a German Jew . . . a fellow who speaks with a foreign accent, all that sort of thing. I remember some people in very good houses talked very nastily behind my back: "Do you know this fellow Siegmund Warburg? He starts in the office at *eight o'clock* in the morning." That was considered contemptible. Most of them came to the office at ten o'clock in the morning. I was awful. They looked down upon me with utmost snobbism. . . .'*

Siegmund Warburg bounced the old guard aside in 1958 by expediting the unfriendly takeover of British Aluminium (Chapter 2), which ranged the newcomer against the establishment, filled the City

---

* *Institutional Investor*, March 1980. From an interview by Cary Reich.

headlines for months, and left him as a strategist to be reckoned with. He said later that his side won because it had more cash at its disposal and was able to keep buying shares on the Stock Exchange. The legend has him weaving spells to bewilder his slower adversaries; probably cash alone would not have sufficed without his will and boldness. The episode was a watershed for the City. Eight years later Warburg was knighted, and aggressiveness in the community was beginning to catch on, slowly. An exacting man, his imprint remains on S. G. Warburg & Co., which is respected and sometimes envied, especially for its skills as corporate (as well as sovereign) adviser, and Eurobond issuer and trader. It is the only British bank to retain a significant place in the league table of Eurobond issuers. Its contacts with central banks and other institutions throughout the world are said to be unusually good. The holding company, Mercury Securities, which includes overseas operations, employs only 1,300 people and disclosed a profit in 1982 of £13.5 million. The balance sheet shows the firm is active as a commercial bank. But it relies less on banking business and more on fee-earning services than its rivals. With a history covering less than forty years, compared with the century or more that many merchant banks can claim, it has needed to be assiduous and clever in creating the connections it needs with people, firms and markets. This is where the hand of Siegmund Warburg is still evident. Literate, sociable and a keen 'student of human nature', Warburg surrounded himself with colleagues whose background might be anything from politics or industry to literature or journalism, and who, like him, saw merchant banking as a subtle game for men of affairs.

Not a few former directors and senior executives of S. G. Warburg are scattered through the City. This is nothing unusual in a business that competes for talent. But a stint at Warburg is not easily forgotten. Opinions are handed round, sometimes by people who have never worked there, but know someone who has. Warburg 'uses a sledgehammer to crack a nut', there is 'a lot of backbiting', it 'isn't everyone's cup of tea', it 'works its people very hard'. Warburg's system of doubling up its office lunches has been a City joke for years. It is less of a joke now that frugality shows signs of coming into fashion. But the idea of cramming two sets of guests into a dining-room, the first from 12.30 to 1.30, the second 1.30 to 2.30, with some directors eating part of the meal at each session, is still good for a smile. 'It's not easy to get a drink beforehand, either, except a glass of sherry,' said a capital-markets director at a bank where they still serve wine. 'If you ask for a gin and tonic, a dusty bottle may appear after twenty minutes. When I was there last I said I wanted a campari and soda, just to pull their legs. Warburgs get away with it because everyone *expects* them to behave like that.'

The drab modern building that the bank occupied in Gresham Street before it moved to new premises in 1984 was in keeping with the dour face it showed to strangers. At a popular level, it makes no visible effort to sell itself. The annual report of Mercury Securities is a meagre document; there are no full-colour views of Lake Geneva or oilfields or men talking earnestly down telephones to gild the information, in the usual manner. The bank recoils from personal publicity for its officials. Siegmund Warburg himself was a hard man to interview. In this respect the bank is old-fashioned, except that the merchant banker's traditional reticence was an instinct, and one feels that at Warburg it is a conscious weighing of options, a feeling that silence is a commercial asset. Sent an innocuous questionnaire by a business magazine, S. G. Warburg took the trouble to reply that it was company policy not to reply to question-naires. *

The visitor to S. G. Warburg at Gresham Street was greeted by an entrance hall with plain counter, male attendants and lifts that seemed to have been designed for cargo, not passengers; it might have belonged to a newspaper. In any case, casual visitors were not encouraged. The first Warburg director that I met, on a strictly anonymous basis, said it was 'dangerous to receive people in your office if you don't want to do business with them. They may announce to others, "I was at Warburgs" as a way of getting introductions. We're choosy who we invite.' The subject arose because of a telephone call that the director dealt with while I sat on the other side of his desk. This was with New York (where it was still not 7 am) and involved a business proposition by two lawyers who might or might not be acting for the US Government, one of whom claimed to have met Siegmund Warburg, then still alive. The director said things like, 'It may be perfectly all right, of course, but there are some suspect characters in that area,' and 'Where did he say he met Siegmund, exactly?' I was aware that I had not been invited to the office, either: we met elsewhere than Gresham Street. When I finally went there, it was for a preliminary meeting with David Scholey, one of two joint chairmen, who has been at S. G. Warburg since 1965, and was regarded as the founder's protégé. Scholey, a bulky man still in his

---

* *Business Matters*, July/August 1980.

forties (born 1935), is a merchant banker's son. Every cuttings library includes a reference to the fact that he plays or played the trumpet and the guitar at jazz clubs. Since 1981 he has been a part-time director of the Bank of England. The fifth-floor room at the bank where I waited for him was dominated by an oval table covered in green cloth, set with eight cut-glass tumblers and two unopened bottles of Malvern water, eight yellow American-style legal notepads, and eight sharpened HB pencils. An antique clock was three minutes fast. A glass-fronted cupboard, perhaps a bookcase, had curtains drawn across, as if the content might be too revealing. The idea of the conversation was that it would be a non-attributable attempt to define what I wanted to know, with a view to talking again later. At one point my pen stopped writing. I picked up one of the yellow HBs and said, 'I'll use a Warburg pencil.' 'A non-attributable pencil,' said Scholey, smiling broadly.

Eventually I returned to talk in a general sort of way to Scholey and the other chairman, Lord Roll of Ipsden, who as Eric Roll had an earlier career as economist and civil servant before joining the firm in 1967; he is in his seventies but looks younger. Roll is also chairman of Mercury, the holding company. I showed them some random remarks I had heard about the bank. One read, 'Junior directors don't have full authority.' Scholey/Roll said that there was another way of looking at it. Warburg wasn't a partnership, but it operated as though it was. An aspect of partnership was that every partner committed his fellow. Each executive director at the bank (there are nearly fifty) needed to know what the others were doing. Every morning at 9.15 there was a meeting of all the directors who were in the building.

Another aid to information-sharing was that letters coming into the bank were summarised, and an abstract of the day's mail circulated. 'Apart from highly confidential price-sensitive things,' said Scholey, 'there is no reason for everybody not to have a clear motion-picture impression of all the business the firm is doing.' I said that if I were a director I wouldn't fancy sharing my correspondence. 'Some people have certainly found it restricting,' said Roll. Every outgoing letter had to have the writer's copy read and initialled by another person – 'just helpfulness,' said Scholey. 'Somebody can see it and say, "I wonder if that third sentence is quite clear?"' A similar arrangement governed a formal signature that committed S. G. Warburg. 'None of us,' said Scholey, 'including Eric and I, has the authority to commit the firm on his own signature. We still have the old-fashioned rule that it takes two signatures. When we go to the signing of an underwriting agreement, everybody else around the table has one representative. Warburg has two.' It wasn't a sledgehammer to crack a nut, it was meticulous attention to detail. Backbiting? No, the atmosphere was merely competitive. Perhaps they were intense, but they were happy. Slave drivers? 'We work ourselves hard.' The two-lunch bank? Roll sighed. Scholey said, 'It would almost be a claim to immortality to write anything about this firm and not mention the two lunches.' But they did happen? 'Yes,' they said, 'every day. Not everyone, every day. We don't have the old bankers' lunches of six of us and six guests. Ours are more a lunchtime meeting with a customer or a friend, and the courteous thing to do is offer them something.'

They said modestly that S. G. Warburg regarded itself as a relatively small business. Much of what it did was to provide advice and services, where its function was akin to that of corporate lawyers and accountants. It could do a certain amount of supplying the raw material of money, but purely as bankers there were other accepting houses that had been financing trade and lending to clients for much longer. It could share in the growth of securities markets, given the right strategy. There was no point in a bank buying vast Eurobond issues if it was incapable of distributing them to investors. 'Increasingly we've built up our distribution capacity around the world,' they said. 'But to nothing like the extent we need to or will do.' Scholey said the reason Goldman Sachs appealed to them so strongly was that it had the best-balanced business of its kind anywhere: on one side, capital-raising, corporate finance and professional services; on the other, stockbroking and distribution. They had nothing to say about any plans they might have in this area. A few months after I met Scholey/Roll, the London Stock Exchange's monopoly began disintegrating with many a groan, and S. G. Warburg was the first accepting house to buy a share in a major Stock Exchange firm, Akroyd & Smithers, paying £40 million for 29.9 per cent, the maximum allowed at that point. In London, Akroyd & Smithers was a stockjobber, a 'wholesaler' of securities. In Wall Street it was already a broker-dealer with a seat on the New York Stock Exchange. Soon there were plans for a New York subsidiary, owned jointly by Warburg and Akroyd, to deal in international securities. This could become part of the bank's already extensive distribution system. Like Jacob Rothschild, S. G. Warburg was on the move. A new game was beginning.

*   *   *

Among the second-division merchant banks in the past, respected but unassuming, was S. Japhet & Co., founded in Frankfurt in 1880 by a young banker called Saemy Japhet. At the turn of the century he moved his headquarters to London, and twenty years after that, still in charge, he was accepted into the fold of the Accepting Houses Committee. While he was alive, no one took the firm away from him. He died in harness in 1954, chairman of S. Japhet, aged ninety-six. After his death an investment company called Charterhouse, which specialised in buying up private companies that needed finance, acquired the bank, and ran it as Charterhouse Japhet without exciting much interest for the next quarter of a century. A few vibrations went through the bank in 1980, a hundred years after it started business, when Charterhouse bought up a second merchant bank, Keyser Ullman, that had never fully recovered from the London banking crisis of the mid-1970s. When the newly enlarged firm settled down after some blood-letting, it had sufficient capital, something over £60 million, to expand its banking business (there are strict ratios between a bank's capital and the amount of borrowing and lending it can do). But the turning point for Saemy Japhet's old firm was not the steady plod of banking but a piece of mergers-and-acquisitions business that got the bank's name into the popular papers as well as City heads, and sharpened its profile in the mysterious way that seems necessary to make people take notice.

The company involved was F. W. Woolworth, UK child of a US parent, American Woolworth World Trade Corporation, though seen for generations by the British as something that was as native as kippers or cricket. 'Woolies', once an exciting place to shop in, became homely and then dowdy over the years. Profits languished and Woolworth shares had a poor record in the late 1970s. More than a thousand of the stores had prime sites up and down British high streets. Imaginative attempts to make the chain more sophisticated never quite worked; a small suburban Woolies often had a curious lingering smell, like a cupboard in an old house. From time to time, property developers cast longing eyes on all those stores, and thought what splendid profits might be made if they could buy British Woolworth cheaply, in line with its share price, and break it up into prime sites for sale. The key to such a purchase was American Woolworth, which owned just over half its offspring. But it resisted such overtures as were made. The British company was almost as old as its parent, and the relationship was emotional as well as commercial, or so it was said by those who knew Woolworth from the inside.

In 1981 a chartered accountant with extensive property interests, Godfrey Bradman, decided to try his luck with the Woolworth connection. Bradman is an unusual figure, a successful financier with a sub-interest in 'social' issues like the environment. He had been a tax consultant in London, advising clients, individual and corporate. As the climate turned against ingenious (though perfectly legitimate) tax arrangements in the 1970s, Bradman ran down that side of his business. He controlled his property affairs through a public company called Rosehaugh, once a tea company in Ceylon, that provided a convenient shell with a Stock Exchange listing when he bought it. His plan was for a consortium to make an offer to American Woolworth and then to the rest of the shareholders, financing the deal by persuading British institutions which had plenty of cash to buy shares and loan stock in the new company that would be formed. He discussed the scheme with his stockbrokers, the well-connected Rowe & Pitman (they are believed to be brokers to the Queen), and asked Charterhouse Japhet to act for him. American Woolworth had troubles of its own, and might be receptive to a serious cash offer. Bradman and his advisers began to visit the institutions. They found four that were interested, a life insurance company, a couple of big pension funds and the Kuwait Investment Office in the City. It was the kind of long shot that a merchant banker might have conjured up on the back of an envelope; instead, it was the nimble Godfrey Bradman who stood to make money. But when he and his advisers went to New York in March to meet the Americans, the project came to a halt. American Woolworth and its investment-bank adviser, who was Goldman Sachs, said the price being offered was too low. In the background, perhaps, was American Woolworth's fear of handing over its beloved subsidiary to a group that for all it knew might treat it as property for development, not a chain of variety stores. The project went off the boil.

The appearance of a brand-new merchant banker called Victor Blank was the next, and, as it turned out, the crucial event. Blank had been a partner for twelve years with a City firm of solicitors, Clifford-Turner, dealing with commercial business. One of his clients was American Woolworth, and when Bradman went to New York to put his proposition in March 1981, Blank sat in on the meetings as a friendly observer. Later that year, and for unconnected reasons, Charterhouse Japhet's chairman, John Hyde, busy strengthening the newly enlarged bank, asked him if he would join the firm as head of corporate finance at a salary of £70,000. He switched from lawyer to banker as many had done before him. Mergers and acquisitions were his specialty. In New York, one or two of the big law partnerships are as skilful as investment bankers at handling M&A work. The unsleeping and filthily rich firm of Skadden, Arps, Slate, Meagher & Flom, where a senior lawyer is always on duty in case a corporate client telephones, is as likely to send business to a banker as to receive it from him. The person responsible for hiring Blank to represent American Woolworth in the UK had been a partner with Skadden, Arps: Robert Pirie, who later left the law firm to run the Rothschilds' New York bank. Pirie says he thought Blank 'the best solicitor in England ... the only one I met who worked like an American lawyer'. Blank is far removed from the languid school of banking. He is a genial, punctilious, almost finicky man who hurries home to his family to keep the Jewish sabbath but gives the impression of having few other fixed points in his working week. Once settled in at Charterhouse Japhet, the Woolworth project drifted back into his thoughts. In New York early in 1982, he looked in at the Woolworth Building, and found his friends there still toying with the idea of a sale, but uncertain how to go about it. What they didn't want was a prolonged battle. Once American Woolworth showed its hand, the British board would be up in arms, fighting the sale. 'It was', says Blank, 'a major *optical* problem. They had to be seen to be handing back the company to British investors who would hopefully carry on the retailing business. They didn't want conditions attached to the sale. They wanted a deal where someone came along, said, "We'll give you X dollars a share," and they could say, "Yes, done, here's our fifty-two per cent," and walk off.'

By this time, the relationship between Charterhouse Japhet and Godfrey Bradman was changing. Blank had consulted Bradman before visiting Woolworth in New York, saying that he wanted to try again, but that he perceived difficulties if a property company – Rosehaugh – were to be a participant. In effect he was saying to Bradman: it may have to be portrayed as a Charterhouse deal, but we'll cut you in on it. The wheeling and dealing had begun. With Bradman's original scheme as a starting point, Blank and a small team developed a detailed plan. They envisaged a consortium on the original lines, including insurance companies and the rest, put together in secret. No retail group would be included, in case the Monopolies Commission saw it as a reason to intervene when the plans were made public. That would mean delays. The consortium's money, together with loans from a syndicate of banks, would be used to buy out American Woolworth's majority shareholding, and then the minority British shareholders. These minority shareholders were to be given the chance to retain a stake in the business. All this would have to be done through a company formed by Charterhouse, which would end up as the successor to British Woolworth, with a Stock Exchange listing. The cost was likely to be several hundred million pounds. No British retailing group had ever changed hands for so much.

Armed with the plan, Blank was in New York again in March 1982 to talk to the Woolworth chairman, Ed Gibbons, and two of his colleagues. This time, nervous about security, they met in an hotel room. The Americans said they were looking for a price around 100 pence a share. The previous year, Bradman had been talking about a figure of 77 pence. For the Americans' holding alone, £1 a share would cost the consortium £40 million more than Bradman's price. Victor Blank said it was not realistic.

Another difficulty was that the consortium didn't exist in any formal sense. Blank, back in London, talked to one of the four possible backers that Bradman had sounded out, Prudential Assurance, immensely rich and solid in its red-brick palace at the City end of Holborn, institution of institutions; it is a major shareholder in the Charterhouse group, with a man on the board. 'The power of the institutions' is a well-worn phrase. In this case an institution was involved from the start in shaping events. The Pru gave its opinion that the key to the operation was that the new company to run the old Woolworths should have a visible management, so that investors could see who they were backing. This identified a problem that then proceeded to plague Blank and his team, as they looked for outstanding retailers whose names meant something, who would allow themselves to be known as part of a consortium which didn't yet exist, but which hoped to do a deal with a nervous seller if the price was right. Consultants were engaged and lists of candidates produced to fill a job that might or might not be available. Nothing could be said in public.

The feeling at Charterhouse Japhet was that the deal would never come off. But Blank persevered, that summer devoting the equivalent of perhaps half a day a week to finding a management team. Peter Firmston-Williams, who had built up the Asda group of stores, had retired as its chief executive. Blank went to see him, and pencilled him in as deputy chairman. As chairman he pencilled in John Beckett, who was not a retailer but had run British Sugar until it was taken over that year, and he left with a parting gift of £200,000. The idea was to have a chief executive as well; no one who was suitable and willing could be found, so Charterhouse Japhet created a shadow board by adding a couple of directors, one from its own board, the other the former senior partner of Rowe & Pitman, Alan Hurst-Brown. There was now the nucleus of a management, but only just. Even more difficult for the price negotiations with New York, Blank had no buyers prepared to pay, say, 80 pence a share. 'We hadn't been to find them yet,' says Blank. 'We were using our judgement as to what price we thought would attract buyers.'

Blank had already warned them in New York that even 90 pence, which the Americans were now arguing for, was too much. He telephoned Ed Gibbons to tell him so, a few days before the British were due to fly over to negotiate the price, 'so that he could say not to waste my time going. In fact, after a pause he said, "I think you'd better come anyway." And at that point in time, having put the phone down, I felt like jumping up and down in the air and doing backward somersaults. I said to my missus that I thought we were going to do the deal.'

I asked Blank what was the reasoning behind the price calculations. He said that at one end was the current price of Woolworth shares on the London Stock Exchange: a little under 50 pence, having been between 44 and 50 for months. At the other was the 'net asset value' of the F. W. Woolworth chain, including the sites, which was something like £2 a share before tax. Between these extremes, the price had to be low enough to convince the consortium that a revitalised business would show a real profit on its investment; both the Pru and Rowe & Pitman had advised that 90 pence a share wouldn't work. But the price also had to be high enough to attract the sellers and make them feel they were getting, in Blank's words, 'some kind of value for the property'. To the outsider it is almost metaphysical. Although everyone kept repeating that property had nothing to do with the deal, the vision of all those High Street sites somehow continued to dangle on the end of a string like a carrot in disguise. 'It's worth saying,' said Blank, 'that the aim of the new venture was to revitalise the retailing business. We recognised that some of the stores might be unprofitable and need to be sold [about twenty were up for sale already]. But we were absolutely committed to its not being any kind of property break-up. We knew we wouldn't get the institutions' support for a break-up. At a time of high unemployment, they wouldn't have wanted to be associated with it. Anyway, we believed there was more profit to be made out of getting the business right.'

So off they went to New York on a Sunday in August – Victor Blank and the senior partner of Rowe & Pitman, Peter Wilmot-Sitwell. They stayed the night at the Hotel Carlyle, ready for an early start next day. Now that the deal began to look possible, everyone was uneasy at the prospect of a leak. British Woolworth still knew nothing. At 9 am on Monday, Blank and stockbroker were to be collected by Ed Gibbons' chauffeur and taken out to the chairman's house at Bronxville. On the way down to the lobby, the lift stopped and a man Blank recognised got in. He was a banker from First Boston in London. They greeted one another and started chatting. Blank was appalled. He knew that the First Boston man had contacts with a London property group, and that the group had been interested in British Woolworth. In the lobby, Blank, still talking, kept a look-out for Gibbons' chauffeur. He was there; unfortunately so was Gibbons. 'Hello,' said the man from First Boston, who knew him. 'Have you met Victor Blank from London?' Perhaps alerted by a wild look in Blank's eyes, Gibbons said, 'Oh yes, we did some legal work with Victor.' Then the First Boston banker said goodbye, and everyone breathed again.

At the chairman's house they drank decaffeinated coffee and looked for an agreement between 80 and 90 pence a share. The men from London said they believed the deal was do-able at 80 pence. The further one moved from that, the harder it would be. The discussion went on for hours. It ended with an agreement that American Woolworth would take 82 pence each for its 199 million or so shares. (This was 5 pence more than Bradman had proposed. But because the rate of exchange had moved against sterling, the Americans, who would have got $1.74 then, were getting only $1.39 now.) Blank had done the first part of a deal that would be rich in fees and glory for the bank – as long as it could do the second part, raise the money.

The company formed in private to replace the unsuspecting British Woolworth was called Paternoster Stores, after the bank's address in Paternoster Row, alongside St Paul's Cathedral. The time had now come to invite the institutions to subscribe, still in secret, for shares in Paternoster. Normally a takeover would not require the vehicle of a new company. But the circumstances were abnormal, the sale of a subsidiary that had no wish to be sold, by a foreign parent that wanted to be rid of it. This was why Paternoster had been created. The trouble was that once Paternoster set out to raise new money, it was brought within the Bank of England rules that are designed to keep the capital market in order. Money-raisers have to form a queue in case a sudden surge of demand interferes with the Government's own borrowing through gilt-edged securities. The 'Government Broker' (the senior partner of the stockbroking firm of Mullens & Co.) organises the queue. Blank went to see him on 7 September 1982. He was told the bank could have two weeks, starting on 9 September, to raise the money.

Further regulations had to be coped with. It is not surprising that investment bankers are often lawyers by profession. Charterhouse Japhet had to consult the Takeover Panel, one of the City's self-regulating bodies (force of moral censure, not force of law), which in this instance was anxious about security. If news of behind-the-scenes activity fell into the wrong hands, someone might make a killing by speculating in Woolworth shares. The Panel told Blank that ideally it would like him to contact no more than five institutions. But his target figure for Paternoster was £165 million from the institutions, with another £145 million to be available in loans from banks. There was no chance of raising £165 million (less whatever Charterhouse itself contributed) from five firms, even if they all agreed to subscribe. The Panel agreed that Charterhouse Japhet could approach 'ten or a dozen' institutions. It wasn't worried about the banks, who were presumably thought to be better at keeping secrets. So, under less than ideal conditions, the money-raising began. The £145 million in loans, largely from British commercial banks, and some of their American counterparts in London with access to sterling deposits, was guaranteed quicker than Charterhouse Japhet expected. The institutions were the problem. 'If we were going to have ten or twelve,' says Blank, 'we needed the money in fifteen-million chunks, and we weren't getting it.' The bank was committing £15 million of its own and clients' money. The Prudential was in for £20 million, £25 million at a pinch, but there was no one else in that category. The Merchant Navy Officers Pension Fund was committed; so were two investment groups. Blank and Peter Hardy of Rowe & Pitman did a double act at meeting after meeting, working their way through the dozen names. The £165 million was a long way off.

Then the price of Woolworth stock began to rise. Someone was taking options on the shares, which is what a speculator with inside information will do, putting down a small amount of money with the prospect of a large profit if the anticipated event occurs. Whether or not the buying was innocent, Blank had promised the Panel that if the price of F. W. Woolworth shares moved significantly, the bank would request American Woolworth to tell the British board what had been going on, and ask them to suspend dealing in the shares. On 21

September, that happened. It made life more difficult in one way, because British Woolworth and its merchant bank, which was S. G. Warburg, could now try to upset the deal. But it also meant that Charterhouse Japhet could solicit as many institutions as it liked. The bank and its brokers scurried around the City, meeting fund managers and leaving them detailed proposals.

Still the promises were coming in too slowly. Blank asked the Government Broker for more time, and was given a few extra days. The final deadline was Tuesday evening, 28 September. Blank worked through the Sunday, talking to two institutions, one of which came in with £5 million. That evening he had to stop for twenty-four hours: Monday was Yom Kippur, the Jewish Day of Atonement, and he spent it in fasting and praying. When he resumed work, after 8 pm on Monday, they were still more than £40 million short of the target.

At this point it seemed hopeless. American Woolworth, bombarded with counter-proposals by Warburg, hadn't wavered. But some of the City institutions, perhaps, had been pushed off the fence in the wrong direction. In the Charterhouse Japhet offices, John Beckett, the Paternoster chairman, was already drafting a press announcement to say the deal was off. Blank, however, wouldn't give up. A few of the fund managers were still undecided. American Woolworth could be asked to put up some money as a last resort. The bank still had all day Tuesday. Blank argued they had nothing to lose by persevering till the last minute.

Others disagreed. Rowe & Pitman – which, as stockbroker, would have closer links than a merchant bank with the institutions – invited Blank to its offices at lunchtime. Senior partners gathered to commiserate. 'They gave me a very nice talk about how there comes a point when you really have to let go,' says Blank. 'They said one shouldn't risk losing friends by pushing too hard. They were saying, Don't get too emotional about a deal that's slipped away – life's life, and there it is. They were being nice to me.'

Blank went off to another meeting with the Prudential. The Pru said it would go to its absolute limit, which was £26 million. Late in the afternoon, a couple of institutions came off the fence on the right side. Charterhouse Japhet put up a bit more of its own money. The target was £20 million away. American Woolworth was asked, reluctantly, if it would cover the shortfall. Rather than see the deal fall through, it said yes. They were uncomfortable times for the parent company. Ed

Gibbons, whose decision it had been to take the plunge and sell British Woolworth, was ill in hospital; he died a few weeks later. A severe programme of store closures and redundancies in the United States had just been announced. But the British deal was on. Planning, persistence and luck had contributed; so had Blank's nerve. Next day directors and lawyers arrived by Concorde from New York. A champagne supper was prepared, to be eaten after the signing ceremony. With so many lawyers at Paternoster Row, the details took longer than expected; they had to eat first and sign later. It was four in the morning before they drove home through empty streets.

Godfrey Bradman, the instigator of the scheme, didn't go unrewarded. 'I lost the kudos,' he says. 'But I took the profit and I had no risk.' Bradman, an intense person with glasses and wispy hair, runs his affairs from handsomely furnished offices in the West End. He accepts with a shrug the dark suspicions that he was after the property, saying they were wrong but he can understand them. Rosehaugh drew off 'a little bit of money' by way of a fee, a little bit to Bradman being about £300,000. The real profit lay in the option granted to Rosehaugh to subscribe for a block of Paternoster shares at the original issue price of £1.50, over the next few years. Charterhouse Japhet itself had a similar option for a larger block. But as Bradman pointed out, the bank had £17 million at risk in the company, and Rosehaugh had none. 'Hopefully,' he says, 'we'll make millions out of it.' Had the option been exercised in the early part of 1984, which it was not, Rosehaugh would have realised £8,500,000.

After Woolworth had been won, Charterhouse Japhet was viewed in a different light. When, shortly afterwards, it was asked by the Government to advise on whether Britain's road-building programme could be privatised, this seemed to follow naturally. Very likely there was no connection between the two. But the bank was seen to have moved into the first division. It became easier to recruit good personnel. All at once there were more clients.

By the middle of 1983, Charterhouse began to think that a merger with the right partner would help keep the momentum. Jacob Rothschild at RIT & Northern had his own reasons for seeking a route back to the ramparts of the City. A year after Woolworth, the two groups joined forces to form Charterhouse J. Rothschild. Soon after, CJR bought out Hambros Bank's remaining share of Hambro Life, and began to explore with Mark Weinberg the possibilities of co-operation or even merger. In any case, CJR was now bigger than any merchant banking operation in the City. Through L. F. Rothschild, Unterberg, Towbin, it was also the only one to have a leading Wall Street investment bank under the same umbrella. Saemy Japhet's bank had become a strand in the new conglomerate-of-the-future, where London bankers of a different colour were at work.

8

BELGIAN DENTISTS

The Eurobond network — No tax please, we're investors —
The creation of Credit Suisse First Boston — Lunch with Dr von Clemm —
Stanley Ross and the grey market — The Order of the DCM —
A David among Goliaths

Every morning, as Europe's financial markets begin to wake up around eight o'clock, traders and salesmen in Eurobonds are dialling one another to gossip about interest rates, politics, deals and the furious inner life of their market. Most of the calls are made from trading rooms with the familiar banked-up dealing boards, telephones and TV screens, on desks arranged in rows, ovals and rectangles. Eurobonds (issued mainly but not exclusively in dollars) are a worldwide commodity, a model for the 'global securities' of the future that make so many mouths water. But they were invented in Europe (see Chapter 3), and London, always at its best when being casual, let the tiny market sprout there without interference twenty years ago. Nowadays a diagram of the morning's phone calls across the Continent would be like an airline map with thousands of routes, all converging on the City.

Even when sitting near the market men and women, it's not easy to pick out their words. Once they start doing business, they talk louder, partly out of excitement, partly because the point of being near one another is to eavesdrop and share information, if only subconsciously. For the morning gossip they tend to whisper, and ten minutes' listening produces only a few fragments: 'According to her, the co-managers were out there before eight' – 'Who's the new guy at Deutsche Bank?' – 'Ten billion yen down the tube in the Singapore branch, it was on the screen.' A man in shirt sleeves shouts across to the head dealer, 'For you, on thirty-three.' The head dealer's lips move. He frowns and nods. When he flips the switch to end the call, I ask him who it was. 'My wife,' he says. 'I'm going to New York tomorrow. She wanted to know if I needed new shirts.' The same pattern of lights flashes at all the dealing positions. Some of the lights that indicate calls on direct lines go unanswered. I ask why, and a dealer says they are one or two merchant banks in the City, not important. Since I've asked, he answers one of them. 'Nobody there,' he announces. A minute later the light is flashing again.

By the afternoon, when New York opens, the dealers' chorus is in full voice, a murmuring stabbed with cries and curses. Open circuits to the firm's trading floors in New York broadcast deals from one to the other as they happen. Electric fans stir the heavy air. Near a printed sign that reads 'Reason? Hell, there isn't any reason. It's just company policy', a young man – they are all young – is wearing a pair of plastic cow-horns. No one is taking any notice. The dealer next to me is speaking into his mouthpiece with exaggerated patience: 'Ford, you know? Brmm-brmm? Ford? . . . That's it . . . That's twelve and five-eighths of eighty-five. That's a good piece of short quality paper under par . . . What? . . . I wouldn't worry up to eighty-five, my dear. If anything goes wrong with the Ford Motor Company before 1985, Reagan goes back to his farm or playing cowboys.' Whoever he is reassuring must have been watching a holocaust movie on television, and become nervous about blue-chip companies. Nearby, another dealer is explaining to a sales desk that he doesn't have a particular bond. He says it twice, sounding bored. Almost yawning, he says, 'What do you expect me to do? Go short of the fucking thing?'

Like all securities markets, Eurobonds have two sides, the new issues and the trading-and-selling. Because issuing bonds is the public part of the market, the leading banks can be identified and listed in league tables. The key statistic for each bank is the value of bonds in the issues for which it has acted as lead manager; again as in all underwriting, the lead bank gets a fee for its pains, and can allocate itself the largest share of securities. About ten banks issue half the forty or fifty billion dollars' worth of Eurobonds that are pumped out to borrow international money for companies and countries in a year. Near the top there might be a couple apiece from France and Germany, 'universal' banks that include investment-banking functions; three or four Wall Street firms; a single merchant bank, S. G. Warburg; and a Swiss-American hybrid, the ubiquitous Credit Suisse First Boston, CSFB, which dominates the market.

But participating in new issues, even as lead manager, is not as profitable as it was. Competition for business has reduced margins. Banks frequently lose money on issues, not for any dramatic reason, but because the profit is shaved away, to give issuers attractive terms on one side, and tempt buyers on the other. It is not illegal, as it would be in

New York, for an underwriter to pass on some of his selling concession as a cash inducement to a buyer. Terms can be slim for underwriters. A director at Samuel Montagu – far from the top of the table, but trying – described how it fought hard to get into an issue on behalf of a French borrower, Crédit Lyonnais. It succeeded in becoming a co-manager. But the terms were so narrow, at the end of the day Montagu found itself without a profit. It actually lost a few thousand dollars. 'Not exactly risk-reward, is it?' said the manager. The chairman of another accepting house said that not long before, they had lost £200,000 on a single issue. I asked why the bank didn't say No more often when invited into a syndicate on poor terms. He said it wanted to stay in the market. It couldn't go around saying No to powerful managers like CSFB.

Compared to the early days of the Eurobond market, things are much harder for merchant banks. Twenty years ago, houses like S. G. Warburg, Hambros and N. M. Rothschild were never off the tombstones. The City had begun the market in a small way when it realised that although there were European investors who owned dollars, and European borrowers who wanted access to those dollars, no local machinery existed to bring the two together. The dollar market was in New York. So it seemed logical to start issuing bonds in Europe and tap the 'offshore' dollars, owned outside their country of origin. The market they gave rise to existed in a no-man's-land. It used local European facilities and stock exchange listings, but was essentially disembodied.

S. G. Warburg is usually credited with fathering the market when it led a $15 million issue for an Italian borrower, the Italian state highways authority, in 1963. Twenty years later, Credit Suisse First Boston was lead manager for a $1.8 billion Eurobond issue by the European Economic Community. In two decades the market had changed from a novelty in which merchant bankers could do conjuring tricks by backing them with their good name, to an established system run by heavyweights. The skill came to lie in distributing the bonds. Trading and selling go on in private; there are no league tables. But the big issuers include the biggest distributors. Because issuing Eurobonds is such a cut-throat business, the surest profit is in selling them. Professionals trade with one another, but it is the sale to the 'end-investor', or to someone as near as possible to the end of the trading chain, that carries the real rewards. This is why the big French and German banks, especially Deutsche Bank, are so prominent, because they have access to customers who like to buy Eurobonds. Once they realised their

214

power, they elbowed out the City bankers from the prime positions. (The City stockbrokers, too small and parochial, were never there in the first place, in any strength.) Wall Street firms like Morgan Stanley and Morgan Guaranty succeeded because they went to great lengths to build up their distribution.

The salesman, hurrying about Europe and Asia to solicit central banks and industrial companies and shipowners, became indispensable to Eurobonds. 'You phone them up,' says a Merrill Lynch salesman, 'you suss them out, you assess them over lunch. You throw in a couple of jokes. If he doesn't respond to you, give him a salesman who is more like he is. But I can change personalities ten times in ten minutes. I can be serious, I can be shocking. I get to know things about a fund manager, about his wife, whether his child is sick. I know who's drunk, I know who's sober. He knows the same about me.' The salesman is thirty-six. 'I am drained at the end of the day,' he says. He doesn't fancy doing the job beyond the age of forty; by that time he hopes to have made enough money to stop working if he wants to. Only Warburg, of the accepting houses, has survived in the Eurobond first division. 'By dint of not being members of the Stock Exchange,' says David Scholey, 'London merchant banks didn't have distribution systems. Some of us set out to build our own placing power.'

The best end-investors for those with securities to sell are private individuals: the shipowner, the film star, the lawyer, the widow. At one extreme, said a Samuel Montagu director, they can be 'substantial individuals, worth literally hundreds of millions of dollars ... their names are bandied about in the market-place.' He declined to bandy them about for me. He said that people studied the job advertisements in the *Financial Times* on Thursdays, looking for clues to unexpected sources of wealth; *portfolio manager wanted* might indicate a new fund, worth getting to know. At the other extreme is someone who buys half a dozen $1,000 bonds and keeps them under the mattress. The advantage of private investors, even large and sophisticated ones, is supposed to be that they (or their advisers) are less choosy than professional institutions. Some, at least, don't care about fractions of a per cent more interest as long as the name of the issuer is something reassuring like Exxon or the Kingdom of Sweden or BMW. They receive bearer bonds, on which – though not in the UK or US – the interest is paid without deduction of tax. This turns out to be the reason Eurobonds have got where they are. Many of the dollars that flow into Eurobonds might flow into US Treasury bonds instead were it not for US withholding tax. From the beginning the Eurobond investor has received his interest payments gross, without any deduction at source. The market belongs everywhere and nowhere; it is responsible to no single tax authority. Whether the investor eventually pays tax is up to his conscience and his nerve. But the absence of any provision to compel him is generally thought to have been the Eurobond's secret weapon.

If world citizens evade taxation in their own countries, it is no business of investment bankers, who caricature the crafty Eurobond investor, and perhaps hope to make him sound innocent and of no interest to politicians, by mocking him as 'the Belgian dentist'. The casual slander conceals a grain of literal truth. 'The market started from the investment of "black" money, if you trace it right back,' said another banker at Samuel Montagu. 'The Belgian dentist is the archetypal retail investor, who kept his money under his mattress and ran to Luxembourg to get his interest coupon cut and collect his cash – the cartoon investor. There's still a fair amount of that around.' The city of Luxembourg, on whose stock exchange many Eurobonds are quoted, is not far from Brussels by train or car. In the mythology of Eurobonds, respectable-looking men with brief cases hurry across the cobbled squares. Figures cluster at bank counters, clipping coupons from bonds, receiving banknotes in exchange. In the evening, after their day out in Luxembourg, they sweep back across the border to Belgian-dentist land. Nowadays few investors still make these personal visits. But the category remains, and whether its members are dentists in Belgium, farmers in France or garage owners in Germany, they are not directly accessible to investment bankers. They are customers of the universal banks, which either buy the Eurobonds in bulk and retail them at a profit, or, very often, are themselves members of Eurobond syndicates.

London-based Eurobond managers who want to get as close as possible to rich investors turn to Switzerland. 'Belgian dentist' is still the label. Many investment banks have branches or affiliates there. Goldman Sachs and N. M. Rothschild and S. G. Warburg and Nomura keep an eye on the Swiss and one another. But bankers from outside tread carefully in Switzerland. The Swiss have a reputation for being touchy. They will be nice to those who are nice to them, but if they feel themselves threatened by pushy investment banks, the eyes turn glassy behind the rimless spectacles, and they are not available when telephoned. The big Zurich banks, by the coldly elegant avenue that runs from railway station to lake, control a great fortune in customers' money. So do the smaller private banks of Geneva, tucked away among trees and fountains. It may be wiser to channel Eurobonds through such banks, and let the Swiss find the end-investors, creaming off their profit in the process. So the Swiss bankers are much courted, stuffed with lunches and dinners if they will accept them, and invited into syndicates when they aren't themselves the managers.

Merrill Lynch has six branches in Switzerland, most of them set up years ago to sell American domestic securities. A visiting Merrill sales-man eyed his glass of Dôle, nodded across the stone square, and said there was a gentleman's agreement not to poach private individuals in Switzerland. 'If we put a sign on our door tomorrow,' he said, 'announc-ing "Come and buy Eurobonds direct from us, no stamp duty, all you'll pay is a half-point spread net," we'd have a queue right down the rue whatever-it-is. But start doing things like that and it's "Goodnight, you're out." Obviously we want to sell a million bonds to a Swiss bank. We're not so interested in selling fifty tickets of twenty bonds each to guys on the street.'

Credit Suisse First Boston is the leading Eurobond firm. In 1983 it was lead manager for issues that raised more than $10 billion, 22 per cent of the $46.7 billion that the market raised in the year. Its nearest rival was Deutsche Bank, with 14 per cent of the market. After that there is no contest. S. G. Warburg was third, with rather more than 4 per cent; Morgan Stanley International fourth, with just under 4. CSFB's pri-macy is an achievement in a market with so much talent and so many sharp teeth. Operating out of London, controlled through complicated cross-shareholdings between itself and banks in Switzerland and the United States, CSFB has a ruthless, cosmopolitan air that perhaps indicates what a global investment bank might be like in future. But its complement of curiously strong personalities, together with an involved history, suggest that, like most investment banks, it is typical of nothing but itself.

The history goes back to an American brokerage house called White Weld. This was founded in Boston in 1890, handled 'old' money for East Coast families, the kind who still go to Brown Brothers Harriman, and by the 1930s was established in Europe and Asia as well as in New York. During World War 2 it remained open in the City. It helped the Government liquidate British holdings of overseas securities, unravel-ling a century of investment in other people's railways and factories, to provide foreign exchange.

Among its good deeds after the war was to move clients' money out of Canton and Shanghai just before the Communists took over. The money was transferred via Hong Kong to Uruguay, and later to Switzerland, where White Weld had set up a finance company, White Weld AG. Here the Chinese money happily rubbed shoulders with other kinds, until one day a candidate running for legal office three thousand miles away in the State of New York declared (in vain) that he intended to stop the Mafia salting away its criminal gains in Switzerland. White Weld's lawyers knew that the partnership was the only one in Wall Street to own a finance company in Switzerland. It would be awkward if the firm were dragged into the campaign, however innocently. The partners decided to sell White Weld AG to a friendly bank, Credit Suisse, the oldest of the country's Big Three. Credit Suisse, sympathetic to the problem, took legal responsibility for the company but otherwise left it alone.

This situation lasted a decade, until the end of the 1960s. By that time the Eurodollar markets had emerged. White Weld, with partners in London, Zurich and Paris, was as cosmopolitan as any of the merchant banks, and was active in Eurobonds. But the market was already changing, as 'distribution' grew more difficult for smaller firms. This was also the period of the 'American threat', when many people, particularly in France, feared that 'Yankee carpetbaggers' were about to take control of Europe's industries. The White Weld partners decided that the less they resembled Yankee carpetbaggers in European eyes, the better chance they had of persuading firms to let them raise capital. So they split White Weld in two. White Weld & Co. remained the New York firm, with its brokerage branches in Europe and Asia. A White Weld Trust ran Eurobond and any other 'offshore' business, based for tax purposes in the canton of Zug, next door to Zurich. White Weld AG was repurchased and given the name of Clariden Bank.

Meanwhile Credit Suisse was one of many European banks that hoped to make a name for itself in the Eurobond market. By 1974, however, it had decided that it would do better to improve its connection with White Weld Trust, and license the firm to do all its capital-raising outside Switzerland. The outcome was a new company, Credit Suisse White Weld. Eventually White Weld in New York sold itself to Merrill Lynch, where until 1983 'White Weld' continued to exist on paper, adding to the famous ramifications of Merrill Lynch's organisation charts. It only remained for the European half of the firm to find itself a new American partner, First Boston, which it did in 1978, when each took thirty-five per cent of the other, carefully defining the areas of the world where either could operate. The new entity dropped the

'White Weld' part of its name and substituted 'First Boston'. CSFB carried on where CSWW left off.

The operational headquarters in London, where CSFB leads in effect an independent life of its own, is a modern seven-storey block adjoining Credit Suisse. Movement beyond the lobby is controlled by stout glass doors equipped with a device called a Memorilok. Staff enter a code to gain admittance. The visitor is let through by an attendant. For the City, this is still a high level of security. I passed through the Memorilok on the way to see the chairman of the bank, Dr Michael von Clemm. Eyes light up or sometimes roll alarmingly at the mention of this name. He is a figure in the Eurobond community, which likes von Clemm stories. The magazine *Euromoney* published a photograph of a long silver car with fins like a missile, seen at an International Monetary Fund meeting in Toronto, captioned 'Guess who hired this monster?' and offering a bottle of champagne for the answer. David Potter, the former CSFB man who left to run capital-market operations at Samuel Montagu, guessed right and wrote to claim the champagne. The headline on his letter was *Vonclemmmobile*. Von Clemm now says he curses the day someone hired the car for him as an office joke, silver cars with long fins not being his style.

My visit was for lunch in a dining-room on the top floor. The room was empty, with a table laid for two. An attendant who offered a choice of drinks brought a tomato juice on a silver tray. The walls were decorated with oil paintings of sailing vessels and nineteenth-century naval encounters, moored above a carpet of deep Atlantic blue. Von Clemm arrived at ten past one and explained that he had been putting out a fire. 'From time to time we have fires in this place,' he said sternly. 'I have to put them out.' He was a tall saturnine American with sunken eyes in a bony face; his hair looked as if a wire brush had been used to make it lie flat. His suit and tie were conservative, even drab. The food was excellent; he munched it studiously, and I remembered hearing that he had helped start (and now owned a share of) Le Gavroche and other well-thought-of restaurants.

There was something intimidating about him. We were soon on to the subject of the Belgian dentist. 'The only difference between a good Eurobond issue and a bad Eurobond issue,' he said, 'is that a good issue reaches the Belgian dentist in one week, and the bad issue, or the issue that ran into trouble because the market went sour, gets to the Belgian dentist in three months.' His point was that the best operators were those with the swiftest channels to private investors, who remained the backbone of the Eurobond market. That was why the Swiss connection, in particular Clariden Bank with its portfolios of investors' money, was so important.

CSFB had a good relationship with its Swiss shareholder, but that wouldn't make Credit Suisse buy an issue from the investment bank if it didn't like it. 'We listen carefully to their portfolio managers,' said von Clemm. 'They may have a hundred reasons for not buying – they don't like the dollar at that moment, or the price, or the name on the paper. Sometimes the Swiss point of view is negative. They don't buy any-thing. Or they just buy gold bars and lock them up.' But CSFB had made an analysis of the market covering the year to August 1982. Nearly $50 billion of Eurobonds were issued in the period. The bank con-cluded that four-fifths of the total ended up in Switzerland. This means that the equivalent of forty thousand people or trusts, each with a million dollars to invest, bought Eurobonds through Switzerland in a year. Or forty million people, each with a thousand dollars. If half of them were evading tax, say at thirty per cent, on interest payments, say, of ten per cent per annum, they would have got away with about $600 million between them.

I didn't try this moralistic sum on von Clemm. I asked what happened when the Swiss were feeling negative about dollar securities. Did CSFB have investors in Asia, or were Nomura and the other Japanese firms there first? This was the wrong question. 'We were handling investors' money in Asia long before the Japanese poked their noses out the front door,' said von Clemm. 'We were in Shanghai and Canton doing New York Stock Exchange business for China before the Japanese had a navy, for Christ's sake.' He thought a moment and conceded that that wasn't literally true. He was keen on facts. At one time he wanted to be a journalist, and for a while he was. Scraps of biography emerged. He said he decided that to be a good journalist in a technically complicated world, one needed to be expert in a specific area. So in between working for the *Boston Globe* he read anthropology at Harvard and Oxford, which is why he is 'Dr' von Clemm, the style he prefers; went to Tanganyika with his wife and lived with a tribe for a year; prepared for a full-time career in journalism, arriving in New York from Africa a few days after a newspaper strike began; counted up his debts; thought of trying for a job at the World Bank; consulted an uncle, conveniently a banker, who advised that if a bank was what he wanted, then find one renowned for its remorseless pursuit of profits; went to work for Citicorp in London; and so became an investment banker by easy stages, joining CSFB's predecessor, CSWW, in 1971.

Von Clemm's theme over lunch was that, whatever anyone else had told me, one couldn't distribute Eurobonds profitably without Belgian dentists. 'In this market,' he said, 'there are Johnny-come-latelies like XYZ who wouldn't know an individual investor if he had a label saying *Belgian Dentist* on his chest – and wouldn't pretend to. They say they aren't going to futz around with little old ladies.' I said that somebody at XYZ had told me it had good contacts with central banks. 'Who hasn't?' said von Clemm with scorn. 'I'll give you their telephone numbers and tell you what they like to eat for lunch. Any damn fool knows that. How many central banks are there? There are a hundred and fifty member nations of the UN of which – how many, sixty? – don't have two cents in the till. Of the ones that do business in Eurobonds, I can tell you that a great number of them were converted by us at this bank. My point is that we all know these people. They can be very nice business. So can the offshore casualty-insurance companies in Bermuda. But it's not distribution, it's trading among professionals. XYZ don't know any Belgian dentists, so they telephone these institutions – so do we, in certain circumstances. XYZ say, "Hello, I can offer you Kingdom of Scandinavias at a discount of one and a quarter." The central bank says, "What are you wasting my time for? I've got four other investment banks talking to me. One guy's offered it me at one and three-eighths." So XYZ say, "Wait a minute, wait a minute, we can talk, can't we?" The central banker or the fund manager in Bermuda is taking them for as much as he can. He's playing on their need to get rid of positions because they can't retail the bonds. He buys them below their true value. In the next few days, when the next set of phone calls come in, he turns out the Kingdom of Scandinavias and buys the next new issue. And where do the Kingdom of Scandinavia bonds go?' Von Clemm pointed down through the floor and said they went to 'Mr Gruebel and his people downstairs.' Mr Gruebel is the managing director of White Weld Securities, an affiliate of the bank that keeps the old name and handles fixed-interest paper. 'We do a huge business in very very young new issues in recently signed new deals, buying them from these so-called institutional investors,' said von Clemm. 'We love it. White Weld Securities is the biggest revenue-producing entity in our group. We do *phenomenal* business. We take the bonds back in blocks, and parcel them out. Ultimately they go to the Belgian dentist.'

It is in the nature of the Eurobond market to be geared to private lives, to the funny ways of individuals, to a mixture of caution and avarice, to the rich wanting to be richer and the insecure wanting something to hold on to. This seemed to be what Dr von Clemm's view from the seventh floor implied. Most bond markets nowadays are geared to institutional investors, powerful fund managers conducting what they like to see as grand strategies on behalf of boards, trustees and shareholders. But Eurobonds have their private clientele. They are a simple way of finding a borrower for one's savings or gains, a good safe name – often an American company, or if not American then some household name from Europe or Japan, or if not a company then a reliable industrialised state or state organisation – who will pay the interest without clawing back thirty per cent on behalf of some grey-faced tax office. Eurobonds are charmingly unencumbered. The market was invented by investment bankers who like controls and bureaucracies no more than do Greek shipowners or émigré Britons in Portugal. It has its Association of International Bond Dealers (set up at a meeting at N. M. Rothschild in 1968), codes of practice and an efficient clearing system that operates from Brussels and Luxembourg. But none of this is anything to do with governments. The market runs and regulates itself, and that, presumably, suits the investors as well as the bankers. Much of the attraction may be in the investor's mind, but that makes it no less real.

'Do you know,' asked von Clemm, 'why our market is cheaper than the US dollar market in New York? It's because we are selling the bonds to little people in small amounts, and these people will buy them at less favourable yields in order to get what they want. In the US debt [i.e. bond] market, I think anyone will tell you that eighty-five to ninety per cent of the business is accounted for by between one and two hundred decision-makers. They are the Equitable Life or the state pension fund of the Commonwealth of Massachusetts, people who buy five or ten or fifteen million dollars of a bond issue in the New York market. That small community of investors controls the pricing of those issues. And since they've got the money, they say, "No, c'me on, gimme a little more, gimme a little more" – to anybody, to Exxon, to Dupont, to the biggest names. So then companies call us up and say, "What can you guys do over there?" Now, how can we do twenty to a hundred basis points cheaper than they can in New York?' The question meant: how can we persuade investors to accept interest payments of up to one per cent ('100 basis points') less than they would demand in New York?

'Very simple,' said von Clemm. 'Because we are selling to a retail, over-the-counter market that is totally diffused worldwide. Down the end of the channels is a small guy buying a parcel of bonds.' ('Small guy' is a relative term: bonds usually come in denominations of one thousand dollars, so if the parcel had a dozen bonds in it, the price would be a year's wages for some industrial workers in Europe. But small for a banker.) 'He doesn't have the negotiating power,' said von Clemm, 'and indeed he doesn't care. Because he's Belgian – or for Belgian read anything else – and he's worried about Poland and Iraq and Iran and the French Socialist election victory and the Russians, et cetera, et cetera, he says: "I want more dollar securities, and my God, here comes Dupont, I don't even want to hear what yield you're offering me, just give me the bonds." So we say, "OK, we'll give 'em to you." '

Von Clemm paused and said, 'Campbell Soup!' as though giving an order to an invisible waiter. 'We did a Campbell Soup issue with a split maturity, seven years and ten years. The ten-year element had a yield of fifty basis points below what an investor could have gotten on that day by buying a ten-year US Government bond. The seven-year deal was seventy-five basis points under the US Government seven-year-bond yield. Any professional, institutional investor, the man-at-the-Pru kind of guy, would have been fired at the next board meeting for buying that. So who were we selling them to? To someone who's looking for something completely different, and is willing to take a sacrifice in yield to get Campbell Soup, a triple A company, a US sovereign risk, in US dollars in small denominations in bearer form, with a guarantee that the interest will be paid free of withholding tax. We're on a completely different game, and to say that ours is a market of institutional investors is a total perversion and corruption of words.'

No two participants agree about the precise anatomy of the Eurobond market. What the spectator sees is an arena where bankers and brokers skirmish endlessly. The fierce competition, more familiar in Wall Street than the City, has given accepting houses a foretaste of the future that awaits them in the domestic British market, when the stockbrokers' monopoly has broken down, and investment banks on the American pattern can trade on the London Stock Exchange. As the Warburgs and Rothschilds began buying their way into stockbroking firms, they knew that eventually foreign banks might be able to do the same, turning securities trading in the City into an unprecedented free-for-all.

The genial exterior of Stanley Ross, chief executive of Ross & Partners (Securities) Ltd, conceals another tough egg in the Eurobond business. Ross & Partners is not an investment bank but a small trading house that specialises in Euro-securities. 'It is no longer the cosy market it was,' says Ross, and adds that one of the reasons is him. Ross dragged into the open a practice found in more than one European market, though not in the United States, and known as 'grey-market' trading. Eurobonds are provisionally traded before they become officially available. It used to be done on the quiet, without any publicity. American firms are still inclined to regard it as a wicked European habit. Ross himself dislikes the phrase 'grey-market' because it sounds shady, and prefers 'pre-market'.

Some investment bankers (though not Michael von Clemm) think he's a bloody nuisance. He thinks they're hypocrites. Investment banks (he says) compete so fiercely for a mandate to lead-manage an issue that sometimes they promise a client too much. It used to be worse than it is. Bonds were seriously over-priced. Behind the scenes there was then frantic trading as they changed hands at lower, more realistic prices. But the life-cycle of the bond was distorted. The end-investor, the Belgian dentist, might be the ultimate loser, paying more than he should. Ross says that Eurobond issues are now more realistically priced. 'We did the end-investor a real service,' he says. But that was incidental. 'Make no mistake,' he says, 'we didn't set out to protect anybody. We set out to make a turn.'

Ross is in his early fifties, a tall stylish man with a taste for dark glasses and champagne and money. Everybody in the market knows him; he is another of its characters. His face is long, his manner direct and flamboyant, with bursts of energy that fire the conversation into fresh orbits. He left school at fifteen; his father was a bus conductor. 'A magazine once referred to me as a "street-wise London trader",' he says, and enumerates the three requirements of a securities trader: think quickly, remember what has been happening, be bold ('you need balls').

After working for years for a stockbroker, he joined an American investment bank in the City, Kidder Peabody Securities, in 1967, and made it the principal trading firm in the burgeoning Eurobond market. But his independent style grated with his Wall Street management, not least in a racy newsletter, 'The Week in Eurobonds', that he wrote and circulated around the world. He even wrote about his superiors in New York. Once there was a telephone argument with them about a technical instruction that Ross didn't agree with. It ended with New York saying, 'Let me tell you something, Stanley, you'd better adopt a low profile.' This gave him a paragraph for his next newsletter. 'I said I'd been instructed by my supremos in New York to adopt a very low profile, and accordingly I told all my dealers that when the telephone rang, they were to lie flat on the floor. Was that low enough? Well, can you believe that New York didn't like it?' Ross seems to have thought himself safe because he ran a successful firm, but he trod on too many toes, and 'to my great surprise I was suddenly awarded the Order of the DCM, which is Don't Come Monday.' He walked away to start his own firm, which is now owned by another Wall Street house, Drexel Burnham Lambert.

His innovation was to tell the market, before an issue was launched, what he thought the bonds were going to be worth. He did this by renting an electronic 'page' from Reuters, on which he displayed his trading prices for Eurobonds to any subscriber who chose to interrogate it. The idea of doing so occurred to Ross in 1979, not long after he set up his own firm, when a bank that was to lead an issue of bonds for a Japanese borrower offered him a block of them at 'less five', that is, at five per cent less than the notional '100' that represents the full value of the bond. The issue was to be brought 'at par', at the full hundred per cent value. Commissions to the lead manager and the other members of the syndicate, together with the selling concession, amounted to $2\frac{1}{2}$ per cent. That could reduce the price of the bonds to $97\frac{1}{2}$ if all the commissions and concessions were used up. But they were already being offered at 95.

'I'd never heard of "less five" before,' says Ross. 'Clearly there was something very wrong with that issue, even in the early stages. About four days later the issue came at par, but trading began at eighty-eight. So I thought, how would it be if I could show everyone what the *real* price was, right from the start – the price at which I would buy and sell the bonds? The upshot was that I put the price on the screen and caused absolute uproar. I thought at one stage lynch mobs were going to come hammering on the door. But it got us noticed. There was now a mechanism to trade bonds before the price was fixed, on an "as-and-when-issued" basis. We made the managers realise that if issues weren't realistically priced, they wouldn't be able to get away with it on the old-boy network, on the basis of "You support my issue, old chap, and I'll support yours next time". We began to make everything much more market-sensitive. Often the issues seemed OK. There were even occasions when we were trading at *plus* two or *plus* three, which showed the issues were coming to market too cheaply. And of course the issuing houses didn't like that either, because it told the borrower he might have done better.'

That same year, 1979, the committee of AIBD, the bond dealers' association, tried to stop pre-market trading, but the rule it proposed was humiliatingly outvoted by delegates to the annual meeting. 'The floodgates were open,' says Ross. Thus the grey or pre-market has come to be accepted, though reluctantly by some, as part of the Eurobond machinery. Several firms now display the prices. Occasionally banks still throw fits of rage when they see an issue they mean to bring at 100 already marked down to $97\frac{1}{2}$, but the practice is unstoppable. Michael von Clemm thinks that Ross has done more than anyone to increase the efficiency of the market. It seems an odd business, dealing in securities that don't yet exist. Ross now has dozens of pages on the screens of assorted financial services, available everywhere ('from Helsinki to Montevideo'); it costs him about £25,000 a year. On a busy day his pages are interrogated eleven or twelve thousand times. 'My salesman is the screen,' he says. 'It doesn't ask for a commission on top of its salary. It doesn't take clients to the races.'

Traders and salesmen are the coming breed, even if Ross is not one of the banking set, merely a David among Goliaths, a phrase he slips into speeches. 'I changed the way our new-issue market functions,' he says. 'Nobody loves me for that. But I don't really look for love and affection. I only look to make a turn.'

9
FRENCH REVOLUTION

Shadow of the State — Pierre Moussa and Paribas — Unthinkable things —
Bankers and Socialists — Outwitting the Treasury —
'When a subject rebels, crush him!' — Business as usual — A trial and a verdict

It has been said that temperament and geography led the English to lend their gold, and the French to buy it. It is a broad half-truth that applies to much of the continent of Europe. London, a capital city that was also a major port, looked outward to trading and financial relationships with the world. The landbound commercial centres across the Channel looked inward. Paris was not the only one. But as a financial centre with a fine range of banks and credit agencies, in a city so impeccably cosmopolitan, the fact that the system was a shade parochial stood out.

The state in France has always taken a close interest in banking matters. Government savings banks and credit institutions came to dominate the system in the nineteenth century. Private capitalists started up commercial banks, but after less than a century of independence the four largest were nationalised in 1945, six months after the war ended. The typical French banker became an employee of the Government, a fate that seemed less alarming in Paris than it would in London or New York. Crédit Lyonnais and Société Générale were encouraged to be as competitive as before, to go through the same capitalist motions, while having to conform to the Government's economic strategy.

The paradox of competition within a closed system is accepted by those who operate it, though regarded with suspicion by those outside. It is impossible to prove that things would have been either better or worse if the banks had been left alone in 1945. Perhaps the act of nationalising them merely ratified what was true already, that French banks saw themselves as servants of the state. In any case, many of the smaller banks, the ones where individualists and entrepreneurs might be expected to collect, were untouched. Nobody interfered with

Rothschild or Lazard. These were the *banques d'affaires*, which corres-
ponded roughly to the British merchant banks, with the difference that
they were also investors in industry, using their own money to build up
portfolios of shares. One of them, the Banque de Paris et des Pays-Bas,
is said to have been a candidate for nationalisation, but to have been
spared because it had interests in other countries, including the United
States; for the state to take it over might have been politically embarras-
ing. For whatever reason, Paribas – the abbreviation later became the
official title – remained in private hands. At first, conditions inside the
firm were anarchic, with strong figures fighting for authority. Twenty-
five years later its internal battles were largely over, and it was a
thriving, outward-looking group, with fingers in industrial pies
throughout France and the world. Besides the industrial-holdings side,
it was both a commercial bank, and an investment bank that raised
capital, dealt in the Euromarkets and advised corporate clients.

In 1978 Paribas came under the direction of a former civil servant,
Pierre Moussa. He had joined Paribas in 1969, at the age of forty-seven,
after a successful career that took in several Government ministries and
the World Bank. Moussa was an *inspecteur des finances*. This grade of
civil servant, achieved by formal examination and informal scrutiny,
constitutes an elite whose graduates cluster in the upper reaches of
banking and economic planning. Its active membership of a few
hundred is spread across private as well as public sectors, since some of
them move on from Government jobs, as Moussa did. The existence of
this small, powerful network, sharing a background and containing
many individual friendships, helps to relate 'state' to 'private' entities in
a way that seems natural to the French. Perhaps the shared background
of schools like Eton and Winchester, where so many of the ruling class
are still educated, provides a faint parallel in Britain. But this is an
informal community, lacking the intellectual stamp and official
seniority that belong to *les inspecteurs des finances*.

The head of Paribas, running a large privately owned bank within a
state-dominated system, was naturally anxious to remain on good terms
with the central bank, the Treasury and the Government of the day.
Moussa, an aggressive seeker after new business, was at first managing
director of the firm, then chairman and chief executive from 1978. The
year before Moussa became chairman, the Paribas group earned FF513
million, about $90 million. In 1980, earnings were FF1,330 million,
about $240 million. It was a very large firm by Wall Street standards,
and probably earned as much as the top eight or ten London merchant

banks together. The spectacular growth of Paribas under Moussa attracted the attention of those on the political Left who didn't like banks to be in private hands. The bigger it became, the more there was to be angry about. Political mutterings seemed of little consequence in 1980. Moussa's personal connections with the French authorities were as good as might be expected of someone whose career had proceeded along classic *inspecteur des finances* lines; he had good friends all over the place. Nevertheless, from time to time the possibility that Paribas might be nationalised by some left-wing government of the future would arise like a bad dream.

Moussa usually heard the fears expressed by one of the bank's subsidiaries outside France. Paribas had been founded in 1872 by merging a bank in Paris and another in Holland. Among the countries where it soon began to operate were Belgium and Switzerland. A century later, Paribas in Belgium was the country's fourth largest bank, and had very large industrial holdings through an investment company, Cobepa, of which it owned nearly sixty per cent. Paribas Suisse (also about sixty per cent owned) was a leading bank that specialised in finance for trade and oil. Colleagues would say to Moussa, 'Do you think it wise to hold more than half our capital?' 'Why,' Moussa would reply, 'are you not happy that way?' 'Yes,' they would say, 'with you. But one day it might be somebody else.' Moussa would point out that he was not very old – 'I think I will be with you for at least eight or nine years, and after that I will choose an excellent successor.' At which point the colleague would say, 'But accidents may happen. What about nationalisation?'

This was an enigma to which no one had a clear answer. Many private-sector bankers shrugged their shoulders over the years and said that the Left was not going to win a national election, and that even if it did, the politicians would have more sense than to take over the remaining banks. Moussa agreed. 'The Left will study the matter as responsible people,' he would say. And he would add, with significant emphasis, 'If the time ever comes, I will pursue it with them.'

The extent of the firm's overseas interests was one reason for Moussa's confidence. Apart from its powerful European subsidiaries, the group (by now organised through a holding company, the Compagnie Financière de Paribas) had banking and other offices in more than fifty countries. Many of its investments in industrial and financial companies were overseas. It had substantial interlocked shareholdings with Mercury Securities, the holding company of S. G. Warburg in

London, and Paribas and Warburg often worked together; there had even been talk of a merger. In New York, the two shared part-ownership of a Wall Street investment bank, A. G. Becker. Paribas was part of an international community. That fact, of course, might damage it all the more in the eyes of those who looked inward rather than outward. But the consensus among the Paris *banques d'affaires* in 1980 would have been that nationalisation was unthinkable.

In 1981, the unthinkable happened. The Socialists came to power; Mitterrand was President. State ownership had been an issue in the election campaign. Guy de Rothschild says he woke up to reality a week or two before the first round of the elections, when the reigning President, Giscard d'Estaing, appeared in a television debate with Mitterrand. 'That is what alerted me,' says Rothschild. 'Perhaps we were all very slow. Giscard said to Mitterrand, "I understand that you intend to nationalise banks?" He said, "Yes." Giscard said, "All banks?" Mitterrand hesitated and said, "All banks". I thought modern socialist parties had given up that way of thinking.' Once they were in power, the Socialists pressed on with a Nationalisation Bill. This covered a number of industrial groups, mainly in the field of electronics, chemicals, metals and glass; and thirty-six banks, headed by the two leading *banques d'affaires*, Indosuez and Paribas. It was time for Pierre Moussa to talk to people and try to make them see reason.

His opposition (he says) was not on doctrinal grounds, 'a sort of religious repulsion. I do not say nationalisation was satanic. I say it was stupid. What I always said to my interlocutors was this. You wish to control the distribution of credit in France. I think you are wrong. But if you do, why take Paribas? We are involved in banking in France for only a quarter of our activity. Another quarter of it is banking outside France, and you don't want to control the distribution of credit in Belgium or Switzerland. A quarter is participations in industry in France. A quarter is participations outside France – for example, stores in Belgium, a brewery in Australia. Why do you want to own those? If you want to make the mistake in the first place, make it. But don't make it multiplied by four.'

A second objection flowed from the first, that Paribas interests abroad might be harmed by competitors, pointing a finger at a national-ised bank. Perhaps European investors and small industrialists, with their suspicious attitudes towards fiscal authorities (not to mention their appetite for no-questions-asked Eurobonds), might feel they had something to fear from a bank that suddenly became state-owned, even if the state was not one's own. Moussa was (and still is) careful not to say that such fears would be justified. But in 1981 he argued that 'competitors of our subsidiaries may well say to people, *Are you really a client of that bank? Do you know who owns it? You are giving them your secrets, like you speak to a confessor or a doctor? You don't know who owns that bank? It is the French Government, sir. You think that is a good idea ...?'*

Moussa is unwilling to give details of his progress through ministries and private offices in the spring and early summer of 1981. A French banker with his own interest in nationalisation says he would guess that if one made a list of thirty people – civil servants, Government Ministers, leading Socialists – whose interest was relevant, Moussa probably talked to three-quarters of them. By July, he was beginning to lose hope. The Government had decided not to nationalise foreign banks in France (as some of the Socialists wanted), but to include the overseas subsidiaries of the French banks they planned to take over. There were possible exceptions for industrial holdings (the question was still unresolved in 1984, though no one thought it likely that these holdings, which were duly nationalised, would ever be handed back). But by the time Paris shut down for the August holiday, Moussa and the other bankers on the list knew they had lost.

Moussa thinks that if the decisions had been left to the Socialist Party's elite, Paribas might have been saved. As it was, a feeling had welled up from humble party members that here was a bank, here was a policy, here was a guillotine ready and waiting. 'It is not an aristocratic party,' says Moussa, with a note of sympathy in his voice, as if democracy would be perfection if only it could be a bit more reasonable as well. 'There are civil servants, officials, ordinary people, who have a very simple idea about capitalism, that it is a bad thing, about the banking system, that it is the worst expression of that horrible system, and about Paribas, that it is the worst part of the banking system. They are people who belong to the old party, who never talked with Mr Moussa – who is very convincing. I would have convinced them, but I didn't get the chance. There were meetings where the overwhelming feeling emerged that the leaders of the party should not be fooled by those capitalists, and that it was a good moment to....' Moussa makes a fierce, chicken's-neck-wringing motion with his hands. He shakes his head – an informal sort of man, with owlish glasses and sudden movements. 'The leaders may have thought there was something in what Moussa said. But they also understood it was necessary to go along with feelings in the party – you know, "People are excited, let's give them something." So Paribas should be completely killed. Full stop. And that idea prevailed.'

The newspaper *Le Monde* published an interview with Moussa early in October in which he suggested partial nationalisation, leaving Paribas' international business in private hands. He knew that the Government could hardly take advice that was so publicly offered. But for months he had been offering the same advice in private, without success. Now he was burning his boats. The article may have been a public-relations exercise, putting on record a plan that men of good will might have entertained, but hadn't. In private Moussa had already turned to a more drastic solution. Beginning towards the end of August, he set out to reduce the control of Paribas over two of its key operations outside France: Cobepa, the industrial holding company in Belgium, and Paribas Suisse, the bank. The idea was to block the French Government's plans for interfering with overseas interests, without destroying the unity of the Paribas group as a whole. In a series of moves which extended from late August to early October, Paribas sold some of its investment in Cobepa to Paribas Suisse, and in Paribas Suisse to Cobepa.

Moussa says that 'our very faithful partners in Belgium and Switzerland were saying, "For everyone, nationalisation is bad. But it is less bad for you than it is for us. In Paris you won't lose your clientele, because where would they go? Whereas in our countries, we shall be considered as *pestiféré* – as having the pest." We hesitated and then decided it was our duty to liberate them, to an extent.'

I asked Moussa who he meant by 'we' when he said 'We hesitated.' He said he meant 'I'. It is a delicate matter. Later, when I asked a senior official at Paribas, he said Paribas officials in *overseas* subsidiaries might have been involved. He thought that several of his colleagues in Paris would resent the implication that they were a party to what happened. No doubt they would. We left the question in the air.

In 1981 it was decided – somehow – to free the foreign associates by 'diminishing the control', in Moussa's phrase. This was perfectly legal. French law said only that the maximum amount of an overseas investment that could be liquidated without prior permission was twenty per cent of the total value of the company. Paribas sold altogether 19.9 per cent of Cobepa to Paris Suisse and vice versa. The effect of this was to reduce its holdings in both companies to less than half. When the Nationalisation Bill was passed and Paribas came under Government control, it would bring only a minority interest in those particular plums.

These moves were duly reported to the French Treasury, which seems to have filed them away without noticing their significance. As far as Moussa was concerned, the job was done. However, other interests were at work. A small Swiss company called Pargesa, originally controlled by Paribas, suddenly came to life. Pargesa – in full, Paribas-Geneva SA – had been dormant for years. Earlier in 1981, when there still seemed a chance of a change of heart by Mitterrand's men, it had been marked down as a vehicle to buy any bits of Paribas outside France that the Government might decide to sell. Overseas associates of Paribas had pumped money into Pargesa. They included the Power Corporation of Canada, an influential holding company, and A. G. Becker in New York, in both of which Paribas had large interests. Another Paribas associate, S. G. Warburg, owned shares in several European subsidiaries of Paribas, including Paribas Suisse. But it was significant that when it came to priming Pargesa with capital and preparing it for its new life, the prudent house of Warburg chose not to participate. This was probably just as well, considering the course that Pargesa, controlled by its new shareholders in Europe, Canada and the United States, now embarked upon. The company set out to buy Paribas Suisse. 'They were friends of mine,' says Moussa, 'but at the time they considered that I was a kind of prisoner, that I couldn't speak freely.'

It was now October 1981. To the French authorities, the Pargesa bid seemed pointless. Did not Paribas own 60 per cent of Paribas Suisse? They checked with Moussa, just to be on the safe side. He told them that 19.9 per cent was in the hands of the Belgians, in Cobepa. This was strange, they replied – how long had that been so? About a month, he said. Why had he sold the holdings? He said it was his right. Ah, said the authorities, very well – but you are going to tell the Belgians that they mustn't sell their shares to Pargesa? He told them that as far as Paris was concerned, he would do what they asked. But he couldn't answer for Cobepa.

In fact, the French directors were now in a minority on the board of Cobepa. The Belgians outvoted them, and Cobepa's 19.9 per cent of Paribas Suisse passed to Pargesa. Most of the other non-Paribas shareholders in Paribas Suisse took the same line – though not S. G. Warburg, which itself had a ten per cent stake in the Swiss bank, but remained neutral. Pargesa had won; the French Government had lost.

A great row broke out. The board of Paribas, composed chiefly of external directors, had not been consulted. In the normal course of business this was unexceptional. Given the political circumstances, some of them were embarrassed. Moussa says that 'at least three' out of thirteen would have resigned. Moussa resigned instead. 'I was no longer a possible chairman', he says, 'because the main thing a chairman of Paribas had to do was protect the bank through his connections with the Government. That task I could no longer fulfil.' The Finance Minister told the National Assembly that Moussa had 'not lived up to his commitments'. Moussa left the bank, and a year later set up a company in Paris called Finance and Development, with money raised in nine or ten countries, to advise corporate and sovereign clients. His view remained that he had acted for the good of Paribas, and that his actions were in no way unpatriotic. But as far as the French Government was concerned, he had defied authority. A Paribas official who is still a friend of Moussa, like many others at the bank, says, 'In France, it is the tradition of the state. When a subject rebels, crush him! No matter *why* he rebels.'

Shortly after the Pargesa coup, authority moved against Paribas – and Moussa – in a remarkable way. The Ministry of the Budget, in effect part of the Ministry of Finance, brought charges alleging exchange-control violations. Moussa was among those charged. The matter was unrelated to the Pargesa story. A year earlier French Customs officers had uncovered what they suspected were illegal transfers of funds to Switzerland (and one unauthorised export of 35,000 gold coins to Canada) by clients of Paribas. This kind of thing is not unknown in France, which has had unbroken exchange control since the 1930s. When an offence is detected, the usual outcome is an arrangement between Customs and the offender, who has to pay a heavy fine. In this case, three or four hundred clients, and a few Paribas officials, were under investigation. As for Moussa himself, no one suggested that the chairman of Paribas had condoned illegal acts; if there were offences within the bank, they had been committed by employees much farther down the line. His responsibility was the nominal one of having been head of the firm. But the fact that the authorities had chosen to use the courts, instead of private fines, to dispose of the matter, aroused suspicions that the Government's real motive was to punish Paribas in general and Moussa in particular. One private deal between a Paribas client, accused of illegal transfers, and the Customs was about to be completed early in November 1981. The client had agreed to pay a fine of about £3 million. But when he presented the cheque, he was told that the deal had been called off, and he would be prosecuted instead.

Many still believe that prosecutions would never have been brought had there not been an intention to punish Moussa, the banker who had dared to rebel. Moussa himself says, 'It is simply that I, and nobody else, was the target.' During his trial in 1984 he demonstrated that more than nine-tenths of the illegal Swiss accounts had been opened before he became chairman of Paribas, commenting that none of his predecessors had been charged.

On the other hand, it has to be said that after the Socialists came to power, there had been increased attempts to move capital out of the country. The Mitterrand Government may have decided it was time to take a strong line against Customs dodgers. Since 1981, there has been a running battle between French Customs investigators and Swiss banks, with the former using much ingenuity to discover the names of Frenchmen locked away in the latter's data banks. But whether Moussa was incidental or (more likely) central to the decision to prosecute, he was caught up in the machinery. The inquiry dragged on. One Paribas official, head of the private portfolio department, killed himself at an early stage, December 1981. Eventually four officials of the bank, besides Moussa, and more than fifty customers, were charged with exchange-control infringements. The case hung over them for a long time. It was the end of 1983 before it finally came to court.

*   *   *

Meanwhile Paribas carried on its business at the same address, with more or less the same management. Its offices are in an angle between the rue d'Antin and the Avenue de l'Opéra, in a solemn grey building that used to be a town hall; Napoleon Bonaparte married Josephine there in 1796. The banking hall is below. The executive offices are above, approached through a kind of enclosed courtyard at an upper level, built over what used to be the inner yard. Green carpets on marble floors, orange trees in tubs, tall french windows leading off, and a lighted ceiling high above, suggest the open air. The small room where Napoleon was married is not far away, panelled and mirrored, on the dark side because it overlooks the narrow rue d'Antin. Moussa used it as his office when he was chairman. The new chairman, the elegant Jean-Yves Haberer, sits elsewhere. Before he was appointed to replace Moussa, early in 1982, he was head of the Treasury. He too is an *inspecteur des finances*, not yet fifty when he joined Paribas, the highest of high-fliers. A senior manager at Paribas says that Haberer is one reason the bank has been unchanged by nationalisation – 'he is very good at resisting the state'. The other reason is that the state was always powerful in relation to banks. 'We still fight as before,' says another manager. 'If there is pressure by the Treasury to put money into failing industries and prop them up, this is not new. The Socialists have brought it to a fine art, perhaps. But there is no direct intervention in our business. Instead of having a lot of shareholders, we have only one. It stops there, luckily.'

The sentences seem to contradict one another, no doubt because the bankers of Paribas sometimes feel themselves on thin ice. All insist, as one would expect them to, that nationalisation has not dimmed their purpose. 'From the start, in 1872, we were a *European* bank,' says Pierre Haas, chairman of Paribas International, which runs the overseas banking. 'Our strategy in the last twenty years has been to have a major presence in all financial centres.' Since nationalisation, Paribas has become more deeply involved (alongside Merrill Lynch) with the Sun Hung Kai banking and securities group in Hong Kong. Certainly the Paribas bankers there sound as anxious for profits as anyone else in that boiling city. In New York, Paribas bought out S. G. Warburg's share of A. G. Becker. 'Increasing our share in a Wall Street bank wouldn't seem to be the first choice of a Socialist government,' says a Eurobond manager. 'But it caused no ripple.' 'We still have the culture of a small, deal-oriented business,' says Robert Carvallo, an executive vice-president.

Haberer himself has been quoted as saying that his only instruction from the Government was to develop the bank and make money. Paribas earnings since nationalisation seem to be healthy and don't suggest the group has been damaged. Haberer insists that the bank has lost no clients, and that on his first visit to New York as chairman, he found Wall Street indifferent to the change of ownership. Pierre Haas says that Paribas clients 'asked a few questions, but they have seen they are handled by the same people in the same way. If the performance is good, they don't care what is behind it. If the service is bad, even if you are free, you may go down the drain.' The relationship with S. G. Warburg, though, has changed. In 1983 the two unravelled most of their interests, leaving Paribas with 6.5 per cent of Mercury Securities; previously it was 24 per cent. Warburg's stake in various Paribas companies was repurchased for £12 million. 'Although we are still very close to them,' says Haas, 'we have unbundled our participation because obviously they could not stay in a nationalised Paribas, which no longer has a market for its shares. The state was ready to accept Warburgs. But for them it had no interest.'

Running through most of the dozen conversations I had at Paribas was a stoical acceptance of the way things had turned out. 'We were not nationalised because we were bad,' says Pierre Haas. 'Our business was doing exceedingly well.' Another banker said, 'We were nationalised because it was one of the myths of the Left – the same that you have in the [British] Labour Party.' A senior manager said, 'In a strange devious way, the Government has proved that nationalisation does not destroy a bank.' Another said, 'Because the duly elected government of a democratic country could not accept a blow in the face, Moussa had to go. But the shareholders of Pargesa and Power Corporation of Canada and the rest are still friends of the bank. Therefore, as friends of the bank, they like to work hand in hand with us.'

The Paribas Suisse affair seemed to have lost its sting. There had been real fears that nationalisation would effectively destroy Paribas. Whether the bank had been in some way diminished was a matter of debate; but it was still very much in business. Behind the scenes, tidying-up went ahead. In 1981, pieces of Paribas had been sold to shareholders who were themselves part of the same entity. The entity having survived intact, everyone had to think again. Switzerland's central bank wanted to know what Paribas Suisse would call itself if its Paribas connection was no longer important. The question alarmed Pargesa. An understanding (though perhaps not a permanent one) was reached. Pargesa sold Paribas sufficient shares in the Swiss bank for the two to be equal partners. Paribas Suisse kept its name and remained, rather uneasily, with a foot in both camps, state and private. Paribas continued to describe it as a subsidiary; Haberer refined this in an interview and said it was 'considered like a subsidiary'. Compromise was poured on troubled waters. In 1984 Paribas regained control of the subsidiary in an amicable deal with the foreign shareholders. It hardly seemed to have been worth the trouble.

*   *   *

Moussa says that when the Socialists marched to victory in 1981, most of the banks marked down for state ownership would have regarded it as a mutilation – 'As if one would say, You will live, but I'm sorry, one of your legs has to be taken off.' Three years later, he concedes that the reality is less traumatic. He explains this by reference to the calibre of new men brought in by the Government, such as Haberer at Paribas. But one could hardly expect him to be enthusiastic. He is convinced that many of the survivors at nationalised banks fear their firms are not what they were. 'Maybe they were afraid to lose the whole leg,' he says, 'and find they have lost only the foot. They still consider they have been mutilated.'

I met Moussa first in a London hotel, in his shirt-sleeves, and later at his temporary offices in Paris. Donaldson, Lufkin & Jenrette, the Wall Street firm, occupied another floor in the same building. At the second meeting I mentioned that a senior officer at Paribas had told me he thought that but for the affair of Cobepa and Paribas Suisse, Moussa would have 'stayed in the system. He would have gone along with nationalisation.' 'Well,' said Moussa, 'I would not have said that running a nationalised bank is so terrible that I would rather become a beggar. But I have said several times, very sincerely, that a man who has had the luck to be the manager of that immense thing, Paribas, is not the best person to be asked to run the nationalised Paribas. It is still something great, but in my view it will never be the equivalent. So I would not have been eager to accept, unless I felt it was my duty by my associates.' But the episode was behind him now. So, at last, was the celebrated court case. It had lasted two months. The court took a further two months to reach its verdicts. Moussa was found not guilty. So were about thirty other defendants. Two Paribas officials were given suspended sentences; a third had fled the country. The bank itself had to pay $20 million. Clients, about sixteen of them, were punished with fines or suspended sentences. The state had had a sort of revenge. But it had hardly emerged with credit.

As for Moussa, the rebellious subject was uncrushed. His plans, unpublicised while the case continued, had been laid already for a new international bank to be based in Luxembourg and run from London. He called it Pallas, after the Greek goddess of wisdom, and raised $100 million of equity capital for it in Europe, North America, India and Australia. Pallas, said Moussa, would be an investment bank, a commercial bank and a *banque d'affaires* rolled into one. In London it bought a half share of Dillon Read's European operation. After marking time since 1981, Moussa was a man in a hurry. The last time I saw him he was talking on the telephone to someone in English. I think it was a Rothschild.

10
HAPPY DAYS

Lone wolves — Lord Keith and his first million — Anatomy of the entrepreneur —
Goldman Sachs and how much is too much? —
Chinese walls and conflicts of interest — Barton Biggs behind closed doors —
Richard Jenrette and the ivory tower — The pragmatists

Most investment bankers work for somebody else, although they tend
to behave as if they didn't. They dislike to be seen as the plodding
servants of impersonal institutions. They are survivors from supposedly red-blooded times when it was every man for himself. They will
tell you they never take a risk for its own sake, which may be true.
Nevertheless, they like the connotations of risk, and the other side of the
coin, reward. They enjoy a degree of freedom.

Charlie Smith, not his real name, is a senior manager with an American 'merchant bank' in London. It isn't really a merchant bank, more a
vehicle for its parent in the United States to use for raising offshore
capital and making offshore loans, outside American jurisdiction: legal,
international and profitable. But compared with Charlie's previous
employer, a British clearing bank, it's hot stuff. He was an even more
senior manager there. 'The core deposits at British banks are sleepy,'
says Charlie. 'Unless a customer started cordially to dislike me, I would
pretty well have had to kick him in the face to make him move somewhere else. But if I screw it up with an American corporate client, he's
off.' Charlie says it was a shock when he left the protected pastures of a
clearing-bank head office. 'I had two secretaries and a personal assistant,' he says. 'Here I have to answer my own bell. I work in a different
fashion. I have the power to lend up to twenty million dollars on a single
name. That's well beyond what I could do before.' Lending a small
fortune on the judgement of Charlie Smith is what he likes. Just for a
moment, as he says Yes to twenty million, he is Smith the lone wolf.

All the great bankers were individual performers – Nathan
Rothschild, Pierpont Morgan, Siegmund Warburg, André Meyer. A
managing director at Wall Street's Dillon Read told me proudly how he

once made money for his firm by putting one department of a commercial bank in touch with another. What could be more lone-wolfish than that? He had tried it twice before, with other banks, unsuccessfully. 'They said, "Go away, dummy, don't be ridiculous, you can't get paid for putting us in touch with ourselves." But the third time it worked. It was basically a part of the bank with x million dollars, looking for the right sort of borrower over three years. I went to another department that was looking for funds of a particular kind, and said I had just the client. They said they were interested, given the right conditions. They were flabbergasted when I told them they were lending it to themselves, but they did the deal. They paid the fee.'

Some people think the days of the banking entrepreneurs are over. Firms are too big, governments are too nosey, capitalism is too hesitant. I went to see Baron Keith of Castleacre, the former Kenneth Keith, merchant banker and industrialist, a force in the City during the sixties and seventies. One or two bankers had suggested him as an archetypal City entrepreneur of a generation or so back. Sixty-eight years old in 1984, his distinguished career includes the chairmanship of Rolls-Royce, and he still holds many directorships. He helped create the merchant bank of Hill Samuel from two existing firms, and used it as his power base in the City. A large man, physically restless behind his desk, as though afraid it might trap him between visitor and window, he attracted adjectives like 'electric' when City journalists wrote about his business coups, as they often did. Now the head is a shade older, the drawling Churchillian speech more measured. I arrived ten minutes late on a summer afternoon at his office in Victoria, having been delayed by widening ripples of traffic-jam from Buckingham Palace, where hundreds of men in striped trousers accompanied by women in huge hats were filing into the grounds for a royal garden party. He didn't seem to mind.

I asked him to talk about making money in the City. He blinked and said that, in his day, that was the reason for going there. He qualified as a chartered accountant and joined the City firm of Peat Marwick in 1936. But accountancy offered no chance of acquiring capital, which he didn't have, and he was only biding his time. This took ten years to come, because the war, in which he rose to lieutenant-colonel in the Welsh Guards, intervened. *Who's Who* notes that after it he married a viscount's daughter. In 1946 he went back to the City, to join a firm called Philip Hill. 'If you wanted to go into the long-established merchant banks,' he said, 'you either had to be of the family, or married into the family. Philip Hill was a financier. He and his partners all ended up rich. We worked away and we were able to make money.' I asked if this wasn't difficult at the time. Britain's first Labour Government to have real power was in office, taxing the rich and alarming Fleet Street; the Government's leading bogyman, Aneurin Bevan, stormed about the country, telling miners and steelworkers that no one was going to have 'luxury homes' while ordinary people lacked a decent roof over their heads. Wasn't there penal taxation aimed at the likes of struggling young capitalists like Keith? 'Ah, well,' he said, 'there was no capital gains tax. You made wise investments. Bought and sold. There were great opportunities to make money. We were employees of Philip Hill, but we were able to buy shares. Interest charges on the money we borrowed to buy them was deductible. The rates for money were low.'

All the time that Mr Attlee, Mr Dalton, Mr Bevan and the rest of them were tinkering with society, gentlemen in the City were doing business as usual; the social millennium hadn't arrived after all. Like royal garden parties, the Stock Exchange went on for ever. 'We were interested in making money, you see,' said Lord Keith. 'I'm not certain these fellows today are. They may say they are, but the fact is that damned few have done it. They're interested in bigger and better salaries, bigger and better pensions. They're not so entrepreneurial as they used to be. People are concerned about perks and company cars. I was much more concerned about what heavy metal has one got at the end of the day.' He swung his arms about. 'I'm blatantly entrepreneurial,' he said. 'We were eager young men.'

I said, what about the old charge against the City, that it had always failed to invest money where it was needed, in developing British industry? 'We did a hell of a lot of constructive financing,' he said. 'We were instrumental in getting Arnold Weinstock into General Electric – that was later on. But the more progressive firms – the smaller, more aggressive ones – came to us. Somehow it all worked.'

What about the stock market side, trading for one's own account and building up a fortune? Was 'insider dealing' sometimes a factor in those days? 'Oh, yes,' he said, though he implied that that was a high-flown term for it. 'Really, I suppose, till the sixties, or certainly the fifties, people weren't so worried about dealing with information to which, as Lord Keynes said, you wouldn't normally be entitled.' That made him laugh. 'The whole thing has changed,' he said. 'Wall Street has changed, the City has changed. You've got bigger, monolithic institutions, which are less entrepreneurial.' He said that Hill Samuel – his old bank – prided itself now on being a financial-services institution. 'Well. These things are all good and splendid. But if I was going to go into the City today, I'd look for something thoroughly entrepreneurial, that was interested in making money.' Sometimes, as then, he seemed to hang on the word 'money', drawing it out. (I thought later that if he was reborn into the City around 1990, when the Securities Revolution will be well under way, he might do very nicely again.) He agreed that things were difficult in 1984. Capital gains tax, had it existed after the war, 'would have prevented us making money *trading*, which we did. That gave us our basic capital as individuals to go on. Philip Hill prospered, we prospered. We made the thing spin.'

I asked how much capital a hungry young merchant banker with a reasonable amount of luck could have expected to accumulate in those happy days beyond recall. 'I suppose,' said Keith slowly, 'after the war ... I don't know, but. . . .' He sat silent for ten full seconds. 'I suppose, between nineteen forty-six and fifty-six. . . .' Another long pause drifted between us like smoke. 'I suppose, one way and another, I accumulated a million pounds. Somehow I made ... money.'

Perhaps the entrepreneurs of banking are not what they were. Purists argue that if it is not the banker's own money at risk, then he lacks the real stick and the real carrot. Michel David-Weill of Lazard says that partners are likely to think more about profits and less about size and glory. 'Glory,' he says, 'is not what this business is about.' (They say the same of spies: that an agent with economic motives is safer than one with high principles.) There are not many partners left. London has had no merchant-banking partnership since 1970; the large sums involved on the lending side of the business exposed firms to risks they couldn't shoulder as groups of individuals. In New York, where investment banks are not lending institutions, some firms have been able to continue as partnerships, accumulating sufficient capital to back their positions as traders. One or two of them are among the largest financial-service firms in the West still to have partners in control. At Salomon Brothers they controlled capital of hundreds of millions of dollars, before the firm merged with Philbro and the capital was broken up and distributed among the managing directors, as they then became. Until that shower of gold, the Salomon partners, although well remunerated, lacked easy access to their capital. They were at one remove from the carrot.

The same is true at the remaining full partnership among the Bulge firms, Goldman Sachs. The partners' capital there stood at $500 million in 1984. Roy Smith, managing director of Goldman Sachs International in London, and a full partner of the firm in New York, told me that partners draw 'a modest salary* plus interest on our capital, computed at a low rate'. The firm has about the same number of partners as Salomon, seventy. I said it suggested that on top of his modest salary, a Goldman Sachs partner was drawing about three-quarters of a million dollars a year in interest. He said, 'That analysis would lead you to the correct conclusion, that guys aren't starving.' But why stop at three-quarters of a million? He said there was 'a question that lurks behind the eyes of all the major guys in the firm. That is, they don't think it's healthy to pay out too much money to the younger partners. Won't they be distracted by having to think about what to do with it? Will some of them use bad judgement and go out and buy yachts or big houses they don't need and change their style of life, lose their keen edge? What happens to people when all of a sudden they get locked into a room with a lot of money? Maybe they change.' It wasn't exactly a policy. 'There's never been any articulation of the policy I've described as a policy. I don't know whether there is a policy or not. It's been our tradition. It's part of the way we do things. Who knows what's coming tomorrow?'

Other Wall Street firms exercise caution too, knowing that bad years can follow good years. And interest on capital is not the only source of remuneration. Partners may have valuable investments in, say, property (Goldman Sachs owns the large building it helps to occupy in Broad Street) and oil and gas leases. Still, the firm appears to go out of its way to keep the carrot trimmed. It struck me as mildly inconsistent to find this happening to a bank at HQ, Capitalism. Inconsistent was not how it appeared to the American who had the most to say to me about banking and entrepreneurs, Dr Michael von Clemm of Credit Suisse First Boston. Von Clemm, who has lived in London for many years, said the trouble with bankers was that they were becoming bureaucrats. 'If you want a theme for your book,' he said, 'it is that young men used to come to the City to get rich, today they come to get a job. It's not black and white. There are Hambros people who like to buy interests in things. There is Jacob Rothschild who broke away from the Rothschild bank. People haven't gone from being pure *entrepreneurial* investment bankers to being pure *bureaucratic* investment bankers. But there has been one hell of a shift.' Thank God, he said, there were still

* $80,000 according to *Institutional Investor* – 'Inside the Goldman Sachs Culture', January 1984.

acceptable ways of becoming wealthy in some parts of the world. Unfortunately investment banking wasn't the best way to do it. Historically it had been so, at least in the United States, where the investment banker was once richer than the industrialist.

It was not long after Christmas; yellow January rain lapped at the windows, darkening the skyline. The financial gossip columns had been reporting that year-end bonuses in the City offices of Wall Street firms had sent ecstatic young bankers tumbling into Moorgate and Poultry, all of them richer than rich. Von Clemm said this wasn't relevant. It was true, he said, that the bull market was producing fat bonuses for everyone connected with securities. When it began, in the late summer of 1982, it was like a miracle, not to be relied upon to happen every year. 'I've been in this bank for thirteen years,' said von Clemm, 'and I've waited thirteen years for it to happen. If I averaged out my earnings over those thirteen years, well. . . .' He shook his head at the thought of how depressing that would be. 'In any case,' he said, 'bonuses are totally different. The numbers may look large to you, and therefore may lead you to think that something is going on which is the equivalent of the way the Xs and Ys' – he named a couple of elderly bankers – 'made their pile twenty or thirty years ago. But in profit-sharing you're not taking any risk, unless you call coming to the office at seven o'clock in the morning, not knowing whether you're going to get anything at the end of the year, a risk. Of course, that's a kind of risk. But it's not what we mean by entrepreneurial capitalism. I come to the office at seven and try like hell to do business better than anyone else, knowing that if the firm makes a ton of money I'll get some sort of handout. But I haven't actually risked anything.'

Von Clemm said that one should consider those bankers who had accumulated capital, and then gone on to multiply it, within the last three or four decades. He cited Lord Keith – 'the Kenneth Keiths of the world who could make a million bucks overnight, trading on a security. Go back and look at some of the things that made him a very rich man. Then look at the von Clemm generation in their late forties. Do they behave like those other fellows did? The answer is No.' Von Clemm has kept a hawkish eye on his own situation. Credit Suisse First Boston appears to the outsider a paradigm for capitalism in action. But it is a sort of bureaucracy, and von Clemm says he is a sort of bureaucrat. He owns some equity capital in the firm, as do his senior colleagues. It is too little to mean much in a bank that does business on the scale of CSFB. In the sense of profiting directly from a deal, he is more of an onlooker than a participant. 'Because of tax,' he said, 'I can't accumulate personal capital in the business to keep up with the growth of the risks. When I started, a twenty-five-million bond issue for ICI was a huge deal. We have just completed a $1.2 billion issue. Let me tell you that my capital – and I've been, quote, successful in this firm and in this field – my capital hasn't moved one-twentieth, one-fiftieth, of that shift. And the same is true for everybody I know. A combination of attitudes and the tax system is what has prevented us.'

I mentioned Goldman Sachs and its policy or tradition of not distributing profits. 'You've just come to my point,' he said. 'What a *presumption* that anyone should decide that half a million dollars or whatever is about as much as old von Clemm can handle.' He knew of British merchant bankers who earned £100,000 in the 1930s. Allowing for inflation, that was equivalent to two or three million pounds half a century later. Allowing for income-tax levels, it was more again. Such rewards were unimaginable in the City today. But he thought that even twenty years ago he could have made a million dollars in a year. He would just have been in time. Now the banker's world had changed.

A few individuals break away from large firms and set up on their own. James Wolfensohn (ex Salomon), Geoffrey Bell (ex Schroder) and David Craig (ex Morgan Guaranty Ltd) are among this select crew of escapers. But all it proves is that some people would rather work for themselves. The Tokyo securities houses, where everyone works for salaries modest by New York standards, are among the most competitive in the industry. Perhaps the Japanese are different, dedicated to the team. Then what about the team at Goldman Sachs? Their capital stays locked up, but they hardly seem short of motivation. Or Jacob Rothschild, who inherited sufficient money never to need to work if he chose, which should have left him with no financial incentive? His own conclusion is that a private fortune enables him to concentrate on developing a business instead of having to make money for himself. That stands the conventional argument, about money being the spur, on its head. He says that his Wall Street colleagues pull his leg and call him 'the last amateur', because he takes only $60,000 a year from the firm (although he also has shares in the Wall Street business), while they are drawing millions. Yet Rothschild is regarded as an exemplary entrepreneur.

In the past, when bankers and brokers made fortunes from unregulated markets, it was often at the expense of investors. Western stock exchanges are now more strictly policed. The United States has its

Securities and Exchange Commission. Britain has an unsatisfactory system of self-regulation, soon likely to be subject to state supervision. Yet within whatever the local framework may be, the same old currents can be seen, moving beneath the surface. André Meyer (1898–1979), the Frenchman who ran Lazard Frères in New York, operated in what had become, certainly during his later years, the world's most highly regulated financial centre. But it is said that he was nevertheless able to benefit by using privileged information. 'He was a practitioner of the art of merchant banking, in a class by himself,' says Stanislas Yassukovich, a grey eminence of the business in London. 'The cynic would say that his success at the end of the day in making money usually boiled down to a form of insider trading. He had enormously profound knowledge of the US corporate sector. He was very much an instigator of mergers and takeovers. And he took advantage of his knowledge.'

Cary Reich's biography of Meyer* glances at this subject in its account of how Lazard Frères made a great deal of money in the 1960s by trading in the securities of firms involved in mergers, speculating on the outcome. This activity has become even bigger business. But nowadays investment bankers, in all situations, are careful to emphasise that a 'Chinese wall' separates the corporate-finance department, which may have privileged information about a company it is advising, from the investment and trading officers, who could make use of that information, whether to enrich clients or the bank itself. In the case of a merger, a bank must decide that it can advise a company or speculate in its stocks: it can't do both. Reich suggests that in Meyer's day, some of the profits 'came from mergers in which Lazard was also acting as an adviser to one side or the other'. He quotes the dealer in charge of risk arbitrage then as saying, 'The rule was that in any deal in which Lazard was involved as an adviser, I was expected to use my common sense. The rule was, simply, don't get Lazard in trouble.'

'Privileged information' is a grey area, not easily defined. At one end it may be precise and criminal – 'insider trading', the act of using the information improperly, to profit from dealing in securities. Most investment bankers take elaborate steps to avoid any taint. A criminal offence in the United States, it carries heavy penalties. A few sharp operators in the industry, although rarely in senior positions, carry red-blooded individualism too far, and are regularly caught doing it. Common sense suggests that a few more get away with it. In Britain

* *Financier* (William Morrow & Co., 1983).

insider trading has been illegal only since 1980, but frowned on with increasing severity for a period before that.

The very words 'insider trading' contain a guilty nostalgia for the unregulated past. It is wrong, but well within living memory in the City it was all right as long as it was done discreetly. It's doubtful if the majority of non-financial people, at least in Britain, would see much wrong, still, with a merchant banker or stockbroker profiting from information he picked up while talking to a client. It is how they expect financiers to behave. Insider trading even has its intellectual apologists who see it as a feature of the past that met a need in a different system. 'It's like all these things,' says Michael von Clemm, 'it's subjective. You call something an abuse and do away with it. The individual therefore has less of an opportunity to make money for himself. He therefore becomes less willing to take risks. I would propose to you that not all the money made on insider trading – which we would regard as illegal today, but which wasn't illegal then – went on horses at stud or dairy farms in Hampshire. Most of it was kept in the game and cycled on into other deals.

'If I could make a hundred thousand pounds in three days – trading in securities where I had a pretty good idea that something favourable was going to happen – my inclination as an old-style merchant banker would be to put that hundred thousand pounds into some founder shares in a new microprocessor manufacturing company in Nottingham or some-where. And if I don't have the opportunity to make large amounts of money quickly on the one hand, I'm not going to risk large amounts of money quickly on the other hand. So you take away both sides of the equation when you remove the so-called abuses – which is fine, you can say, "Ah-h! Nobody has a head start on anybody else in the stock market, isn't that wonderful!" But then you look on the other side and you say, "Who puts up money for people to start new business?" I would suggest to you there's less money for that today, and it's harder to come by. You have to deal with the investment committees of large insurance companies, with bureaucratic organisations. They try to take up the slack for what is now missing, for what was present as little as twenty years ago.'

In practice, of course, all investment bankers are anxious to show that the industry has changed, as indeed it has. The 'Chinese wall' is intended to cut off improper circulation of information within the bank. Departments are often sited on different floors to put physical distance between the trader and the corporate-finance banker. Stanislas

Yassukovich says that at the European Banking Co., the investment bank of which he is managing director, 'our people have to sign all sorts of frightening documents, making them subject to instant dismissal if they're caught in any way taking advantage of information they have as a result of working on deals'. At Morgan Stanley in New York, Barton M. Biggs runs the asset management subsidiary, with $9 billion of other people's money invested, from separate premises (though Biggs says there is no significance in this). High security is in force; Biggs had to negotiate electronic devices on two doors to reach his private office. He explained that as soon as Morgan Stanley knew that it was to raise capital for a corporate client, that company's securities went on a restricted list. This meant that his managers couldn't buy or sell the stock for investment clients. They couldn't even tell clients that the stock was on the list, because it would reveal that Morgan Stanley was privy to secret information about the company, and the investor might work it out for himself.

I asked if it wasn't difficult to exercise this discretion. Barton Biggs said, 'We train our analysts. If the Kuwait Investment Office, say, rang up and asked about a stock that was on the restricted list, the manager here would answer with a string of banalities.' I didn't like to ask the logical next question, what happened if a string of banalities made a client suspicious? In practice, the fund manager who is making the call will recognise the coded message as soon as the salesman or analyst says, 'I can't comment right now.' But the fact that a stock is on the restricted list may not be very helpful, according to another Morgan man. 'If I told you every time it happened,' he said, 'and you bought that stock, you'd lose money.' Sometimes they use low cunning and put a stock on the list just to confuse people.

No doubt the system is as secure as a reputable firm can make it. But is any financial centre, packed with ingenious capitalists, quite as prim in practice as it is in theory? Investment banks have to be practical. They operate essential bits of the financial machinery, which they didn't invent; they are latecomers in a long story. Something I heard at another Wall Street firm, Donaldson, Lufkin & Jenrette, lit up a corner of the real world that bankers have to make the best of. The firm is comparatively new, founded 1959. It has a fine staircase and handsome old paintings on the wall. Donaldson and Lufkin and Jenrette were classmates at Harvard Business School. Richard H. Jenrette is the chairman, a prepossessing man. He said that DLJ began by doing investment research, then branched out into broking and portfolio management for clients. Now it is an important investment bank, raising capital and offering the full range of services; it manages more than $18 billion of clients' investments. But Jenrette said that the firm hesitated a long time before it became more than a broker-cum-investment counsellor. Wall Street firms were broadening their range; it was the period when brokers were deciding they needed also to be capital-raisers, and vice versa. Jenrette's firm, perhaps because it was new and less sure of itself, feared a conflict of interest between the two sides of the business: the 'banking' side privy to information about clients, the 'investment' side unable to pass that information to other clients. 'In other words,' he said, 'DLJ in the sixties and early seventies took a purist approach. Whatever security we were recommending, we could say, "This company is not a client of ours. Therefore you can expect our advice to be totally impartial." We were sitting here in our ivory tower.'

It began to dawn on them that the conflicts of interest implicit in the new Wall Street didn't bother the institutional clients. On the contrary, said Jenrette, 'many institutions seemed to relish the potential conflict, on the theory that maybe at an XYZ or an ABC [a couple of leading Wall Street firms], something was getting under the Chinese wall. Instead of the big institutions saying that XYZ's research on a company was tainted because it was the investment banker to that company, we found they were delighted to receive it. They knew of the conflict. But they felt they were big boys and could handle it. They felt that XYZ was an honourable firm. It wouldn't blatantly tout stock that was over-priced. I think that subconsciously many of the institutions felt that at an XYZ, maybe the research people would meet the investment banking people over the dinner table or at the cocktail hour. Therefore the XYZ analysts would have this kind of knowledgeable underground network. Therefore one should listen to them.'

Immediately after 'Mayday' and the end of fixed commissions in 1975, Wall Street's future looked bleak. Firms needed all the income they could get. Donaldson, Lufkin & Jenrette emerged from the ivory tower and became an investment bank like the rest.

As far as modern times and manners allow, investment banking is still a business of every man for himself. Financial institutions conform, on the whole with good grace, to the fine print and prying inspectorate of ten thousand regulations. It isn't freedom as Pierpont Morgan would have understood it. Banking, like business in general, proceeds via endless compromise with tax authorities and regulatory bodies, to keep its patrimony intact. The rapacious old ways have to be abandoned, or disguised as not-so-rapacious new ways. The system has enemies. But the lone wolves of investment banking aren't dead, only wounded. The Eurobond market has flourished because there is no authority to breathe down its neck. It runs itself. 'What would happen if the authorities here put on a withholding tax?' asks a merchant banker. 'We would do it out of Zurich instead. People would up-sticks and move.' If investment bankers don't always conform to the rules as entirely as they like to suggest, it is merely evidence that the ancient war between officialdom and privateers continues, however often the privateers have had to retreat and make concessions.

Their own personal capital may not often be at risk, but they still play a mean game of beat-the-officials. I was visiting a foreign investment banker in his London office. As I took off my coat I said I supposed he was busy, since investment bankers usually are. He said, No, not at the moment. 'We've made a lot of money this year,' he said. 'Now I'm sitting here thinking of ways to make it seem less.' I took it to mean he was hoping to do some creative accounting, perhaps shifting earnings to make it appear they arose in a low-tax area; it is reported to happen quite often. Later in the conversation, when I had the tape-recorder going, I made some reference to what he had said. 'But that sort of thing isn't for attribution, is it?' he said, all smiles, and I had to agree that it wasn't.

INDEX